Africa – The Ultimate Frontier Market

Frontier Market

A Guide to the Business and Investment
Opportunities in Emerging Africa

by David Mataen

HARRIMAN HOUSE LTD

3A Penns Road
Petersfield
Hampshire
GU32 2EW
GREAT BRITAIN

Tel: +44 (0)1730 233870
Fax: +44 (0)1730 233880
Email: enquiries@harriman-house.com
Website: www.harriman-house.com

First published in Great Britain in 2012
Copyright © Harriman House Ltd

The right of David Mataen to be identified as Author has been asserted in accordance with the
Copyright, Design and Patents Act 1988.

Set in Palatino 10pt/8.5pt and Rockwell

ISBN: 9780857191724

British Library Cataloguing in Publication Data
A CIP catalogue record for this book can be obtained from the British Library.

Printed and bound in Great Britain by CPI Group (UK) Ltd, Croydon, CR0 4YY

To my mother, Annah Selian Minik. For raising me
to become a man of virtue.

Contents

Acknowledgements

In researching, writing and getting this book published, I have come to be in debt to many people.

I begin by thanking my wife, Laila, for her matchless patience and support. She read through the initial manuscripts and became my first sounding board – even at the time when she had no early idea the effort was all towards a book. When I was researching, validating and referencing the book, she endured long hours of loneliness. Above all she believed in the vision against the absence of any hard or credible evidence to go by.

In the course of writing this book, my son Lepatei was born. I would like to thank him for not crying too much at a time when I hardly had four hours to sleep and every minute of sleep counted for much. I also would like to thank him for inspiring me to write on and to delve deeper into the soul and character of emerging Africa as he lay on the couch, a symbol of the young, fragile but inexorably growing and flourishing future of Africa.

I am deeply indebted to Mr Paul Spence. A great friend, an intellectual interlocutor and a constant source of encouragement. I thank him for reading and editing the first version of the manuscript in its roughest and rawest form. And for sharing many thoughts, perspectives and opinions which immensely helped improve the quality and rigour of this book.

In researching for this book, I arrived at a stage of intense personal understanding and appreciation of the wonders of technology – its virtual, universal and accessible ability to simplify both human interactions and the conduct of business. In particular, I would like to single out and thank Mr Larry Page and Mr Sergy Brin, the founders of Google, the world's leading search engine, for giving the world, in my view, the top technological tool of modern times.

Mr John Gachora, my high school classmate and life long friend, I thank for agreeing to write the foreword to this book. This is a role he was specially cut out for – doubly by his intimate and nuanced knowledge of African business, and by his abiding friendship with the author.

To the team at Harriman House Publishing, I owe profound gratitude. To Mr Stephen Eckett who received a speculative manuscript submission from a debutant writer from Africa about Africa and had the courage to consider and accept it for publication. To Mrs Suzanne Tull for managing and executing my contract in the most professional and efficient manner, also for illuminating my thoughts about publishing and distribution rights. To Mr Craig Pearce, editor extraordinaire – for taking my raw, uncut manuscripts and making the finest diamonds of African investing literature. To Ms Rebecca Blackman, I thank for her skilful and insightful marketing design and multi-delivery strategies which afforded this book the best market position it ever could get.

Finally, I thank God Almighty for His grace and favour, freely given.

About the Author

During David Mataen's 13 years in financial services spanning commercial banking, stock brokerage, management consultancy and investment banking he has had the singular opportunity of becoming a scholar of African investing. His travels and tours of duty across the continent, though not to each and every corner, have allowed him to put his hand on the pulse and feel the heartbeat of African economies.

Being born, bred and educated, and having worked in Africa grants David the luxury of being first witness to the comings and goings in the continent, especially its commerce and economics. In his two and a half years as a contributing columnist to Business Daily, a publication of the Nation Media Group, he wandered far and wide intellectually and picked up invaluable insights, broad perspectives and sound reflexes that have become a foundation for his analysis of business on the continent.

Add to this his habits of extensive reading in finance and economics, and intense fascination with systems and their mechanics, which has favoured him the unique privilege of discovering just a little more of Africa's economic soul. David's travels outside of Africa gave him glimpses of a future Africa, when it grows up, and of what it has to do to reach that point. Above all, he is a hopeless romantic about the future and the intuitive signs of the future that appear in the course of ordinary life and business in the present.

David is currently the head of Corporate Finance at Faida Investment Bank in Nairobi, Kenya.

Foreword

There is no doubt that Africa has become the new growth story. Not so long ago, the debate on Africa was dominated by international aid and Aids. More recently the debate has shifted. At the World Economic Forum and other conferences, the debate is now focused on the significant opportunity that Africa presents. Whether it is the success of the World Cup in South Africa, or the addition of South Africa as the "S" in BRICS, there is no denying that this is Africa's decade.

But Africa has had a long journey to its decade, and more importantly the journey continues. There are countries still waiting for their version of the Arab Spring. There are countries still at war. There are countries where governance remains just a word. And there are countries still being founded. In a few countries, the question of nationalisation and indigenisation remains. In most others, the issue of marginalisation continues to dominate political debate.

However, one cannot deny that Africa has made enormous steps towards this decade. Political reforms have been crisp. Between 1991 and 2009, the number of African countries with a democratically elected government increased from eight to thirty-two. Furthermore, the number of countries at full civil war decreased to just two. The Mo Ibrahim Index, which assesses governance quality, shows that between 2000 and 2011, governance across Africa as a region has improved. Economic reforms have been fast, with a number of the continent's countries ranking high on the reforms index. Regulatory, legal and judicial reforms have stayed at pace. Financial reforms have seen several countries develop credit bureau agencies enabling the development of and access to credit. And, most importantly, common markets regimes have strengthened.

Investors have taken note of these reforms. Between 2010 and 2011, Africa foreign direct investment grew by 27%, the largest growth recorded by any region over this period. Furthermore, in South Africa, for example, M&A activity has increased from R588bn in 2010 to R602bn in 2011. Multinational corporations have been focused on growing their presence in Africa. The Asian trade corridor has experienced fast-paced growth. Chinese manufacturing firms are setting up shop in Africa. Chinese government institutions have set up bases in several African countries.

Africa's abundant natural resources continue to attract the world's attention. Recent oil discoveries in Ghana, Uganda and Namibia show that Africa will continue to play an important role in international trade. Discoveries in Mozambique and Tanzania have revealed one of the largest natural gas finds in the world. The mineral wealth of the Democratic Republic of Congo (DR Congo) remains largely untapped.

Whereas commodities and natural resources dominate the story, we are seeing diversified multinationals taking interest in Africa. The recent acquisition of South Africa based Massmart by the US retailing giant Walmart is a testimony to the growing importance of Africa's middle class. Africa boasts over 50 cities with populations above one million.

Furthermore, McKinsey and Co, a leading management consulting firm, estimates that by 2020 there will be 128 million households across Africa making $5,000 or more per year. Financial institutions have also noticed this opportunity. American banks such as JP Morgan, Citi and Bank of America have continued to invest in their corporate banking business in Africa. Barclays, the majority shareholder of the South Africa based Absa Group, has made clear its intentions to invest and grow its African business where it operates across multiple markets. South African banks have made growth into the rest of Africa a priority. Standard Bank has recently refocused its strategy towards growth in this region, selling its Brazilian and Russian entities.

To reap success in Africa however, investors must adopt a long-term view. Things move slower in Africa than in most other continents. There are many cultural nuances that can determine success or failure. There are political undertones that one must not ignore. Land rights, a cocktail of both modern and tribal land laws. Social requirements vary from country to country. It is thus important to understand these underpinnings even as one navigates the massive opportunities that Africa offers.

Fortunately, in *Africa – The Ultimate Frontier Market*, David Mataen has provided a go-to place for investors looking to understand Africa with a view towards tapping its long-term potential. Through well researched work, Mataen walks through Africa in generations. Understanding where Africa has come from allows for a better projection of where it is going. In this decade for Africa, Mataen's book is a must-read.

John Mburu Gachora
Managing Director, Barclays Africa Corporate and Investment Banking

Preface

"Four billion dollars doesn't count as an 'every day low price', but Walmart, the world's biggest retailer, hopes it has found a bargain. That is how much the Arkansas-based 'beast of Bentonville' has offered to acquire Massmart, a retailer with 288 stores in 14 countries in Sub-Saharan Africa.

"This is the clearest sign yet that Africa is now near the top of the agenda for the world's leading businesses. The continent still has problems, but it is no longer 'hopeless', especially for anyone wanting to be part of a fast-growing consumer market. Last year, while the global economy struggled with the aftermath of the financial crisis, Africa as a whole continued to advance and is expected to grow at least 4.3% this year (2010). Some economies such as Nigeria and Ghana are racing ahead. As the middle class and urban working class expand rapidly, food consumption is expected to grow strongly, along with sales of other consumer products.

"The bid for Massmart is an attempt to gain a first-mover advantage by one of the world's most sophisticated companies, and it is likely to be seen as the moment when the beasts of the corporate world recognised that Africa is the next big growth market."

'The beast goes on safari: Can Walmart make it in Africa?' –
The Economist, 2 October 2010

"Much has been written about the rise of the BRICs (Brazil, Russia, India and China) and the shift in economic power eastward as Asia outruns the rest of the world. But the surprising success story of the past decade lies elsewhere. An analysis by The Economist finds that over the ten years to 2010, no fewer than six of the world's ten fastest-growing economies were in Sub-Saharan Africa.

"On IMF forecasts Africa will grab seven of the top ten places over the next five years. In other words, the average African economy will outpace its Asian counterpart. Looking even further ahead, Standard Chartered forecasts that Africa's economies will grow at an average annual rate of 7% over the next 20 years, slightly faster than China."

'The Lion Kings? Africa is now one of the world's fastest growing regions' –
The Economist, 8 January 2011

The data in Tables 1 and 2 shows the world's ten fastest growing economies between 2001 and 2010 and the forecast for the fastest growing economies for 2011 to 2015.

Table 1 – the world's ten fastest growing economies for 2001 to 2010 (annual average GDP growth, %)

2001-2010	
Angola	11.1
China	10.5
Myanmar	10.3
Nigeria	8.9
Ethiopia	8.4
Kazakhstan	8.2
Chad	7.9
Mozambique	7.9
Cambodia	7.7
Rwanda	7.6

Source: *The Economist*, IMF

Table 2 – the forecast ten fastest growing economies for 2011 to 2015 (annual average GDP growth, %)

2011-2015 (IMF forecast)	
China	9.5
India	8.2
Ethiopia	8.1
Mozambique	7.7
Tanzania	7.2
Vietnam	7.2
DR Congo	7
Ghana	7
Zambia	6.9
Nigeria	6.8

Source: *The Economist*, IMF

Frontier economics and a quest for information

Quite a bit has been said and written in the recent past decade about Africa's, or Sub-Saharan Africa's (SSA's), economic potential – there has been a groundswell of interest in Africa and its economies. (For the purpose of this book, the term *Sub-Saharan Africa* has been used interchangeably with *Africa* and *emerging Africa*. I have done this because the countries of SSA – the territory south of the Sahara – have similar economic circumstances including stage of development, nature of economic and social challenges and, more specifically, rate of economic potential and opportunities.) However, most people in the developed West, the Far East and emerging Asian countries are only just waking up to the idea of an Africa draped in full commercial glory. This is because for many years Africa was ignored, if not actively sneered at, being thought only capable of tribal wars, biting poverty and hopeless disease.

Those who bothered to try economic activity in Africa were seen as rugged pioneers and courageous individualists, given the sheer optimism of their outlook against a dark and forlorn backdrop of wretchedness and botched experiments. And so it was that for decades on end Africa was bypassed by agents of commerce seeking new fortunes in other emerging economies.

Yet, business still carried on in Africa out of view; subtle, unremarkable and sometimes inscrutable. Occasionally this caught the view of researchers, journalists, outliers, and most certainly management consultants. For the main part though, Africa remained unexplored, unattended and neglected. That has been changing, and the new attention Africa is now receiving – though it remains fairly cautious – still amounts to a shift in outlook. Suffice it to say, the worm has started to turn!

In the 2000s alone Sub-Saharan Africa became one of the most talked about regions of the world in terms of emerging investment opportunities, sources of new growth and newly qualifying investment destinations – a quintessential *frontier market*. The term frontier market is commonly used to describe capital markets located in developing countries that are less advanced; they are countries where investable stock markets are not as established as those located in emerging markets. Frontier markets are considered risky but in some instances the pay off can be high.

The *Financial Times* Lexicon described a frontier market as a type of emerging market. It said: "A frontier market is considered to have lower market capitalisation and less liquidity than many emerging markets." Frontier markets are generally deemed to appeal to investors because they offer potential high returns with low correlation to other markets. They are ultimately expected to become more liquid and take on characteristics of the majority of emerging markets.

No doubt, there seems to be an increasing consensus that Africa is now developing into something the rest of the world would be happy to look at more keenly and with economic interest. The world is warming up to Africa as the final investable frontier: enquiries have been increasing, reconnaissance trips are more frequent, and coverage in world press is more positive.

There is a swelling appetite for information on Africa – positive information about Africa – on a broad cross-section of issues such as economic growth, social progress, political stability, implementation of modern governance systems, entrepreneurship, market expansion, commercial and trade opportunities, and financial investments. Unfortunately, there is a massive gap between this appetite and the availability of credible information.

As an avid consumer of financial and economic information, I have personally trodden this arid road in search of quality knowledge numerous times and each time I have felt the profound lack of information, especially about the rising economic appeal of SSA and its economies. Yet, something is going on here, and the more it goes on the more people want to know.

This thirst for knowledge has inspired the establishment of certain magazines, journals and websites dedicated solely to informing about Africa and its rising appeal. Some examples are *Africa Investor, Africa Business News, The African Report, Africa Business Journal* and *TradeInvestAfrica*. Indeed CNBC in 2007 started a channel for Sub-Saharan Africa – CNBC-Africa.

This lack of good information about African economic development has also motivated the writing of this book. *Africa – The Ultimate Frontier Market* does not pretend to fill the void of information on Africa on its own, neither does it claim exclusivity on its coverage, perspectives explored or depth of analysis. It brings to you Africa and its economic appeal from a consumer markets perspective through the eyes of an African capital markets practitioner; it aims to present the market opportunities in emerging Africa.

How this book is structured

This book is split into three parts. Part I examines how the Africa of today came to be. It builds up historical, demographic, cultural, social, government policy and economic perspectives with a view to providing an understanding of the driving forces behind Africa's rise. It provides a richly developed background to the dynamics that are currently in play in Africa's emerging consumer markets. The time period that Part I covers falls between the independence period and the implementation of structural adjustment programmes which came with restructuring, reforms and privatisation – therefore between the 1960s and 2000s.

Part II addresses efforts that have been made to lay down enablers for business and trade across the continent. These could be by individual country or regional, isolated or concerted, short term or long term, but are all collectively viewed as deliberate attempts at creating an enabling environment for the promotion and successful operation of business in single country economies or in regional economies. In terms of period, this section falls between 2000 and 2010.

Finally, Part III uses the backdrops set out in Part I and the possibilities brought about by the positive changes addressed in Part II as the foundation for identifying the broad themes and organizing principles for the range of expected economic, business and commercial outcomes in African economies going forward. It then proceeds to outline the opportunities in the specific consumer sectors expected to have the greatest growth trajectories and the broadest impact on African consumer markets – building the investment cases and rationale for value and wealth creation. Part III looks at the period from present day to 2030, meaning it is futurist in approach. The maturities of the implied opportunities cannot be placed on a definite timeline, of course, and so some may peter out earlier than projected while some may hold out for a longer term, even beyond 2030.

This book looks at Sub-Saharan Africa as a whole, as an asset class, or alternative investment opportunity, without isolating national economies, though it draws on examples from national economies as evidence of premises promoted or arguments set out. This is because while Sub-Saharan Africa is not one distinct unitary geographical expression, almost all the dynamics, trends and opportunities are similar and transcendental – cutting across from one economy to another and increasingly reinforced by regional economic and trading blocs and common markets. If national economies are not exactly similar in terms of their size, stage of economic development, population size, and levels of social and economic development, when comparing the collection of countries against other world regions, the internal differences between African nations are insignificant. It is very feasible for African nations to catch up with each other and converge; this confirms that Africa is not an event, but a process.

I acknowledge that the trends and dynamics developed or alluded to in this book may not necessarily be affecting all SSA countries simultaneously and the overlying opportunities identified may not all mature contemporaneously. But to return to a central feature of the book, I believe the close similarity and proximity of economies should be recognised. There is ongoing economic integration within the framework of common markets and monetary unions, and other attributes of economic contagion will accelerate the realisation of trends and opportunities already being experienced in satellite economies within the neighbourhood. As such, events in Kenya would immensely influence its neighbourhood, as much as those in Ghana, Nigeria, Côte d'Ivoire and Sierra Leone.

In researching references, attributions, examples, illustrations and citations, statistics for some Sub-Saharan Africa countries are less readily available than others. In this regard the reader will find disproportionate emphasis on a few countries. This does not constrain meaning nor transfer application from Sub-Saharan Africa to individual countries or regions; it only serves as a sample of the whole.

Who this book is for

This book is targeted at all classes of investors in African economies, be they within or outside the continent: active investors, prospective investors, aspiring investors and students of investments. These investors may fall within two broad category types: *professional investors*, financial and equity participants, or stock market investors; and *trade investors* – roll-up-the-sleeves entrepreneurs and strategic investors. It is also targeted at investment intermediaries in financial markets: executives and employees of commercial and investment banks, stock exchanges, brokerage houses, investment research houses, management consultancies, asset and fund managers, financial advisors and all those charged with proffering investment advice and recommendations.

It has, however, been written in a style and approach to also fit general readership. An average grasp of economic and financial terms, acronyms and abbreviations in general usage has been assumed, for example GDP (gross domestic product); PPP (Public-Private Partnership); inflation to depict the general rise in consumer and asset prices; and GDP growth rate to represent the rate of economic growth in an economy.

Exclusions made by this book

This book deliberately excludes South Africa because its advanced economy, and its physical and social infrastructure, are years ahead of the rest of Africa. It has dissimilar internal dynamics and a more complete interconnectedness with the rest of the world. Basically, South Africa is an emerging economy whereas the rest of SSA economies are frontier economies.

Apart from South Africa, another exclusion from the book's coverage is the mining sector. There are various reasons for this, chief among them being that it is largely operated under systems of state capitalism in partnership with giant multinationals, to the exclusion of local private sectors. The mining sector also does not have much impact on job creation, being extensively mechanised, and its products are sold in export markets abroad as raw materials without any impact to the local consumer markets. Besides these points, and most importantly, the mining sector is not present in all African countries, not even the majority of them. Where it has been present long term (except in very few glowing exceptions such as Botswana) it has tended to result in less progressive governance systems that have seen the propagation of corruption. It has also provided less and less incentive for economic liberalisation and therefore the private sector has generally remained stifled and less empowered by mining.

Finally, I have deliberately excluded the challenges, constraints, problems and threats to business in general in Africa and to the realisation of the specific opportunities identified in particular – there is far too much literature on this already. This does not mean that Africa is suddenly without problems and challenges to business, commerce and investments. Africa still faces the greatest challenges of any area in the world. These do not, however, detract from the opportunities that abound now and in the future in the African consumer markets.

Challenges are not necessarily negative, either; the challenges and constraints faced by African economies form the underlying basis for developing unique business models with which to access and appropriate the opportunities identified in this book. After creating home-grown solutions to mitigate constraints, African entrepreneurs will have built the bridges that enable them to step over the challenges to the opportunities, thereby cultivating long-term competitive advantage for themselves.

I hereby invite you to explore Africa as it proceeds toward greater economic and commercial relevance!

David Mataen,
Nairobi, Kenya, June 2012

THE MEGATRENDS

I

Introduction

Of course, Africa's movement into a position where its business environment generates a warm buzz in halls of academia, business conferences, and the world's business and financial press has not happened in a short period of time. The set-up for Africa's economic and commercial proposition has its genesis in various factors. These are sometimes disparate across time and sometimes they act together in unison or overlap, to bring into being an underlying framework for business incubation. When put together these factors make possible the prevailing positive economic and business case for Africa.

I have called these factors Africa's *megatrends*. They are the forces that, acting together over the long term and in the main part out of view of the casual observer, provide the context in which doing business on a global scale has become possible in Africa.

What is a megatrend?

To understand what a megatrend is, it is first good to define a trend. When talking in terms of countries, a *trend* is an emerging pattern of change likely to impact state government and require a response (i.e. adult children taking care of parents).[1] It is a

❝ A megatrend is a large, social, economic, political, environmental or technological change that is slow to form. ❞

pattern of change over time in some variable. Having trend data for the variable implies multiple instances of that variable. For example, one revolution in Africa is an event; two or three revolutions would call for comparative case studies; 15 revolutions in countries in Africa within five years would constitute a trend. One of the most obvious trends is the increase in world population. A potentially even larger trend, but much less obvious – or even agreed upon – would be the gradual warming of the Earth's atmosphere. Another is the continuing decline in the cost of microchips and consequently of computers.

The term megatrend was made popular by John Naisbitt with his bestselling book *Megatrends*. A megatrend is a large, social, economic, political, environmental or technological change that is slow to form. It is a major movement, pattern or trend emerging in the macro-environment; in business then it might be an emerging force likely to have a significant impact on the kinds of products consumers will wish to buy in the foreseeable future. The term is commonly used to indicate a widespread (across more than one country) trend of major impact, composed of sub-trends which in themselves are capable of major impacts. For example, global climate change will have a major impact on all the countries of the world and can be disaggregated into global atmospheric warming, sea-level rise, decrease in stratospheric ozone, etc.[2] Thus, it is a megatrend.

Once in place, a megatrend influences a wide range of activities, processes and perceptions, both in government and in society, possibly for decades. A megatrend marks a general shift in thinking or approach affecting countries, industries and organisations. Megatrends evident today include a growing interest in health, leisure, lifestyle and environmental issues.

The eight African megatrends

The megatrends I have identified as the drivers of Africa's current and future economic realities are the following:

1. Population growth and demographic shifts
2. Cultural revolution
3. Regionalisation of markets, consolidation and evolution of intra-African markets
4. Rapid urbanisation
5. Commercialisation of essential services
6. Deregulation and liberalisation
7. The growth of credit
8. Capital market development

Some of these megatrends have had longer incubation periods than others. Some have cause and effect relationships with each other. Some of them will peter out sooner in terms of their effects on society and the business environment while others will linger on far into the future. Some transcend Africa to have a global impact but affect Africa no less, such as demographic changes and urbanisation. In fact their effect on African society and geography is what perhaps gives them the global profile they enjoy currently because of the massive contribution current happenings in Africa make to their global aggregate changes.

A thorough grasp and understanding of these megatrends and a rational analysis of how they cascade to affect society, its tastes and preferences, its ability to consume, its demands and commands, will significantly inform future expectations and the design of markets in Africa.

What follows is a detailed analysis of each of these megatrends, highlighting its background, perspective and its driving forces, and setting out its implications for today's Sub-Saharan Africa marketplace. For each of the eight megatrends, the analysis is arranged as follows:

Background and perspective

Explanation of the megatrend itself, description of its components and context, and some relevant data to support the premises introduced.

Driving forces

Description of the driving forces making the megatrends possible, sustainable or likely to increase in strength. Examining the megatrends that drive socio-economic change in Africa, though useful to consider in understanding Africa and the composition of its markets, is not enough on its own. I will give a thorough analysis of the driving forces that made the megatrends possible, and that will continue to sustain the relevance of the trends in the future, in order to show the foundations for the megatrends identified.

Implications for today's Sub-Saharan Africa marketplace

Linking each megatrend with the realities of the present and emerging African marketplace, summarising its underlying contributions and implications for why African markets are the way they are currently or the way they are shaping out to be in the future. In situations or circumstances where there has been overlap or interdependence between one or multiple megatrends, this will be demonstrated. In the final analysis all the megatrends come together in a complex nexus of the cultural, economic and commercial reality that is the Sub-Saharan Africa marketplace.

POPULATION GROWTH AND DEMOGRAPHIC SHIFTS

1

Background and perspective

Sub-Saharan Africa has been experiencing phenomenal population growth since the beginning of the 20th century, following several decades of population stagnation attributable principally to the slave trade and devastating epidemics like smallpox. The region's population has increased from 100m in 1900 to 770m in 2005.[3]

As the population of Africa has grown exponentially over the past century it consequently shows a large youth bulge, further reinforced by increasing life expectancy, which is now at about 50 years in most African countries. The total population of Sub-Saharan Africa is estimated at 864.6m as of mid-2010 (total African population is estimated at 1,030.4m). The population of SSA has doubled over 28 years and has quadrupled over 55 years (UN estimates).[4] The latest population projections for Sub-Saharan Africa envisage a figure of 1.83 billion being reached by 2050.[5]

The most populous country in SSA is Nigeria, with an estimated population (without the benefit of reliable national census data for a long time) of 158m, followed by Ethiopia with 85m and the Democratic Republic of the Congo (DR Congo) with 68m in population. Niger, Burkina Faso, Uganda, and Liberia have annual population growth rates above 3.3%, while in Mali, Benin, Guinea, Somalia and Tanzania growth rates are above 3%. Table 1.1 summarises the population figures for the ten largest SSA countries.

Table 1.1 – population figures for African countries, mid-2010

Country	Population (m)
Nigeria	158
Ethiopia	85
DR Congo	68
Tanzania	45
Sudan	43
Kenya	40
Uganda	34
Ghana	24
Mozambique	23
Côte d'Ivoire	22

Source: Population Reference Bureau, 2010 World Population Data Sheet

Driving forces

African cultural laissez-faire

In pre-modern Africa the land was the centre of society, it was almost a deity. The people depended on it for practically everything. They fed off it, they made shelter from it, they sought protection in it and they relished it. Cultural festivals were held throughout the year, in fact becoming the basis for an annual calendar. Everything revolved around the land.

That is why land was so fiercely defended and fought over. Powerful communities projected their influence in the societal pecking order not by the extent of tangible possessions but by their expansionism: a consistent ability to expand, integrate and defend their territory.

Accordingly, where family units in Western societies considered the combined earning power of the family, the availability and cost of day-care, the destabilising impact of newborns, the availability of education capacity, projected inflation, economic cycles and taxation regimes impacting net disposable incomes, family units in Africa concerned themselves only with the land and its ability to support them. Where that ability was undermined African communities reacted by acquiring more land from neighbouring tribes, or driving deeper into virgin lands such forests, mountains and hillsides, and marshland. So while in Western societies a newborn belonged to a family, in Africa a newborn belonged to the land. Therefore the dynamics of population growth in the two scenarios were totally unrelated.

It is against this background of simple civilisations that uncontrolled child birth developed, and even heightened to a contest between communities. Regular checks would be made by rival communities on the numbers of babies born in enemy tribes and they used these figures as a case for increasing the rate of childbirth in their own tribes. Similar counter-actions across tribes would touch off a proliferating baby-race.

Dietary changes leading to enhanced fertility

Dieticians and nutritionists will tell you that a good, varied diet is important in improving human fertility.

In pre-modern Africa both male and female fertility were never assured. Instances of infertility were far too common in certain communities, especially the nomadic pastoralists who lived in marginal lands where access to an abundant and variety of food was a challenge. Agricultural communities which farmed arable land and wetland fared slightly better in this respect because access to a rich variety of food types helped sustain a very high level of fertility within the communities.

In Africa today the introduction of cash-trade and establishment of trade infrastructure across a large number of communities has opened up trade and enabled the availability of a wider variety of food types than ever before and at affordable prices.

The efforts, albeit gradual, to extend dietary education through the media of public clinics and hospitals, educational institutions, mass media and public meetings has helped change the dietary habits of many in society with the effect of boosting fertility in African communities generally, but among marginal communities in particular.

Medical advances enabling people to live longer

Traditional African societies lost young children and strong active adults alike to disease and epidemics that unremittingly hit communities. For example, between 1880 and 1920 smallpox almost decimated the population of northern Kenya,[6] In the Congo River basin, malaria, yellow fever and other tropical diseases made it difficult for human life to survive the vagaries of the harsh, humid African equatorial climate.[7]

What is more, African communities and their leadership regarded these chiefly as curses, bewitching or bad omens, meaning that afflicted individuals got minimal or no care. Among the Maasai of Kenya and Tanzania, people who became critically ill would be thrown in the bush to die there, or left alone in abandoned homesteads as the rest of the family would move on to find new habitation elsewhere. The sight of death was dreaded but was almost always seen as a certainty for those who fell sick.

Before the arrival of modern medicine (brought by missionaries and colonial administrations) and the dispersal of medical services across Sub-Saharan Africa, the average life expectancy was 42 years and infant mortality rate per 1,000 births stood at 149.[8] Medicine as a practice was introduced to Africa by Christian missionaries, first in isolated places and on a small scale. Colonial governments went a little further by laying the foundations for national medical infrastructure. This also did not go too far, owing to a

❝ Heightened dissemination of medical services, steps towards universal healthcare and lately provision of healthcare as a business have together allied to increase the lifespan of individuals and communities. **❞**

deliberate focus and bias towards settler communities and their servants, rather than native populations.

Independence governments, acting by themselves, were spectacular disappointments in their efforts to spread medical care to their citizenry. Where there was no capacity expansion, the colonial infrastructure was maintained. Where some sort of capacity addition was witnessed it was through tokenism and pork-barrel politics which rewarded communities that backed ruling parties and political classes. In certain sorry states visited by civil strife and other chaos, even the colonial infrastructure was uprooted by disease.

Where tangible success can be identified in the extension of medical services to African communities is within the complex of religious institutions with international networks; global pharmaceutical companies seeking new growth and footprints in frontier markets; targeted development assistance in turnkey projects from world healthcare institutions like the WHO; and leading health sector NGOs.

Governments only later became active, riding on citizen activism that fed the social and political resurgence of the 1990s that saw many independence administrations toppled at the ballot and the ushering in of a new breed of progressive African leadership. Of note too is the UN Millennium Development Goals (MDG) initiative which set target deadlines for achievement of, among other things, universal healthcare by 2015.

While the MDGs may not be achievable in Africa as conceived, its supreme benefit is found in the principle of unintended consequences. Under UN and World Bank supervision African governments have had to earmark large chunks of their national budgets to healthcare provision as a prerequisite for accessing vast resources under numerous programmes designed to collectively achieve MDG targets. One such programme that has benefited is the Global Fund to Fight AIDS, Tuberculosis and Malaria. The latest initiative is private sector healthcare provision, an initiative backed by medical insurance.

By 2008 life expectancy for the African population, excluding HIV and AIDS, had improved to 54 years according to the UN.[9] This represents a leap of 11 years from the independence era of the 1960s.

Heightened dissemination of medical services, steps towards attainment of eventual universal healthcare and lately provision of healthcare as a business have together allied to save lives and increase the lifespan of individuals and communities which live responsibly.

A major explanation for why population growth in Africa has spiked only in the past couple of decades is that healthcare provision was only then reaching societies and communities which hitherto had none.

Antenatal and early childhood care

Childbirth has never been an issue in Africa. In fact the best exemplification of nature's creative combination of multiple production and natural selection was to be found in traditional African societies. Men married many women in polygamous family settings. Families begot large numbers of children.

Besides the requirement for many hands to work and defend the land, the underlying imperative for bearing many children was the very real spectre of death and child mortality. Parents always worried how many children would reach adulthood. A random check on families in rural Africa would reveal this fact. National census sheets in Africa have provisions for total children birthed into a single family and another for those who are still alive. With minimal variations, these two figures always turned out vastly different.

Measles would kill a sizeable portion of all children below the age of five years. Malaria had its own quota; Polio, Tuberculosis, Kwashiorkor, Marasmus and other similar complications all took their toll as well. As a result, in the 1960s, 267 children out of every 1,000 children born in Africa would never live to see their fifth birthday.[10]

With the gradual introduction of antenatal clinics and early childhood care in Africa, this picture has been changing for the better. Government and church mission clinics provide free or hugely subsidised pregnancy services to women in rural Africa and those living in slums or low-income settlements. General practitioners, nurses and clinical technicians receive basic training in dispensing of these services. Standardisation and simplification of the procedures involved have resulted in almost universal availability of antenatal care across Sub-Saharan Africa. The emergence and current advance of gynaecology and obstetrics as standard medical practices in Africa is testament to the improving healthcare for pregnant women and young mothers.

Early childhood management has been made routine in all medical centres, even where only first aid can be administered. Large paediatric wings with comprehensive childcare facilities have been established in most large hospitals; while dedicated paediatric hospitals have been emerging in urban centres and progressive areas of rural Africa.

As a consequence, between 1990 and 2009 average child mortality has fallen from 180 per 1,000 to 129 out of 1,000 across Sub-Saharan Africa.[11] Still some countries are ahead of others – in Mauritius and Botswana child mortality has been reduced to near developed-world rates at 12 and 13 out of 1,000 respectively.[12]

Many more children born in Africa now have the chance to grow into adults, therefore boosting Africa's population numbers significantly.

Social permissiveness and moral decadence

Barely three decades or so ago, Africa was one continuous, unpunctuated rural real estate sheltered from the rest of the world by its remoteness of communication and infrastructure. The city of Nairobi had a population of 1.3m[13] in 1990, Kinshasa in the Congo had 3.8m people,[14] and urbanisation of Africa as a whole was 28%,[15] which indicates that the majority of African populations lived in the rural areas.

Most children attended rural schools and grew up to engage in the economic and social activities of their families. Migration was almost non-existent and the little there was was generally rural to rural in type. In summary, traditional African social systems and norms were functioning, and families were raised under strict rules of morality and etiquette. Children were imbued with the ways of the straight and narrow, and society enforced these rules to the letter. Infraction or malfeasance were punished disproportionately, not only as a corrective system but importantly as a deterrent to any other elements that might be having such dispositions. Sexuality among the youth was anathema and was out of bounds. Child pregnancy would scarcely happen and when it did it was met with the full weight of societal wrath.

Over the years, Africa has opened up. It has opened up to Western systems of education, which have led to young people travelling away from home and living among themselves for most of the year in schools and training institutions. It has opened up to Western media and entertainment. It has opened up to Western economic and cultural systems. It has opened up to Western civil liberties.

The result of this is a cultural mélange that is neither African nor Western. It is a fact that it is still taking time to fully define itself but for now, provisionally, it has had huge and costly social implications. It has presided over the collapse of the African way of life, particularly its checks and balances.

Wherever you turn now, the old social norms are considered relics from a past way of life. Most of the aspects of this state of affairs are positive, or at least progressive and innovative. Some may not be so, but when put together with other forces at play in society they contribute to making possible the current and future realities of the African economic marketplace.

Runaway pregnancy among the youth is one of the changes. In Uganda, teenage pregnancy is the highest in Sub-Saharan Africa at 25%,[16] while in Kenya teenage pregnancy and childbearing

> **" Wherever you turn now, the old social norms are considered relics from a past way of life. "**

remains very high at 18%, with regional differentials.[17] By way of comparison, teenage pregnancy in the USA is 5%, in China it is 0.5%, in Japan 0.4% and in South Korea 0.3%.[18] Amongst many families in the slums and rural Africa there are unmarried teenage girls nursing babies in succession, some with entire families of their own, with no fathers, under the watch of their parents.

The growth in child pregnancy in Africa is a phenomenon that has become one of the main reasons for the continent's population growth.

The 1980s demographic bulge

Between the late 1970s and the early 1990s Africa experienced a baby boom, a period when the mothers of Africa gave themselves to child bearing at an unprecedented rate. The average rate of population growth recorded was 3% across Sub-Saharan Africa. Kenya as a country posted the highest rate of population growth ever recorded anywhere in the history of mankind and

Rwanda wasn't too far behind that. Ethiopia, Nigeria and the Congo, even though buffeted by famine, social strife and government misrule, still recorded high figures.[19]

A critical mass had thus been reached by virtue of the factors present – the forces amenable to bringing into being and sustaining human life converged at that critical juncture in the continent of Africa and a demographic bulge occurred. The earlier progenies of this demographic bulge would have reached about 30 years of age by 2000, and the later ones about 18 years. This means that the ripple effect of this baby boom has been underway for well over 10 years in 2012 and the baby boomers are now having babies of their own.

> **" The forces amenable to bringing into being and sustaining human life converged at that critical juncture in the continent of Africa and a demographic bulge occurred. "**

Various factors come into play to compound the current baby boomers and should result in this boom being even more significant than the previous one. Fertility levels have soared and teenage pregnancy is on the rise, for reasons previously explained. If good antenatal clinics and early childhood care made it possible for many baby boomers to survive and mature into adults, then steady improvements and better spread of clinical services make it even more possible for their offspring 20 years hence. The result is that a second demographic bulge could take Africa within striking distance of deposing Asia from its long-held perch at the top of the world demographic table.

Absence of national population control initiatives

Following the demographic bulge described above, governments across Africa were advised by donors and development partners to establish national population control programmes. These had the broad mandates of sensitising their citizens to the dangers of uncontrolled population growth, educating them on the economic and social impact of bringing forth new lives without corresponding economic empowerment to bring them up, and about the deteriorating collective welfare effect of unchecked child birth. In simple terms the governments were told that population growth without corresponding or higher economic growth was a clear recipe for poverty.

For a very brief moment, these programmes were splashed across the local press, with a few road shows in rural regions and in areas of population clusters like industrial towns and slums. Posters were displayed in clinics, hospitals and other public places. Mothers with babies and pregnant women were visited in hospitals. Additions to school curricula were introduced to give school children an early foundation in population studies.

Unfortunately the initiatives did not last long and soon petered out. The donors never intended to fund the programmes indefinitely. They only meant to help African governments establish the programmes and once in full operation take them over and provide for them in the state budgets.

This is not to say the programmes had no positive initial impact at all; in a handful of African countries they did. In Kenya fertility patterns during 1977-89 revealed a reduction in the total fertility rate (TFR) of 1.2 children between 1977 and 1983.[20] The number of children per woman came down from 7.2 to 6.5.[21] However, it is difficult to isolate how much of this was as a direct result of the population control initiatives.

African governments on the other hand had never really embraced population control, either as a principle or as a practice. Most presidents and senior government officials were themselves polygamists and heads of large families. Those who did embrace the principle failed in the practice. It was a major test in prioritising for governments which couldn't even extend basic primary education and basic health care to 70% to 80% of their populations. And so population growth is occurring once again.

The social aspect of the dominant economic activities

African traditional communities were a broad dichotomy between agricultural and ranching communities. Agricultural communities tilled the land and had permanent or semi-permanent abodes. They were intensive in their land tenure and land use. The ranching communities roamed the plains in search of new pastures and water for their livestock.

This order of economic wellbeing also set the order of social interactions. Families in agricultural communities lived in one place together throughout the year. The family garden, which was never too far away from the homestead, was cultivated in a team effort enabling married couples maximum time together to build families. The livestock keepers on the other hand were peripatetic with skeleton staff mainly of able bodied males and

> **"** Embracing of modern lifestyles has contributed to the increase of incidences of child birth among a majority of African people. **"**

young boys, while leaving the women in makeshift homesteads which served as forwarding addresses. Time together for married couples was reduced often to only three months in a year, drastically reducing opportunities for family building.

With time the ranching communities have settled down to permanent homesteads and reduced their seasonal migration to only critical periods when rains fail or delay for too long. They have taken up subsistence agriculture and engage in rural trade. With this landmark change in their way of life, their time at home has stabilised and their population numbers have shot up precipitously in recent decades.

But more fundamentally, the general crossover from subsistence agriculture and livestock keeping to regular employment in cities and trading centres for many of the African folk, coupled with living in modern houses where a man and woman sleep in the same bed every night, has increased contact between them and with it the probability of conception.

Embracing of modern lifestyles, therefore, without underplaying the overarching concept of sexuality and virility, has contributed to the increase of incidences of child birth among a majority of African people. This is the reason slums and planned settlement schemes are heavily populated across Africa.

Projected demographic outcomes

The Population Reference Bureau estimates that the Sub-Saharan Africa population will rise to 1.83 billion by 2050 from 864m in mid-2010, a 110% increase in 40 years. This represents a rate of 2.5% population growth per annum, more than double the current annual world growth rate of 1.2%.[22]

Table 1.2 serves to illustrate the current population numbers and the projected changes up to the year 2050 for a sample of Sub-Saharan African countries. Importantly, this data signifies two things: that population growth is a continent-wide factor and not isolated to one country or region; and the momentum already in place is sustainable in the long term.

Table 1.2 – population figures up to 2050 for African countries

Population	Mid-2010 (m)	Mid-2025 projected (m)	Mid-2050 projected (m)	Increase by 2050 (%)
Nigeria	158.3	217.4	326.4	106
Ethiopia	85	119.8	173.8	104
DR Congo	67.8	101.4	166.3	145
Tanzania	45	67.4	109.5	143
Kenya	40.1	51.3	65.2	63
Uganda	33.8	53.4	91.3	170
Ghana	24	31.8	44.6	86
Mozambique	23.4	31.2	44.2	89
Cote d'Ivoire	22	30.8	47.2	115
Niger	15.9	27.4	58.2	266
Sub-Saharan Africa	864.6	1,207.4	1,830.8	112

Source: Population Reference Bureau 2010 World Population Data Sheet

Three African countries are expected to be in the top ten countries which will contribute most to world population over the next 40 years. They are all projected to add new net population sizes far exceeding their current estimated populations. Nigeria, fourth globally, will contribute 168m new people; DR Congo will contribute about 98m people; and Ethiopia will add 88m new people.

Conclusion/marketplace implications

The most distinct character of Africa's population growth is its long-term sustainability. The continent, now and in the future, boasts the most youthful demographics of any in the world. Its net contribution to world population, in absolute and percentage terms, continues to rise, especially against a bleak contrast of negative growth rates and greying populations in Europe, North America and Japan.

This has three major implications for business and economics going forward:

1. It assures a growing and replenishing consumer hinterland into the long term. This should be compounded by rising GDP income per capita and further democratisation of credit.

2. It lays massive overbearing demands on infrastructure, both mainstream physical such as transport and communication, as well as social, such as schools and health facilities.

3. It provides a compelling basis for supersized long-term capital investments in (production) scale, (distribution) capacity and (modernising) technology.

CULTURAL REVOLUTION

2

Background and perspective

Historically Africa was the last cultural bastion of the world. Heterogeneous communities and ethnic groups lived alongside each other for centuries as self-sufficient nation states, not always in peace and harmony. The lack of communication and common ideals created a barrier to interaction. Westernisation came late and in most of African regions where it encountered deeply-rooted cultural traditions it was rebuffed. Traditional systems, norms, practices and legacies were therefore preserved even after the independence period.

In fact large parts of rural Africa have only in the past two decades begun to come unstuck and even now some remain incorrigibly steeped in traditional customs in the face of the inevitable. Notwithstanding, something new seems to be taking place within African societies. It may not have been characterised by notable single events, but undoubtedly a cultural revolution is underway.

Driving forces

Education and enlightenment

Ever since the establishment of systems and infrastructure for the mass education of the African people by independence governments, education has become one of the greatest cultural influences on African societies. Currently, it is the most widespread and by far the most enduring legacy of foreign interaction with African societies on African soil.

Primary education has been universalised in almost every African nation,[23] while public secondary education is subsidised by governments. The infrastructure for education – including schools, a schools inspectorate and a ministry of education network of offices – has expanded over the years. As an example, in Kenya the vote for the ministry of education alone consumes about 26% of the national budget.[24] Nursery and primary schools are now ubiquitous across Africa, within easy reach of every village and densely populated slum.

Children are started very early in school, even at the age of three years these days. And for some of them it will not be until they are young adults, of ages between 24 to 26 years, that they leave the formal educational system. Most

> " In short, schools and prevailing school systems are the leading shapers of emerging African societies more than any other force at play. "

linger on in further education, tertiary education or professional certification until they are, on average, 30 years of age.

The school system is designed to be intensive and exacting of its youthful clients. Classes run through the entire day, Monday through Friday in a week and for a minimum of nine months in a year. Besides, there is prep and homework to be completed in the evenings.

Children from all communities and all social classes congregate together at school. They begin in their formative years when they are highly impressionable to habit-forming tendencies through adolescence, when they are volatile and susceptible to character-shaping traits, to adulthood when who they are or have become is virtually ingrained. In short, schools and prevailing school systems are the leading shapers of emerging African societies more than any other force at play.

Up to 90% of primary schools used to be day schools. Now, there is an almost equal split between day schools and boarding schools. All other education above primary was and has remained predominantly boarding system. This means that children share life experiences together and grow up together in the same environment, which binds and cements them into a micro-society built on strong bonds of loyalty to one another and duty to the ideals that make them different. They slowly and imperceptibly drift away from their parents' traditional and tribal cultures and fuse into a new culture based upon their educational experiences.

Westernisation: the continent-wide embrace of global pop culture

Western pop culture is speedily becoming the universal culture of the world – this is not limited to one continent or region. However, in Africa it is happening even more quickly than in other areas. The youth adopt Western culture with great eagerness and without scrutiny. The middle-aged accept it grudgingly, but accept it nonetheless. The old rebuffed it violently initially, but with time they have come to a position of indifference.

Western pop culture rides on the wheels of music, movies and entertainment, magazines and journals, and pop idols. These all bring to bear Western languages, speech tones and variations; Western panoramic and ambience preferences; Western dressing styles; Western demeanours; Western public and private place dynamics; and Western reflexes.

It bears repeating at this juncture that the youth of Africa keenly receive and internalise these influences. A random drive deep into the heart of rural Africa reveals the scale and breadth of diffusion of Western pop culture into the core of Africa. American pop idols and English football players enjoy instant name recognition to inspire jealousy in local politicians and church priests.

One of the leading agents of Western pop culture is the Hollywood entertainment industry. The frequency with which movies are released, and the overwhelming variety and constant innovations in entertainment value therein, are keenly watched in Africa. One

> **"** Western pop culture is speedily becoming the universal culture of the world, in Africa it is happening even more quickly than in other areas. **"**

unique factor drives Africa's ability to tune into Western entertainment almost without cost. This is the vibrant bootleg operations going on in full disregard of intellectual property rights and copyright in many a nondescript back-street of African capitals. In Lagos, Nigeria; Yaoundé, Cameroon, Nairobi, Kenya, for example, before a new movie has premiered abroad, bootleg copies are already being hawked in the streets and bulk deliveries made to the regional capitals. These bootleg copies are cheap – a CD having anywhere between 9 and 24 movies can retail for only 62 cents. The efficiency of the bootleg operations, and the dynamism of distribution which makes it almost instantly synchronised across Africa, bring home to Africa the glamour, splendour and grandeur of Hollywood real-time at a miniscule fraction of what it might cost to obtain these films through official channels.

A proliferation of cheap DVD players in supermarkets, consumer electronic outlets and even corner shops has flattened the acquisition costs of home entertainment. Urban social halls have also been fitted with DVD players and 24-hour viewing rosters drawn up.

Another agent is English Premier League football. This has become a sensation like no other in Africa. So much so that it became the sole basis and business model for a pay-TV channel, GTV, which rolled out simultaneously in 22 African countries and which momentarily glimpsed success only to be knocked out by the global financial meltdown.[25]

The youth of Africa religiously follow English football matches, are fanatical about England's top football clubs and have a cultic admiration for its leading players. It is in and of itself a mighty cultural revolution across the length and breadth of Africa. It has caused the redesign of youth groups, seeing them arranged into fan clubs that transcend borders, uniting them in a common goal, purpose and identity and basically providing fodder for conversations among them. Club fan-bases have attained denomination status in a new football religion that has come into being in youth-Africa. Christiano Ronaldo, Wayne Rooney, Didier Drogba, Samuel Eto'o and Michael Essien are its high priests.

Not only has it brought into business pay-TV channels (even though DSTV is the only one currently operating), it has also created an entirely new business concept in Africa: sports bars. All over Africa sports bars have proliferated, from estate neighbourhoods right into the high streets of the downtown core. They sell beer in large quantities and sustain local beverage companies in business.

A third agent of the dissemination of Western pop culture in Africa is television itself; TV consumption is becoming universal. CNN, BBC and Al Jazeera rule the news segment and bring the latest news items into living rooms all over the world. Sitcoms, soap operas and the latest fad reality TV shows are just the same – they are screened and carried by all network stations, and even though not contemporaneously (for now), end up being viewed all over the world and all of Africa. They feed and sustain similar buzz conversations in Africa as in the rest of the world. Growing acceptance of paid-for TV in Africa is bringing home dedicated activity channels such as Food Channel for food information, recipes, entertainment, trend information, dining advice, and food discussions; Style Network for fashion and style tips, celebrity fashion style and information; Entertainment Channel – a source for entertainment news, celebrity gossip and pictures.

Further to this, in Africa a new phenomenon in entertainment is taking shape. This is Nollywood – the movies made and shot in Nigeria or western Africa. They have quickly joined the African mainstream and now too form part of the unifying single African emerging culture. The films often feature the travails of new arrivals in large cities – an experience that is recognisable to people across Africa. They show ordinary people struggling to make sense of a rapidly changing, hard world. "The overarching theme of Nollywood films is Africa's troubled journey to modernity."[26] "Nollywood is the voice of Africa, the answer to CNN" says Lancet Idowu, one of the best-known Nigerian directors.

"Film (or TV) is now Africa's dominant medium – it links distant societies, fosters the exchange of ideas and drives fashion trends. It also profoundly shapes how Africans see their continent. They derive many of their opinions on neighbouring countries from the movies."[27] All the cultural forms discussed here aggregate to shape opinions and form the new reflexes for the African populations in cultural convergence.

National language policies and the evolution of ad hoc languages

Even the smallest African country (with the exception of Somalia) has at least five indigenous languages spoken that are distinct from each other. Language barriers make cross-tribal communication difficult, as no tribe, out of self-preservation and protection of its own sovereignty, is willing to learn the language of the other. But language has always been the most efficient medium for human interactions – including trade and business. Without it advanced forms of interaction between people are not possible and nation states are untenable.

This is the logic that encouraged policies to develop and enforce national languages in newly independent African states. The tribal sensitivities informing national policies in all African societies meant that it was difficult to find domestic languages with widespread acceptance across all ethnic communities. It was easier therefore in most states to adopt the language of the colonial master because of its neutrality of ownership and because it was already fairly well-travelled across society.

But there was always the resentment towards colonial masters and adoption of their language was regarded in some quarters as an unwelcome continuation of colonialism. In this regard some societies were lucky. The societies of eastern and northern Africa found themselves in a good position because they had homegrown languages that fitted the bill in the form of

Swahili and Arabic. These languages not only enjoyed neutrality of ownership but also had fairly widespread appeal and could be functional as languages of trade and exchange.

National language policies are perhaps the chief man-made force in bringing ethnic communities together and melding them into one unified society. They simultaneously supply a single media of communicating to the whole nation at once. They have allowed cross-cultural, cross-ethnic communication, enabling Africa's people to mix freely and come to understand each other better. They have reduced use of tribal languages, which are concomitantly beginning to recede or disappear in areas of high tribal mixes, and they have helped in bringing down barriers of mistrust and doubt across ethnic lines. Common languages have given the African people a new identity, a sense of nationhood and unity, and they have made possible single, homogenised markets across African states.

Where official national languages are shared among neighbouring countries, this has enabled cross-border communication, trade and co-operation; they make commerce possible. Take for instance something as plain as mass advertising, which is made easier by everyone in a country or region understanding one language.

> **Where official national languages are shared among neighbouring countries, this has enabled cross-border communication, trade and co-operation; they make commerce possible.**

It is important to see that African societies have gone from a position of total inability to communicate among themselves (making the contact of businesses impossible), to the present situation where national languages have helped put societies under single communication platforms. There could be a position in the future where the African continent as a whole is able to communicate in one or two languages.

Generational gaps: the youth depart from the old

Polygamous societies in traditional Africa made possible inter-generational cascades in a single family. The children born into these families were numerous and the age gaps between the youngest and oldest could be large.

In fact a man could have three generations of children in one homestead. The age difference between the father and the first born child would be between 20 and 25 years, while that between the father and the last born from

" The chemistry of youth seems to transcend national boundaries, and violate tribal or communal barriers of language and traditional components of tribal cohesion. "

the fourth or fifth wife could be 70 to 80 years, leaving the difference between first and last born between 45 and 60 years, or three generations.

The differences in terms of social orientations of these three generations (four, if you include surviving parents) of people living under one homestead is enormous. The young being in the majority have the numbers and emotional energy to gravitate together and form a world view immensely different from that of their parents. They are more amenable to new lifestyles, more susceptible to fads and more open to adventure and discovery. The generational gap that arises is not only more pronounced, but keeps widening as the young increase the velocity of change while the old are frozen in time.

In rare instances, generational quantum leaps occur between the young and their parents. These have customarily been on the back of massive technological changes that transform society. Mobile phones and the internet have been the forces behind the current generational leap in Africa. The chief reason behind this is the polar differential in educational levels and aptitudes, where the old are generally uneducated and the young are generally well educated.

It takes some basic level of education to write and send a text message, which telecommunication experts, such as Europe's leading futurist Dr Patrick Dixon, tell us has been by far the greatest telecoms success in Africa. Likewise, for internet utilisation, be it composing and sending emails, chatting, surfing the net and using search engines, or even such sophisticated uses as collaborating online on a project or database update, it takes education, technological aptitude and most importantly a rudimentary conceptual awareness and appreciation. While the youth use all of these at lightning speed, the old don't understand – a classic generational quantum leap.

These generational leaps minimise talking points, undermine communication flows and reduce, if not eliminate, spontaneity of engagement between the young and old. This cements the conviction of the younger generations that the old do not understand them, and conversely the elderly gripe that the youth are insouciant and intractable. It is much easier for two young people who are absolute strangers from opposite sides of the continent to meet and hit it off well at first encounter than it is for a youth and an aged person from the same tribal community or country to do so. The chemistry of youth seems to transcend national boundaries, and violate tribal or communal barriers of language and traditional components of tribal cohesion.

The youth of Africa therefore see themselves as a unique tribe distinct from the disparate tribes to which their parents so sentimentally subscribe.

Ubiquity, ease of access and affordability of global brands

Global brands, especially luxury brands, were rare in Africa before a decade and a half ago. They were never available even in upscale shops, and only spotted on extremely rare occasions being worn by politicians and flamboyant businesspeople. Wristwatch brands such Tag Heuer, Philip Patek and Rolex would have been easily counted on the wrists of Africans and only readily seen on the pages of glossy high-brow journals and newspapers. Luxury clothing lines such as Gucci, Dolce & Gabbana, Levi Strauss, Hugo Boss and Versace were available but a single suit cost the equivalent of a motorbike. Luxury auto types, such as Mercedes Benz, BMW, Jaguar, Range Rover, Porsche and Ferrari, though visible on African roads, were exclusive to the business dynasties and government officials.

When mobile phones were first introduced into Africa, they were treated as status symbols just like luxury watches, cars and clothing. In the year 2000 in Kenya, Motorola and Ericsson handsets (which were bulky, had poor reception and low battery power retention) were owned by only 15,000 individuals.[28]

Television sets in many African households were black and white. In vast administrative divisions (which are now complete districts) only one black and white television set would be found in either a prison canteen or a public recreation area sponsored by, for example, a mineral extracting company.

White goods like fridges, gas cookers, microwaves and laundry machines were non-existent in the 1990s. Most African young men can only remember seeing small Ignis fridges in local dispensaries where vaccines and needles were kept.

> **"** African youth no longer recognise any basis of difference between themselves and those of the developed world in terms of the access to brands and products they enjoy. **"**

Now every conceivable global brand and consumer electronic device is available in Africa. A Sony television is almost a standard piece of furniture in every urban home or apartment, accompanied unmistakably by a DVD player or home theatre. LG and Samsung fridges are common in urban homes too.

The most culturally impactful segment of global brands is the one that has become available and affordable to a great majority of people, especially the young. This segment comprises casual wear, wristwatches, mobile phones and passenger cars. The youth of Africa now wear and accessorise in exactly the same way as those of North America and Europe. They wear Tommy Hilfiger, Versace, Lacoste and Giorgio Armani casual wear; and sport NY Bulls and Boston Red Sox caps; as well as a wide variety of internationally acclaimed sports club t-shirts and other replica clothing.

There are several factors which have made these changes possible. Firstly, manufacturers are globalising their sales and distribution and have to differentiate their prices according to the buying power of the economies they enter. Secondly, there is a robust second-hand market that enables reach-me-downs from developed markets to find ready markets in Africa. Thirdly, there is a sizeable community of developing countries' diaspora who send goods and clothing back home to family and friends. Fourthly, international travel and tourism has been on the rise between developed and developing nations. This year-round pool of travellers do a lot of shopping which finds its way back to developing countries, Africa included.

As a result the African youth no longer recognise any basis of difference between themselves and those of the developed world in terms of the access to brands and products they enjoy. By virtue of the feeling of close similarity to Western youth, the African youth are already feeling liberated and beginning to demand cultural openness akin to that in the West.

Tribal clusters weakened by urbanisation

It has been stated before that the rate of urbanisation in Africa is growing at a faster rate than anywhere in the world. Demographers anticipate that more than 50% of African population will be living in urban areas by 2050.[29] Great metropolises like Lagos, Cairo, Johannesburg, Nairobi, Kinshasa, Accra and Lusaka are eating into their rural neighbourhoods at alarming rates, increasing the urban sprawl.

Nairobi today has a population of about 3m, close to 10% of the population of Kenya.[30] Kinshasa has about 8m people, easily 12% of the population of DR Congo.[31] Lagos ranks with Mexico City, New York, Bombay and Tokyo as one of the world's most populous cities; all feature some mind-boggling numbers between 18m and 25m people. For Lagos, at approximately 17m, that is more than 11% of the entire population of Nigeria.[32]

In rural Africa ongoing road development is opening up the countryside at a faster pace than had been observed before. Trading centres are springing up at road intersections, hilltops, agricultural produce collection points and at any other places where conveniences like sustenance, rest and relief can be found. As a consequence the distance between trading or urban centres along the nexus of trunk roads and inter-city connectors across rural Africa has narrowed appreciably.

Urban centres are magnets for all manner of people from wholesalers and general merchants, small retail traders, land and produce brokers, used items vendors, consumables and electronics hawkers, street urchins, and commercial sex workers, to roustabouts and layabouts. They come from all over the country, young and old, every tribe and religion, and from all shades of political and cultural persuasion. Their numbers swell as the pace of rural-urban drift is currently in full momentum and the rate of child birth is also much higher than in their rural neighbourhoods. So much so that they decisively influence political outcomes in formerly rural constituencies where the effects of the transition to increased urbanisation have been greatest.

While in the 1980s and 1990s one would find administrative districts or constituencies in Africa predominantly peopled by one community, up to 95% and more, rural Africa is now becoming more cosmopolitan.

The resulting tribal mix is causing the gradual but terminal decline of tribal languages, affiliations and instincts. On the other hand it is nurturing the integration of a people who do not feel too strongly about who they are or have been from a tribal or cultural point of view and are willing to pull together to define who they are going to become.

An irreversible cultural revolution is taking place in Africa inspired by the modernising effects of infrastructure and the move towards urban life.

Intermarriages across tribal boundaries

A strong desire for self-preservation and an irrepressible sense of jingoism among traditional African tribal communities meant that cross-ethnic marriage was not merely inconceivable – it was an abomination. The young married within the community and arranged marriages were common to ensure control of choice and background. In fact this practice still goes on in some African communities on a diminished scale.

Education and enlightenment, as discussed in depth in a previous section, have allowed the youth from different communities to interact. The search for employment opportunities or prospects, wherever they could be found, leads people to travel far from their homes to live and work among people from other communities. Rural-urban drift, which is mainly a youth affair, allows a high concentration of youth from diverse tribal backgrounds to interact at much higher frequency than before. They find that there is nothing fundamentally different about them and, besides, the instincts of youth and their new found freedom pull them together. Intermarriage is the inevitable consequence. This is in many cases not premeditated, but happens out of conveniences such as cost-sharing or out of unplanned childbirth resulting from casual sexual relationships. Of course, still a sizeable number of new marriages are begun through conscious decisions to tie-up a relationship after reasonable considerations.

The greatest and most long-term effect of this particular phenomenon is not that people finally breach tribal barriers and reach across imaginary divides but rather it is in the logical consequence of these actions – the offspring of cross-ethnic marriages. Children born into mixed marriages not only show signs of becoming a large demographic component of future Africa's population, they are already beginning to shape the future of Africa's people. In short, they are homogenising African societies.

Intermarriages such as I am discussing here did not begin recently. There are a handful of individuals from generations of 40 and 50-year-olds who are of mixed parentage. However, the speed of intermarriage has increased with the social and economic forces at play in modern Africa. It is difficult to put a definite figure on it, but intermarriages within African communities and across national boundaries have become more common. Children out of mixed marriage are no longer an irrelevant minority. In fact in urban Africa they are becoming the majority. And in keeping with the statistical projection that 50% of African population will be urban by 2050, this mixed-tribe population segment will be the clear majority all over Africa in the coming decades.

This demographic segment has no fealty to a tribal or ancestral lineage. They speak the national language or the emerging languages. They only subscribe to national or urban identities and sensibilities, as opposed to those of their parents' tribes. They are fairly enlightened, even though most are not very educated. They neither hope nor expect to inherit anything from their parents. They are socially and politically aware and lend themselves to activism and advocacy (of any nature, unhelpfully). They are the avant-garde, super liberal, eclectic of tastes and willing to try anything. What is more, they are the epitome of consumerism. Finally, as a growing mass in the African population, their power to influence others is enormous.

Conclusion/marketplace implications

Put together, all the forces discussed here point to a coalescing and homogenisation of ethnic societies into national societies, and national societies into regional societies, with scope for a future single continent-wide society. Some nations are a long way ahead of the others in this cultural revolution, but there is no mistaking the general trends and influences acting to create a confluence of cultures and lay down the foundations of a single future African culture.

By understanding the characteristics and dynamics of this evolution in African societies, we gain a clearer grasp of the tremendous cultural makeover happing in Africa and of the definitive implications of its consumer characteristics. Not only does it make possible vast single markets, it also homogenises consumer awareness and therefore tastes and preferences, and brings down the barriers to business communication.

REGIONALISATION: EVOLUTION OF INTRA-AFRICAN MARKETS

3

Background and perspective

For a long time African countries only traded with the West. The logic behind this was that the developed world should have ready solutions for all African problems and so trade routes followed the well-defined arteries of colonial relationships. Former British colonies traded more with Britain and amongst themselves, under the post-colonial outfit known as the Commonwealth. Former French colonies did likewise and co-operated under the French-Africa summit. Summits are held annually or biannually to refresh the relationships and for the former colonial masters to reaffirm their commitments to the former colonies while in actual fact confirming that the colonies are still faithful and not seeking succour elsewhere.

An umbrella outfit known as the Africa Caribbean and the Pacific (ACP) was established to integrate the trading and co-operation terms between the erstwhile colonies of the world on the one hand and their former imperial colonisers on the other. This second club of former imperial forces was later organised as the European Union. The ACP-EC partnership agreements were based on two core lopsided principles under the Lomé Conventions. Firstly, the ACP countries had privileged and tariff-free access to European markets for their primary, unprocessed commodities under a generalised system of preferences.[33] Secondly, steeply graduated and punitive tariff escalation was imposed for any level of value addition on these primary resources.[34] The unmistakable message here was to dissuade any attempts at industrialisation in the ACP countries.

Meanwhile, African countries hardly traded among each other. They looked at each other with scorn and mistrust,[35] each one generally not seeing the others as having anything to offer. They engaged in pseudo-ideological rivalry, skirmished about boundaries, squabbled about contraband crossing each other's borders, aided and abetted each other's guerrilla or secessionist movements, and sabotaged each other internationally.

The situation changed when the East opened up in a spurt of accelerated economic growth. The Cold War ended, culminating in the re-unification of Germany in 1990. A new global economic order came with new concepts of business process redesign, downsizing, rationalisation and growth-driven investments. The effect of this was that Africa was abandoned by the West as the world's collective focus was trained eastwards, whether to the Far East or Eastern Europe.

African countries, stranded, shorn of capital and ready markets abroad, were left wondering what to do next. It wasn't long before they [African states] realised that there was something economically meaningful they could do among themselves and intra-African markets became a reality. These markets are still in the formative stages but progress is being made.

Driving forces

Growth and expansion of manufacturing and service capacity

Industrial and manufacturing capacity constraints have long been the dominant issue in Africa's ability, or lack thereof, to supply itself. For as long as many can remember consumer products and edibles were processed and distributed only by Unilever and Colgate Palmolive, or their local subsidiaries. Take Unilever as an example. In east Africa, Unilever was for a long time known as East Africa Industries (EAI) and had only a single plant in Nairobi's industrial area serving the entire eastern, central and southern African hinterland including Kenya, Uganda, Tanzania, Rwanda, Burundi, DR Congo, and Somalia. In west Africa Unilever was present in Nigeria and Ghana as Lever Brothers Nigeria and Unilever Ghana respectively.

> **It wasn't long before African states realised that there was something economically meaningful they could do among themselves and intra-African markets became a reality.**

In eastern Africa, EAI for a long time remained the sole player in the edible oils, kitchen supplies and toiletries industry. The formal markets it catered to formed a very small portion of the total populations and even worse failed to grow with the population for a long time. Consequently, their installed capacity was too small for too long. Supply chains remained slow and product development was lethargic. Meeting the needs of the consumers in these markets remained a constant challenge. Delivery across boundaries was a lengthy process and replete with risks, and distribution networks were vastly underdeveloped.[36] For all of these reasons multinational corporations (MNCs) did not address more than 30% to 50% of local markets and as such informal economies in Sub-Saharan Africa continued to cater to 60% to 70% of the labour force.[37]

The majority of people chiefly depended on local abattoirs for animal fats, which they used for cooking and skin care. Most depended on bar soap or squeezing their clothes against rocks on the riversides to clean them. They used village-processed spices to season their foods and twigs for dental care.

> **❝ A great deal of capacity has been added to supply chains, research and products development, manufacturing and distribution. This has made possible common regional markets. ❞**

The MNCs did not see a market opportunity among these people. That was until local consumer product start-ups thought differently. Bidco Oil Refineries in Kenya, Mukwano in Uganda and Rivers Vegetable Company in Nigeria, for example, have, within a period of only 15 years, grown to surpass the local Unilever subsidiaries. Their combined installed manufacturing capacities more than met the current and steeply growing future demands of Africa's consumer markets. They have local roots and are nuanced in the dynamics of local markets, and what is more they have a wide range of products for every taste and preference, and packing quantities for every price range.[38]

These local suppliers have intensified competition, increased market penetration, accelerated product development, streamlined supply chains and heightened marketing activities so much that they have awoken the large MNCs like Unilever from their slumber.[39] In some African countries Sara Lee (the new parent of Colgate & Palmolive) and Reckitt Benckiser have sold out and exited; for example Sara Lee shut down in Malawi, Zambia and Mozambique, while Reckitt ceased manufacturing operations in Kenya in 2007. In others they have sold old brands to the new companies, who have infused new life into them. Bidco Oil Refineries took over Kimbo cooking fat, east Africa's long-renowned cooking fat brand from Unilever; and Elianto from CPC Kenya, a local subsidiary of Corn Products International, a United States food company. These two brands have since proved very popular with consumers.

Out of this contest to supply Africa's emerging consumer markets a great deal of capacity has been added to supply chains, research and products development, manufacturing and distribution. This has made possible common regional markets based on regionally integrated supply chains that depend on regional sourcing. The newly assembled capacity to produce was enough to meet regional demand and regional distribution franchises built under prevailing common markets conventions. Kenya now has more than ten edible oil companies, all built up after 1995.

Increase in local subsidiaries of MNCs

Most MNCs gave Africa a wide berth for a very long time. Some never even considered Africa for a minute; many never saw an addressable market, most focused too much on the problems to see the opportunities. The MNCs operating or having marketing arms in Africa from the 1960s into the 1980s could be counted on the fingers of both hands. And these, where they were present, were relics of colonialism, or merchants of imperial commerce. Besides that, nothing multinational, nothing global, was going on.

Things started to change in the 1990s when consumer markets in Africa began to exhibit signs of life and the rest of the world was less lively than it had been before. Latin America underwent what journalists have dubbed 'the lost decade' as military regimes enjoyed undeserved popularity. The Far East was coming off the boil as its economic growth lost momentum. Eastern Europe and central Asia were still changing rapidly from the convulsing events that led to the death of communism and were too close to western Europe to be considered exotic and alluring by MNCs.

Further, it was not just the West that had MNCs of its own anymore. The Far East, the Middle East and even south Asia had by the 1990s developed their own national and regional champions with the heft to venture abroad. They had put together enormous scale, durable brands and the cross-cultural skills to spread across the world and thrive.

So it was that, in a very short time period, MNCs descended into Africa. It is not necessary to mention all of them, but a few glowing examples are instructive. In mining and exploration the global colossuses make the roll call: BHP Billiton, Rio Tinto, Vale and Xstrata are all present. In banking and finance, the principals of global financial architecture are in attendance: Citigroup, HSBC, Goldman Sachs, Morgan Stanley and Merrill Lynch. In consumer electronics, Sony, Nokia, LG,

" Multinationals have established a long-term presence in regional offices from which they are serving the rest of Africa. **"**

Ericsson, Samsung and Philips are present. In ICT, Microsoft, HP, Google, IBM, Lenovo, Alcatel-Lucent, Siemens, Huawei, and ZTE came too. In pharmaceuticals, Pfizer, Merck, Bristol-Myers Squibb, Hoffmann-La Roche, GlaxoSmithKline, Sanofi-aventis, Novartis, Schering-Plough and Abbott Laboratories tugged along.

These multinationals have established a long-term presence in regional offices from which they are serving the rest of Africa, usually in Nairobi for the eastern and central African region, and either Lagos or Accra for the western African region. Johannesburg doubles as home for offices serving southern Africa, and sometimes for the whole of Africa for corporations which have yet to venture further inside Sub-Saharan Africa.

Increased transport and logistical network interconnection improving distribution

In 1960s Africa, it is not much of an exaggeration to say that the only networks crossing national boundaries were rivers. Transport and logistical interconnectivity very often did not go much beyond cattle tracks, animal trails and poachers' beats. There was nowhere to go and little to carry across.

Colonial governments had not bothered to interconnect African nations. In fact, in some they had not even connected the country with itself. In Mozambique for example, tarmac roads hardly left urban centres on the Indian ocean coast; 50km outside of Maputo there was very little infrastructure.[40] The exception was, of course, adjacent countries where the colonial presence was by the same power. In this case a railway might be considered, as it was with the East African railways (for many years known as the Uganda Railway). The British who ruled Kenya and Uganda wanted to connect Uganda with the coast at Mombasa and therefore built the railway that cut across Kenya. It was used to transport Uganda's copper from the Kasese mines.[41]

Slowly, infrastructure started springing up in a disconnected manner. The common thread that pieced together Africa's earlier inter-country connectivity was mining or soft commodities. The TAZARA Railway that connected Tanzania with Zambia

❝ In 1960s Africa, it is not much of an exaggeration to say that the only networks crossing national boundaries were rivers. ❞

in the 1970s was built essentially to deliver Zambian copper from the Ndola copper belt to the port of Dar es Salaam for onward shipment to export markets abroad. This provided an alternative route to the Mozambican seaports that went through the hostile white-supremacist controlled Rhodesia (present day Zimbabwe).[42] The Malawi rail connection which terminates in the port of Nacala, Mozambique, was used to deliver Malawi's sugar, tobacco and tea to European export markets.

When independent African governments took over, often by violent means, they were too embroiled in understanding the concept of nationhood and modern systems of governance – and therefore their own internal components – to give much consideration to cross-border relations. Inter-country trade, the very need for connectivity, had to wait a little longer. Countries which were gripped by civil wars saw the most devastating impact on infrastructure. For example, at the end of the civil war in Chad in 1987, the country only had 30km of tarmac road (this had been rebuilt to 550km by 2004).[43] These countries gradually came to their senses though and minimal trade flows began crossing borders. Countries which were left with excess manufacturing capacity or which quickly embraced capitalism found that they had something that the neighbours did not and therein lay the genesis of modern Africa's inter-country trade.

The greatest impediment was the utter absence of transport infrastructure. So in the 1970s and 1980s border posts were established, road links constructed and inland customs services introduced between African countries. But the greatest efforts to interconnect African countries gained traction only fairly recently in the mid-1980s and early 1990s when regional trading blocs had become fashionable. Examples of these blocs are: Economic Community of West African States (ECOWAS) in West Africa; East African Community (EAC) for Eastern Africa; Common Market for East and Southern Africa (COMESA) in east, central and southern Africa; Economic Community of Central Africa States (ECCAS) in Central Africa; and Southern Africa Development Community (SADC) in southern Africa and the Indian ocean islands.

It is a sort of chicken and egg situation. Creation of regional trading blocs has given intra-African trade a great boost. But this would never have been possible without some sense of dependable and reliable inter-country connectivity. This delicate interdependence has catalysed rapid transport infrastructural development in the continent of Africa, which has in turn deepened the capacity of internal markets through increased velocity of intra-African trade.

Increased communication capabilities

Difficult as it is to imagine, the entire republic of Kenya, with a population of around 30m people, had only about 300,000 fixed telephone lines as recently as the year 2000.[44] The central-southern African nation of Malawi had a total of only 41,000 telephone lines at the same time.[45] As of 2000, 38 out of 54 countries in Africa had less than 250,000 fixed telephone lines each. Only Algeria, Egypt, Morocco and South Africa had more than 1m fixed lines each.[46] A big majority of these were in government offices and foreign missions.

To make the communication situation even worse, finding a dial-tone on your handset was not guaranteed and completing a five-minute telephone call without cross-airs or intermittent call drops was a stroke of good luck. National telecom incumbents did not invest in sustaining the capacity that was in place or increasing the capacity for the future. Given the operators' yearly roll out figures of new connections, queues of those waiting for connection would take decades to service. As if all that inconvenience and incompetence was not enough, the operators charged some of the highest calling rates in the world.

These telecom companies were all owned and operated by governments, which never saw them as communication service providers but as bureaucracies to be sustained for the protection of public employment and for preservation of systems of corruption. To this effect, therefore, these corporations were forced to employ 10 to 15 times more people than they needed. The idea that there should be investment in automated systems that would make workflow efficient and people redundant was anathema. Telkom Kenya had a staff of 19,800 in 2000;[47] that is a meagre 15 lines per employee against a global standard of 651 per employee.[48] Before acquisition by France Telkom in 2007 it had 17,300 staff, a number which has now been rationalised to about 2,200[49] in a record three years, improving the ratio of lines per employee to 136.

That is just one part of the story. The other part is even more horrifying. This had to do with inter-country telecommunications, which were non-existent. For the better part of the past three decades, placing a call from one African country to another was just not possible. The reason was that African countries did not own communication satellites of their own and there was no satellite capacity in the rest of the world to be dedicated to African countries. There was just not enough commercial satellite capacity in the world and where there was it was way too expensive for the telecom companies of Africa to afford.

Later, calling across international boundaries became possible by a complicated system of call carriage, transfers and termination that would involve at least four or five carriers or network operators. For example, anyone calling Kinshasa, in DR Congo, from Nairobi, Kenya, some 2,400km apart, had to dial into Telkom Kenya, which would deliver the call to a satellite orbiting somewhere above the Mediterranean, which would pass it on to another orbiting above Belgium, which in turn delivered to the local fixed line operator in Brussels which bounced it off yet another satellite orbiting above the Atlantic, which pushed it to the international exchange in Kinshasa, which then routed it to The Office Congolais des Postes et des Télécommunications (OCPT) and which finally terminated the call on the local telephone number dialled in Kinshasa. Such a relay trip made phone calls very expensive and the poor quality of the line made conversation nearly impossible.

In summary, the absolute absence of telecommunication connections and capacity between African nations made it nigh on impossible to transact business and execute trade between them. To do international business it was necessary to physically travel to the other country, which was impractical and time-consuming because of the lack of inter-country transport systems.

Improvements since 2000

Fast forward to the last ten years; in this decade there has been a telecommunication revolution in Africa. It all began with the liberalisation of the telecoms sectors, which led to an expedited privatisation of government-owned telecom operators, then the introduction of privately-owned and operated second national operators.

The real impetus then came from mobile phone penetration across Africa. What telecom operators were unable to achieve in 40 years of operational monopoly, GSM mobile phone operators achieved and surpassed in only a decade. Kenya has moved from only 300,000 telephone lines in 2000 to 21m in 2010,[50] 97% of the difference being mobile phone connectivity. In 2000

Nigeria only had about 500,000 main lines,[51] but in ten years this has become just over 100m connected lines, according to statistics from the Nigeria Communication Commission. Sub-Saharan Africa is now estimated to be at 50% telecommunications penetration, with more than 90% of that from mobile telephony.[52]

The main advantage came from the fact that the mobile operators were being introduced into already liberalised sectors where competition was encouraged. The unmet, pent-up demand from decades of under-investment by the telecom firms supplied the massive initial lift-off that these operators needed, and the momentum was sustained by the highly innovative, private sector models of telecoms systems and market penetration that were executed.

Mobile phone operators have taken it even further by enabling seamless on-net call transfers across the continent at local call rates, such as Airtel's first in the world transcontinental system, *one network*, which is now fully operational in all 16 African countries where it is present. Those without cross-border networks are co-operating with players in other countries to enable seamless call transfers at the cost of local calls. Fixed-line telecom operators have also modernised their networks and most have now moved from analogue to digital systems.

Meanwhile, international submarine fibre-optic capacity has been expanded and costs have come down drastically – the whole of Africa is now fully ringed by fibre-optic cables with multiple landings. The necessary terrestrial extensions into the continent have advanced substantially. Only a few landlocked countries are not currently connected to an international fibre-optic cable at a coastal landing nearest to it.

The role of the internet also cannot be over-emphasised; email, interactive corporate and business websites and Voice over Internet Protocol (VoIP) have introduced a new dimension of business communication and interaction in Africa. E-commerce is slowly becoming a reality.

Global telecommunication advances and the adoption of these in African countries played a significant role in making intra-Africa trading and the evolution of Africa's regional markets possible. There may be no recent statistics on the increase of cross-border calls made between African countries, but the systematic dismantling of barriers to communication has paved the way for possibly the fastest expansion of use in the history of telecommunications.

Currency exchangeability enabling reliable and transparent pricing

Before the 1990s and apart from the 14 west African countries (12 former French colonies, one former Portuguese and one former Spanish colony) which use a common currency (the CFA), all other African countries maintained insular local currencies and strict exchange controls regimes. Trade between countries was thus hampered by inward-looking exchange policies which prohibited translation of local currencies into any foreign currency.

Efforts to correct this were attempted in the 1980s by establishing regional trading and development banks and monetary unions which either had their own units of accounting or managed exchange rates between local currencies. The Rand Monetary Area of 1974 between South Africa, Namibia, Botswana, Lesotho and Swaziland came into being initially to circulate the rand in other member countries, and later yielded ground to the Common Monetary Area of Southern Africa in 1986 largely to establish a fixed exchange rate between member countries.[53]

The PTA Bank (COMESA regional trade and development bank) established in 1985 was founded essentially with trade facilitation and trade finance high up on its charter. The COMESA (Common Market for Eastern and Southern Africa) clearing house was established in 1984 and to ease the financing of trade among the 23 east and southern African countries in an environment of limited foreign currency, a regional unit of account – the PTA Unit of Account – was introduced with the PTA bank as the issuing treasury; distribution and monetary management support came from the central banks of member states. Nations were encouraged to trade in this quasi-currency as it was made fungible in all member states and therefore currency exchanges and the losses therein would be eliminated. The PTA Unit of Account died a natural death and was replaced by the COMESA dollar.

Much more trade is happening among African countries in their own currencies. This positive evolution has gone a long way to nurturing regional trade and deepening regional markets.

The 16 nations of francophone west Africa have made huge strides and developed their regional markets, and the CFA franc has stabilised as an internationally recognised regional currency akin to the euro. The rest of African countries took measures to float their exchange rates. It was not until exchange controls were repealed, and currencies allowed to freely float against all world currencies in the wake of structural adjustment programmes of the late 1980s and early 1990s, that mild acceptance of local currencies for intra-country trades began to emerge. Inter-currency exchange rates began to be tracked and observed more, until sufficiently reliable track records were available. Now, much more trade is happening among African countries in their own currencies. This positive evolution has gone a long way to nurturing regional trade and deepening regional markets.

Conclusion/marketplace implications

Figure 3.1 – increase of cross-border trade between countries of Sub-Saharan Africa, by imports ($m)

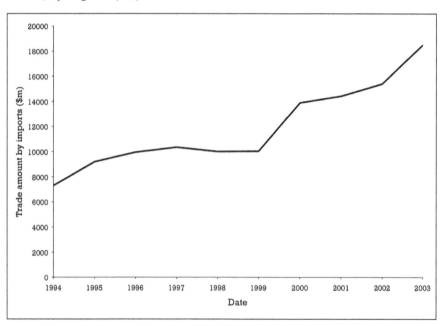

Source: Compendium of Intra-Africa and Related Foreign Trade Statistics – ECA, 2005

As more African economies pull down the barriers to trade and distribution, more and more opportunities are opening up for intra-African trade. As can be observed in the graph above, intra-Africa trade experienced a quantum leap between 1999 and 2003 and sustained a steeper rise thereafter, a period characterised by exchange liberalisation and flotation of currencies.

Since then African trade has grown in leaps and bounds, gaining fresh momentum with each major regional or global economic event that revealed further structural weakness in Africa's dependence on overseas markets. Economies are opening up, demand is rising for manufactured and processed products, the variety of products and services traded is growing, and the amount and speed of cross-border trading is rising quickly. A deep, viable, interconnected and interdependent domestic market is emerging in Sub-Saharan Africa – revealing demand to be met, deficiencies to be satisfied and virgin hinterland to be developed.

RAPID URBANISATION

4

Background and perspective

Africa is urbanising rapidly and is expected to become predominantly urban by 2020. Its urban population increased from 15% of the total in 1960 to 35% in 2006, and is projected to hit nearly 60% by 2020. The rate of urbanisation is now estimated at around 4% annually, the highest rate anywhere in the world. Rural migration accounts for 25% of this, with the balance coming from urban demographic growth and administrative reclassification of rural areas into urban areas.[54]

The story of rural-urban drift is as old as colonialism in Africa. Many young Africans or entire families have been lured to the bright lights of the urban centres over the years. For a long time, the forward march to urban areas has posed a major challenge for urban planning by African governments. The flow of people into towns and cities overwhelms existing infrastructure and efforts to stem the tide of new inflows are often in vain. Calls for people to return to the countryside and till the land go unheeded, mainly because they are not backed by compelling incentives that would give such moves the comfort of compensation.

Governments have traditionally concentrated on developing urban areas only, leaving rural areas to their own devices. New electricity connections happened in urban areas; new road building took place in urban centres and only traversed rural

“ Africa's urban population increased from 15% of the total in 1960 to 35% in 2006, and is projected to hit nearly 60% by 2020. ”

areas when connecting major urban nodes. In fact, in Kenya there was a national economic policy that restricted economic development to only an area of 50km radius from the Kenya to Uganda railway line. This policy created a ribbon of development cutting across the country from the south-east coast to the western border, along which about 90% of the nation's development was to be concentrated, consequently becoming a magnet for population. Looking at the Kenyan population distribution map reveals that more than 50% of Kenya's population lives in this ribbon.

In the most recent two decades another kind of urbanisation has taken place; rather than the traditional urban areas continuing to pull people away, rural areas themselves are urbanising. Under IMF-inspired national Poverty Reduction Strategy Papers (PRSPs), thinking has opened up towards economic stabilisation strategies where areas of low development would be assisted to come to parity with the relatively advanced areas; national economic policies have been revised and rural areas have been incorporated into plans for national development. Funds were therefore devolved from the centre and sent to the peripheries where local committees would prioritise development agendas based on the criteria of urgency, extent of impact on livelihoods, breadth of geographical effect and, of course, availability of funds.

As a result, public services are finally, though still intermittently, beginning to arrive in rural Africa. Other agents of development like schools, medical centres and agricultural produce collection points have also aided development as they have created networks for social and economic interdependence, which have necessitated the extension of the basic essentials and enablers of economic development: water, electricity and state security.

The rate of urbanisation in Africa currently exceeds that in Asia – at 4% it is the highest in the world. Another interesting way to measure the trend is to look at the reducing distance between urban centres. In west Africa, for example, the average distance between agglomerations has fallen from 111km to 33km in 50 years (from 1960).[55]

Driving forces

Pursuit of employment opportunities in urban areas

All over Africa there is an annual ritual of migrating youth. Finished with education and in search of jobs, they arrive full of energy and confident of the life and prospects that lie ahead of them in the urban centres.

The stream of people heading to the towns and cities is seemingly undeterred by the accounts of disillusionment and hopelessness given by their forerunners. They refuse to be put down by the statistics of unemployment. In residential zones, they add to the already overburdened demand for services: water, electricity and security, but this does not deter them either.

❝ In west Africa, the average distance between agglomerations has fallen from 111km to 33km in 50 years. ❞

These migrators then become urbanised themselves. They get into the groove of urban life, develop urban tastes in movies, discos, parties and theatre. They evolve an appetite for urban cuisines and recipes. Within a short time period, they get so absorbed in the tempo of urban life that they become hooked. So, whether or not someone gets a decent job, going back home is not normally an option that is considered – youth migration to the urban centres in Africa is a one way journey, there is normally no return made.

Pursuit of urban utilities

At independence in the 1960s African countries only had some basic water collection, retention and pumping capacity to service urban centres. Electricity generation capacity was even worse. Kenya in 1963 only had two power plants with a combined generation capacity of 21.8 MW, before Kindaruma hydroelectric power station was commissioned four years later with 44 MW capacity.[56] In Mozambique, even though the 2,000 MW Cahora Bassa hydropower plant was completed a year before independence, only 150 MW was to be retained in the country, as the rest was transmitted to the energy intensive Gauteng industrial belt of South Africa.[57] Before 1968 when the first Kainji Dam was commissioned, Nigeria never had any serious source of electric power.[58] The pattern is clear; power plants had been built by the colonial governments to cater only to the part of the population in urban centres.

Therefore, in the 1960s the newly-installed majority-rule governments found themselves with a development conundrum. Independence made everybody equal and suddenly governments were now obliged to provide piped water and electric power connections to the length and breadth of their countries. The development of this infrastructure was constrained by corruption, warped economic development policies and priorities, absence of domestic savings and a lack of interest from major foreign investors in Africa (until the 2000s). Therefore a large part of the populations of these African countries were denied the basic essentials of life.

By 2010, roughly 23%[59] of Sub-Saharan Africa was electrified, but it should be considered that these figures are distorted by South Africa, with an electrification rate of 70%.[60] Even where electric power has reached, the cost of connection has remained prohibitively high. Many rural communities are still cut off from the power supply that prioritises urban centres, mining or industrial concerns or the rural homes of powerful government officials.

Development is concentrated in urban centres where it is a lot easier to get connected to an existing water system, sewerage system and power distribution network. In urban areas, 43% of households have connections to piped water and 18% have sewerage connections.[61] This is in contrast to rural areas, where figures are much lower.

These factors have pulled many families from rural areas to urban centres in pursuit of a better quality of life; the pursuit of basic services has been a major force for the urban drift of erstwhile rural populations.

Commercial engagements lead to clustering in the search for markets

Besides school-leavers who go to urban centres in search of employment, there is another sizeable group of African people making their way to urban centres for a different reason altogether – commerce. A spirit of enterprise and entrepreneurialism is taking root in Africa. Many people are realising the transformational power of trade and are engaging in business activities. Barriers to common trade between any two people anywhere in Africa have been reduced drastically.

" Commerce is unmatched as the largest employer of African youth so far and is a great force for urbanisation of the youth population. "

Historically, producers and manufacturers pushed their products only through appointed stockists and distributors who served expansive geographies from single locations. Today distribution has become fairly liberalised and wholesalers have proliferated to rival even retail shops in numbers. Another factor is that previously manufacturers only delivered products by their own trucks and stocks could run out for weeks in one part of a country because of logistical constraints. Transportation has steadily been liberalised such that manufacturers can now contract any number of transporters to deliver their products simultaneously. Wholesalers have invested in trucks of their own which give them the flexibility to pick deliveries at their own convenience.

The last factor in this supply chain makeover is at the retail front. Retailers used to register with stockists and had fixed quotas of products they could pick in a week. New retailers had to do the rounds among all stockists of products they desired to deal in, seeking permission to do so. This arrangement made stockists powerful and created opportunities for corruption. The modern wholesalers sell to virtually anybody with cash at hand. They have hugely cut down on wholesaling quantities to enhance sales and they even dabble in retailing themselves. Now, not only are retailers numerous and widespread, but retailing has itself been taken to the road by hawkers. The principle of taking the market to the consumer, rather than waiting for the consumer to come to the product, seems to be catching on.

Hawking requires no premises, it requires no trading licenses and it is not practical to subject it to tax. It delivers wares anywhere and everywhere at knock-down prices that are impossible to compete with. It is a challenge to find statistics on hawking market share in Africa's commercial centres due to its illegality, but it has become a force to reckon with in retailing and merchandising.

For all these reasons it has become much easier to engage in commercial activities: licenses, space and capital are not the same barriers that they used to be. Commerce is unmatched as the largest employer of African youth so far and is a great force for urbanisation of the youth population.

Landlessness encouraging movement to settlements and slums

Before colonial rule in Africa, the concept of individual land ownership was alien; people owned and used land communally. Then settlers came and farmed the land, demarcated boundaries, displaced natives, issued title deeds to themselves and enacted trespass laws. In a matter of very few years a revolution in land affairs had taken place in Africa. The native people had been dispossessed; in rich agricultural countries like Kenya, Zimbabwe, Uganda, and Ghana large chunks of the land had been taken over by the settlers. For example in Zimbabwe almost 70% of the arable land was in the hands of the settler community at independence.[62]

The people had been put in settlement schemes where each household was issued an odd lot of garden to farm. Most ran away into urban centres to look for employment in settlers' shops or in their kitchens. Others became squatters in the vast settlers' farming plantations where they proffered human labour in return for garden strips to farm on their own account. Dense human concentration had begun, and with it landlessness.

This state of affairs became the rallying call for most of the independence movements – it galvanised the people to agitate for land and independence in the 1950s and 1960s. The people thought that if they fought for independence, they would get the land back, but that did not happen. All over Africa independence pacts were sealed between exiting settler administrations and incoming indigenous administrations – the settlers who chose to remain would be left unharmed and even protected, and the ones who left would sell the large tracts of land to powerful individuals in the new administrations. Those who had fought for independence through a variety of means, sometimes risking their lives, quite often ended up with no land for themselves afterwards. They had officially been banished to permanent landlessness.[63]

These people unfortunately have continued to live in settlement schemes where nobody has a title deed. The schemes have grown over the years into congested slums. Whether in the big cities or in smaller towns they are without the trappings of development; they are highly congested and crime infested, with poor sanitation. These areas are hugely combustible socially and politically.

The large number of people all over Africa who live in the slums only becomes apparent during elections or in national census exercises. The slum urban population is big, it is growing and it forms an integral part of the African urban market base.

Rapid urbanisation of rural Africa

Though for a long time little seemed to be happening on the development front in most of Africa, there have been good signs all around that some progress is at last being made. Out of the realisation that no country can fully develop and operate at optimal productivity levels without employing all its people and its resources wherever they may be found, African governments have lately been warming up to the proposition of rural development.

Rural development programmes have been started in all infrastructural and developmental ministries of government. In Kenya there is now a rural electrification programme under the Ministry of Energy, charged with electrifying rural Kenya. In the early 2000s, a rural roads board was established under the Ministry of Roads dedicated to oversee the development and management of an all-weather modern roads network within rural Kenya. A ministry of Northern Kenya and Arid Lands has been established by the government of Kenya to give special and top-level governmental focus to the marginal regions and wastelands of the country.

> **❝ In the rural trading centres that have been connected to power and water already urban tendencies are beginning to be displayed. ❞**

Though a very long way in coming before a tipping point could be reached, isolated sections of rural Africa are beginning to see the light, literally. Piped water or borehole water is arriving with common areas like schools, dispensaries, and communal water points connected as a priority; and local trading centres too. Homes are also increasingly being wired up electrically.

In the rural trading centres that have been connected to power and water already urban tendencies are beginning to be displayed. Cottage industries are springing up, such as local bakeries, fast food joints, etc. Urban-style entertainment is also making its way to rural areas. Cinemas and music venues are popular.

Urbanisation of the minds, tastes, preferences and thinking of the rural folk is the ultimate effect of these trends.

Industrial and residential conurbations leading to sprawl of metropolises

The few African cities are very large for their countries' sizes. They are populous and boast a disproportionate concentration of industrial capacity. The majority of them were never planned as commercial centres or capital cities; they just emerged as accidents of development. Nairobi, for example, was an ordinary railway station. It just happened to find itself on the foot of the eastern rift-valley escarpment. So the railway engineers had to stop over longer, to re-engineer the course, mobilise resources and draft sufficient personnel to tackle the herculean lift and elevation of the terrain ahead of them.[64] They built stores, offices and engineering yards. People moved to the settlement in search of employment and it gradually developed into the city it is today.

The fact is that most early African cities were accidental (later cities like Lilongwe in Malawi and Abuja in Nigeria are exceptions); not enough planning went into them and not enough land was set aside for the future expansion needs. A slight spurt in economic growth and they filled up, bursting at the seams and gasping for space. Unplanned, yet unstopped, they have gone ahead to eat up the neighbouring lands be they agricultural, designated forests or protected wetlands. They have sprawled far and wide, irregular in form.[65]

Rural areas neighbouring these cities have had to urbanise quickly. Land values skyrocket, enticing landowners to cash in, and congestion occurs as more people come to the area. Some die-hard farmers and livestock keepers liquidate and move far away from the swelling metropolises, but these are the anomaly; most agriculturalists embrace the urban lifestyle. Thus the lives of those who remain change forever. They are joined by countless millions of others from all over the country chasing escalating land values, consumer markets and jobs in the sudden concrete-isation of previously rural spaces.

For example, in countries where multiple urban sprawl has been happening even just for up to four major metropolises, the combined effect of urbanisation of hitherto rural lands and populations has been of epic magnitude. Again, it is the urbanisation of the tastes, preferences, and opinions of all these peoples that has long-term economic implications going forward.

Mineral discoveries and establishment of industrial capacity

Wherever there is a mine in rural Africa, urbanisation sets in as a commercial and logistical necessity. As mining is one of the major economic activities in Africa, it is a dominant force in the rapid urbanisation of the continent. Large cities like Kimberley in South Africa; Kasese in Uganda; Dodoma in Tanzania; Lubumbashi and Goma in DR Congo; Huambo in Angola; Ndola in Zambia; Tongo in Sierra Leone; and Obuasi in Ghana owe their origins to mining.[66]

People move to the location of mines in large numbers in search of employment. Traders follow them in search of buyers; eateries and restaurants in search of customers; real estate developers in search of tenants; academic institutions in search of students; health facilities in search of patients; and bars and entertainment providers in search of hedonists. That completes the cycle of urbanisation of erstwhile empty, rural spaces of Africa.

It takes an average of 15 to 20 years from commencement of production of a mine in a location before the site has full urban status.

The global commodities boom of the past decade played out more on the continent of Africa than any other global economic event or cycle. This is because Africa is unarguably the world's home of primary hard commodities. Exploration projects stretched far and wide; every single section of Africa, onshore and offshore, had been turned into an exploration block. Exploration rights were sold, issued, or gifted to anyone who could bring a rig, a geologist and some hard currency. Luckily some promising new and large discoveries were made, adding to the wealth of proven untapped reserves already beneath the surface of Africa.

Extraction capacity has been or is being brought to these new mining sites, and a new cycle of urbanisation on the back of mining advances is evidently underway. Brand new mining towns are springing up in new places: in south Sudan, in north-western Uganda, in Angola, in DR Congo, in northern Tanzania, in Madagascar, in Sierra Leone and many other countries. Semi-industrial processing capacity is following these new finds in the model of global mining business.

Modern land tenure systems in rural Africa leading to uneconomic land holdings

I have tackled population explosion in Africa extensively in an earlier section and drilled down to the very driving forces that have catapulted it to the level of a megatrend. I mentioned earlier that these megatrends are sometimes overlapping and can be re-enforcing of each other, that one can become a driving force of another. The relationship between runaway population growth and urbanisation is a classic case.

The fast population increase in rural Africa is taking a huge toll on the land and is increasingly redefining land use. Changes in land tenure, ownership systems and mode of settlements (from African homesteads to

" Modern land tenure systems have ushered in individual land ownership and use. The large village system was given up for individual family homes and quickly more real estate was used up for settlement. "

modern family houses) compound the situation. Before, African families lived in communal settlements, one of which could carry anywhere between five to ten families. This helped maximise on the real estate allocated to habitation and left large tracts of land available to gainful economic use, be it livestock grazing or agriculture. The system always also left room for expansion or land reserves for fallback, in the event of uncertainties like rain failure or wild fires.

Modern land tenure systems have ushered in individual land ownership and use. The large village system was given up for individual family homes and quickly more real estate was used up for settlement. The countryside was suddenly dotted with shining corrugated iron sheets making roofs of endless new settlements.

Two new generations of people have matured to adulthood since independence and have since moved on to have homes of their own. Land subdivision has gone to the absolute indivisible in central Kenya and the Kisii highlands of Kenya, in central and western Uganda, the whole of Rwanda, the whole of Burundi, the Gambia and large parts of Nigeria. Mauritius not only has the highest population density, but doubly posts the highest rate of urbanisation in African currently.

In Burundi, though the country is still largely rural with only 10% urbanisation, the pressure of congestion on land has forced the second highest rate of urbanisation in Sub-Saharan Africa. Acreage in these parts is down to between one-quarter or one-half of an acre, almost the size of urban commercial plots. The dwelling takes half of it and the rest is hardly enough for a kitchen garden. It is just not possible to sustain even subsistence agriculture under such acreage, let alone industrial or commercial agriculture.

Table 4.1 shows the population density and urbanisation of five African countries. From the data we not only observe a significant level and a fairly well distributed pattern of current urbanisation, but, importantly, a high rate of continuing urbanisation.

Table 4.1 – population density and urbanisation of African countries

Country	Population density (persons/sq km)	Level of urbanisation (%)	Rate of urbanisation (%)
Mauritius	588	42	9
Rwanda	281	18	4
Burundi	229	10	7
Nigeria	141	48	4
Gambia	129	57	4

Population density information from **www.fact-index.com** and urbanisation statistics from Afribiz (**www.afribiz.info**)

The density of settlements is urbanising rural Africa, rendering extensive agriculture untenable and forcing people to reach out to commercial activities to make ends meet. There is now a *small shop* in almost every other homestead and baking activities in the next alternate homestead. Trading in raw milk also takes place.

Rural Africa is quickly opening up to the cash economy and urban tendencies are finding acceptance. Rural slums are emerging, unfortunately with the character, shape and form of urban slums. Being united to the land is what preserves the traditional character of rural Africa. Landlessness is chronic now and getting worse, with the result that large numbers of people in rural Africa have no choice but to embrace urbanisation with all the transformations of tastes, thinking and opinions this involves.

Conclusion/marketplace implications

Examinations of the world economy reveal that urbanisation has a direct correlation with a country's or region's economic growth.[67] The most prominent sign of urbanisation is the rapid and sustained growth in GDP – a key indicator of economic strength. Urbanisation levels are another indicator of a country's or region's industrialisation status – since industrialisation, which is closely associated with economies of scale, is easier to realise in cities. In addition, as the urban market grows, tertiary industry steadily becomes the most important component of the urban economy.

Expanded domestic demand is another impact of urbanisation. Urban households consume at a much higher level than rural households. For example, in 2000, the urban population accounted for 36% of China's total population, but its consumption accounted for almost 55%.

Given the purchasing power of the urban market and the increasing urbanisation levels in Africa, it is manifest that the urban consumer will continue to be the key driver of consumption in Africa. Concentrated settlement (as opposed to dispersed settlement) also makes distribution easier and faster, improving the economics and viability of a wide spectrum of consumer enterprise.

COMMERCIALISATION OF ESSENTIAL SERVICES

5

Background and perspective

Since modern systems of government were installed in Africa, public infrastructure development has been the paramount responsibility of government. That is why they are granted licence under the laws and the constitutions to tax and levy charges on people and businesses. Politicians use development as a constant, albeit sometimes empty, campaign slogan. It forms the basis for every political party manifesto and theme for every campaign rally. It is what African people have awaited for years. Yet tangible development remained insubstantial and elusive for most of the last half century, until barely a decade ago.

In the 1960s and early 1970s, African economies seemed to be doing better in relative terms. Their hard and soft commodities fetched good prices in the export markets; major imports were very much less costly, while their external borrowings were modest.[68] Their populations were also a lot smaller than in later decades and, most importantly, the politicians were less corrupt than those who came after them.

Then 1973 and 1979 brought about the first and second oil embargoes – these external economic events shook African economies to the core.[69] Oil prices rose more than seven times in the first embargo triggered by the Arab-Israeli Yom Kippur war of 1973[70] and almost tripled in the second one occasioned by the Iran crisis of 1979.[71] On both occasions fragile African economies recoiled with a whimper.

Meanwhile, civil wars and social strife that enveloped most of Africa in the 1970s and 1980s thoroughly curtailed the extraction of hard commodities and transportation of these to overseas export markets, sending export earnings into a free fall. Simultaneously, there were global food and soft commodities gluts occasioned by an oversupply from non-traditional sources such as Brazil, Columbia and Vietnam,[72] worsening the terms of trade of African economies. The mandatory devaluation of African currencies through the foreign exchange markets (FEM) as a requirement of the sweeping structural adjustment programmes (SAP) of the 1980s was particularly hard on African currencies. Re-pricing to the dollar had the adverse effects of wiping out national foreign currency reserves, bringing down massive deterioration in African terms of trade and touching off hyperinflation.[73]

Throughout the 1980s and 1990s for most countries, public investments in infrastructure, security and human resources development had gone into reverse. Practically half of all African states were either under military rule or the stranglehold of totalitarian regimes for which power was all about the promotion and preservation of the enterprise of control and exploitation through systems of exclusion. Under mildly democratic and open societies, governments were hamstrung by factors highlighted above.

Driving forces

I have divided this section into two parts:

1. The major factors that led to the failure of government to provide or extend essential public services. These are both structural and negative.

2. The responses of civil society and the private sector to the failures of government. These were either homegrown alternatives or entrepreneurial endeavour.

1. Factors that led to governments' development failures

Woefully inadequate national budgets

Few Sub-Saharan Africa countries make the equivalent of the earnings of Fortune 500 global industrial companies in annual GDP[74] with the result that tax revenues across Africa are low. Research estimates put the size of the African informal economy at 42% of the total economy in terms of GNP,[75] while informal employment in non-farm activities engages 72% of the workforce.[76] The informal economy is opaque, diverse and vibrant. It operates outside of the banking system and of the tax nets. National tax authorities can reach and target the formal economy, which they tax at a high rate, possibly to make up for the lack of tax income from the informal sector they cannot reach.

Systems of taxation are then still too inefficient and costly. In some countries it costs up to 4% to 7% of the total tax revenue to collect and book it.[77] That means that only about 93% to 96% of tax revenue actually gets to the national coffers. Due to the porosity of IT systems that are in place or total lack of such systems in some cases, and collusions with tax administrators, still more of the tax revenue disappears into the pockets of individuals charged with collecting it. Because of the limitations of the money economy, taxation regimes are too punitive and too concentrated on a very small proportion of the economy. This tends to encourage tax evasion and corruption at the major tax capture points like customs, retail shops and government offices.

The seasonality of the major economic activities in African countries, namely agriculture which thrives during wet seasons and mining which thrives during dry periods, means that tax revenues are not consistent all year round. In fact agriculture-dependent economies experience the widest swings in their revenue collections according to the vagaries of weather and other incidentals.

Most of the major players in agriculture (Unilever Tea, Del Monte), mining (BHP Billiton, Rio Tinto) and tourism (Kuoni, Thomas Cook) in African economies are foreign investors or companies with overseas links, who as an inducement to invest in the continent got disproportionately generous waivers on repatriation of export proceeds. These lopsided arrangements, endemic in almost every African economy, end up denying them badly needed tax revenues.

In harsh economic times, African economies do not have capacity for fiscal stimulus. Of course when businesses go bad and people lose their jobs in large numbers, revenue from income tax falls further.

Bloated bureaucracies take a large share of budgets

The most tragic thing about African economies was not that they delivered low tax revenues, but that a large proportion of the revenues was consumed by the operations of government. The size of government and its offices did not have any relation to public finances available or the need for public services; government was too large and run too expensively for the budget available.

For example, government offices were fitted with simple computers, furniture and wall hangings at prices anywhere between 10 and 20 times the normal commercial rates, while the quality of the computers and other IT devices was poor. High-consumption vehicles and sleek limousines could be seen in parking lots of government office blocks – these vehicles would make up the convoys snaking around African cities and the countryside, with an intention to instil awe and intimidate those who saw them.

Expenditure on seminars, workshops and conferences was another way tax revenue was used – posters in hotel lobbies advertised numerous seminars for ministries and government departments, apparently on every day of the week. These meetings hogged conference facilities and filled up hotel rooms. In fact, some African capitals and coastal resort towns, complete with 300-500 room five-star hotels, have been put to use for government meetings full-time.

Functional corruption rendered development budgets ineffective

In a large number of Sub-Saharan African countries, development spending had been fully funded by foreign aid, where in most cases tax revenue was not even enough to meet governments' recurrent (operational) expenditures, for example Uganda, Tanzania, Rwanda, Burundi, Sierra Leone, Liberia, DR Congo, Mozambique and Cameroon. On average more than 80% of the total national budgets of Sub-Saharan African countries are dependent on external sources.[78] The entire development budget and a big slice of the recurrent (consumption) budget were financed this way. The most fashionable name for donors in Africa is *development partners*. They provide finance from pre-feasibility studies, to consultancies, to implementation, to operational assistance and handover.

Governments incorporate these finances in national budgets and proceed to take disbursements in instalments until the allocations have been fully spent. In keeping with the demands for local capacity building and the governments' developmental accountability to the people, these budgets are administered by ministries of governments. The ministries have been models in opacity and inefficiency.

According to the World Bank, between 1980 and 1988 Africa received a disproportionately high level of aid per capita at $22 annually, against only $6 for the rest of the developing world. The contrast widens further when looking at aid as a percentage of domestic investments – for Africa this was 34% versus only 3% for the rest of the developing world. However, the story changes when looking at aid effectiveness or at the impact of aid on gross investment, which was a dismaying 4% decrease for Africa, when the rest of the developing world saw a 2% increase.[79]

With limited exceptions, the cancer of corruption in African countries completely refuses to let go and remains by far the single most cited reason for the failure of aid to develop Africa.[80] Political parties and their leaders strive to get to power largely in pursuit of access to the vast enterprises of corruption in the government-business complex. The classic overlap between public office and private gain is alive and well in African capitals. Politicians either form their own contractor and procurement companies, join some already set up by their cronies under blind bona fides, or go into generous rebate arrangements with some of the most notorious grand old names of African development sleaze.

As a result development budgets hardly evoked the impact envisaged in the long-term development plans laid out in glossy volumes every five or so years.

Non-prioritisation and misallocation of resources

Extension of basic public services was rarely carried out on the basis of orderly prioritisation according to resource availability in the majority of African states. Systems of economic stabilisation where regions with higher economic abilities subsidise regions with lower economic abilities to help bring them in line with the general level of development within economies were rare. Instead, what has tended to happen is that government leaders abuse their access to power and national resources to redirect them to their home regions and those of their supporters, to the exclusion of others. The situation gets worse especially where those parts are of extremely low economic potential while regions with high potential are left to languish without investment.

Documented anecdotal examples abound all over Africa where resources had been voted for economically uplifting projects with high potential only to be re-directed to lesser ones whose cost-benefit balance has been woefully inadequate, and whose only merit was that they were located in the president's home area or that of his trusted lieutenants.[81]

Other examples point to wastefulness and resource destruction in vanity projects designed purely to massage the egos and satisfy the whims of national leadership across Africa. They could be ornately designed cathedrals to rival the biggest in the world, international airports in the middle of nowhere, giant power stations on swift streams, long and winding trunk roads used by goats and wild beasts, or auto plants without steel. They are vanity projects dotted all over Africa, intended to burnish the legacies of many a dictator. They have without exception been white elephants. They have cost African economies dearly out of the already meagre resources at their disposal.

Dismal macro-fundamentals denying direct access to world capital markets

Lack of access to international capital markets remained a major impediment to the growth and development of African countries. Until the year 2000 no Sub-Saharan African country outside of South Africa was able to tap world capital markets. Only Senegal and Botswana were successful in being awarded a sovereign credit rating in 2001 by Standard & Poor's.[82] The reasons for this widespread failure of African economies to tap into world financial markets in the 1980s and 1990s could be summarised as weak macro-economic fundamentals.

African economies had limited export industries and depended on primary, unprocessed commodities which generated low and unpredictable levels of foreign exchange earnings. Foreign reserves in most African economies have long been at low levels, hardly ever growing beyond some odd weeks of import cover, and scarcely rivalling international sales of any Fortune 500 company. These poor levels of foreign exchange earnings made it difficult, if not impossible, for African states to service and repay foreign currency denominated borrowings.

Africa's economies also suffered immensely from a highly inflationary trading and operating environment due to various factors, among which were poor installed industrial capacity unable to meet rising demand while producing inefficiently. Other factors adding to inflation in Africa's economies were crop failures leading to chronic shortages of foodstuffs and raw materials for agro-industry, which is the mainstay of most African economies. Inflation makes asset price stability and forecasting difficult, undermining the development of active debt capital markets based on fixed-income securities.

The exchange controls ensured that African economies lost out on decades of free trade and investment flows the rest of the world was engaging in.

Wide swings in short-term exchange rates and general downward trends in long-term currency valuations in Africa made local currencies unattractive as a store of value for foreign capital. The swings were mainly a result of fluctuations in world prices of Africa's primary commodities, while the long-term downward trend of currency valuations arose out of consistently deteriorating terms of trade for Africa's economies. As their traditional exports got cheaper (out of gluts and commoditisation), their imports – which are mainly capital goods, industrial products and finished goods – got more expensive (out of specialisation, branding and protection of patents). This phenomenon inhibited net private capital flows into Africa's economies for a very long time, denying them badly needed resources to install industrial capacity and buttress economic development. It also occasioned revaluation of foreign-denominated debt causing technical defaults (this occurs when devaluation in a local currency results in lower repayments of external debt in foreign currency terms) adding to the burden of debt service and repayment.

While interest rates remained high in African economies in the 1980s and 1990s owing in the main part to the chronic lack of domestic savings, real rates of interest were either too thin or negative thanks to high underlying rates of inflation. Inflation eroded the attractiveness of African bonds and rendered debt markets in Africa arid. It also ate into earnings of businesses, hampering their ability to service borrowings.

Exchange controls were present in most of Sub-Saharan Africa from independence until around 2010. Some nations still have them in place now. Exchange controls create misalignments in currency trades and exchange rates, but more fundamentally they discourage inward investment and inter-country trade. African nations had put in place exchange controls to restrict utilisation of their scarce foreign exchange, but they ended up shutting themselves out of international trade and investment opportunities which would have added to their reserves of foreign assets. The exchange controls ensured that African economies lost out on decades of free trade and investment flows the rest of the world was engaging in.

The lack of sovereign credit ratings for African states meant that governments could not borrow cheaply and on their own terms from world capital markets, and the same thing went for corporates operating inside African economies. They were therefore left to crowd out each other in shallow, illiquid and unconnected domestic debt markets choked by governments' misuse of credit and hemmed in by the desperate lack of refreshing alternatives.

Multilateral and bilateral donors gave governments a wide berth

One of the biggest shocks that gripped African governments was when donors completely stopped trusting them and pulled away financial support in the 1990s.[83] African governments' penchant for wasting donor funds has always remained a permanent fixture in development affairs. Yet it is safe to assume that some development still could be proved to have been achieved if there were a means to check this. A difficulty for the donors was that for a long time they lacked the means to prove their suspicions and find out if their funds were being used effectively. Another problem for the donors was that they lacked alternative avenues through which to bypass the governments and direct their philanthropy directly to the African people.

> " Governments had to make major social and political changes before they could find themselves sitting at the table with donor partners again, talking development and funds. "

With time, institutions emerged that could help measure not only the amount and percentage of funds that ultimately reached the sponsored projects, but also the overall impact in terms of social welfare effect of the same projects. Transparency International and USAID, especially, formed the vanguard of this drive to make Africa's and world governments responsible and accountable. The World Bank also started monitoring aid effectiveness and utilisation efficiency. It was out of the initial outcomes of hard data on utilisation of donor money that painted African governments in a bad light that matters came to a head. Mild scepticism was overnight transformed into hardcore cynicism and mistrust. When this data emerged, donor funds suddenly stopped as a consequence.

It did not help matters that African governments did not act quickly and positively to remedy the situation and work towards resumption of donor-funded programmes and budgetary support. This was because the individuals in governments received tax revenues that could pay for what they considered most important and also at the time no credible alternative framework through which development funds could be channelled was obvious. The governments thought that donors, multilateral (the World Bank and IMF) and bilateral (individual donor nations, such as the USA, UK and Germany) alike, would eventually come back, offering aid to them once again.

Unfortunately for them, that moment did not come in the way they had expected. Some governments had to make major social and political changes before they could find themselves sitting at the table with donor partners again, talking development and funds. What's more, the faces on the African side of the table had started to change with the old guard being replaced in largely peaceful processes by youthful and urbane individuals; this came to be famously referred to as the "new breed of enlightened African leadership".

2. The emergence of social-commercial entrepreneurs

It is no wonder that the gaping lack of basic needs satisfaction and decay of state service delivery had accumulated over time across Africa by the time donor funds ceased. Everywhere one turned, there was no water connection at all, or the existing one was broken; agricultural extension services collapsed; rural medical services either had ceased or were no longer regular and cost sharing (partial payment for the cost of treatment) had been introduced.

Educational opportunities, especially at the nursery and primary levels, could not keep up with population growth and with the demands of an increasingly enlightened populace. Patchworks of past development began crumbling and falling away.

" Problems that were ignored by African leaders and governments eventually led to the privatisation of development. "

Perhaps the best illustration of the state of development in African countries was provided by residential estate roads in all big cities, where receding, residual asphalt cover and open man-holes in the middle of the roads remained as fading evidence of there having been a tarmac road and sewerage system in the vastly receding past.

A large developmental deficit and widespread stagnation emerged among African societies which needed to be plugged. Nature abhors a vacuum and this is equally the genius of capitalism – it fulfils a need where there is one. Problems that were ignored by African leaders and governments eventually led to the privatisation of development.

Various models of this privatisation came to the fore in the course of time, but among them two have emerged as serious alternative options for fixing the developmental deficit that had become the hallmark of Africa's public services. These are:

1.   The NGO/CBO (community based organisations) model

2.   The commercialisation of services model

1. Developing social programmes that bypass governments and link people directly with donors (the NGO/CBO model)

Non-Governmental Organisations (NGOs) in Africa started life as activist movements championing either human rights or pushing equality of gender and social classes. Later they expanded their charters to include civic education and basic advocacy as tools for public policy analysis and overhaul. They have also provided basic services to communities, such as training farmers on various production and processing techniques, as well as marketing and management skills.[84] On balance, in these broadly defined roles NGOs have served Africa well and proudly. To qualify this statement, the *Africa* referred to in this context is the mass of people who are unprotected, unserved and ignored by governments all over Africa.

But it is the social sustenance role of these organisations that had the greatest relevance to the topic at hand. NGOs realised that governments in Africa gave short shrift to rural Africa and especially marginal lands where resources were scarce and tax revenues were either non-existent or difficult to realise.

On the other hand NGOs had developed nationwide, and some continent-wide, infrastructures which they deployed to disseminate their services, sometimes to the furthest corners of rural Africa where governments have never reached. They have stretched these infrastructure channels to their limits, especially during times of emergency like natural calamities (floods, drought, volcanic eruptions), thereby bringing them to optimal efficiency levels. They have expended time and resources to carefully understand Africa's underdevelopment both by geography and social reality. Examples are the Red Cross and the Red Crescent, which is present at every point of disaster and catastrophe.

Being funded from abroad themselves and having the institutional memory of dealing with exacting donors, budgeting for and seeking earmarked funding, accounting for disbursements and filing detailed progress or social impact reports, NGOs were found to easily upstage governments' donor relations and welfare delivery systems.

Also the activities they engaged in were already similar in target-group and utility to government services (in theory): they were meant for the collective wellbeing and welfare of society. Thus it would not be deemed going way off the business model to add related products to their product range and value proposition.[85]

For these reasons, NGOs emerged as worthy counterweights to ineffective African governments of the 1980s and 1990s. As donors withdrew official development assistance from governments it was easy to redirect it to NGOs and CBOs which had meanwhile refreshed their mandates to cover mainstream development and sustainable resource utilisation.[86]

Between the 1980s and 1990s NGOs proliferated in Africa. Today rural Africa is a different place entirely to what it was before, thanks principally to NGOs, CBOs and religious-based organisations. Supporting schools, public libraries, vocational training and technical institutes, educational scholarships, dispensaries, boreholes, dams, and social and entertainment halls, NGOs are fully engaged in rural Africa. In addition, they provide numerous employment opportunities to the rural inhabitants. Some even maintain rural roads and contribute to community initiatives to boost rural security. They act as de facto governments, where real government has never arrived or, if it had been there before, where it has left without ceremony. What is more, to complete the final leadership link, those heading up NGOs are making successful bids for elective office as members of parliament in Africa's legislative assemblies and it will not be long before the NGO sector grabs top leadership in some African capitals.

> **"** Supporting schools, public libraries, vocational training and technical institutes, educational scholarships, dispensaries, boreholes, dams, and social and entertainment halls, NGOs are fully engaged in rural Africa. **"**

2. Converting the deficit into an opportunity and developing business models around it (the commercialisation of services model)

Where there was a deficit of government services, as long as a business model could be developed and sustained, the private sector stepped up and found ways to commercialise some basic essential public services. The thrust of any business model within this realm was found in the word *essential*.

People are in need of essential services and will use them whether they are provided by government through taxes or if they have to pay for them from their own pockets. Private sector investors therefore recognised a need that had to be met and a captive market of users with no alternatives. This can be illustrated using three examples which are prevalent wherever you go in Africa.

Water

From the failures of governments to guarantee availability, quality and hygiene of water in taps in African homes, offices, hotels and restaurants, has been spawned one of the most prosperous and fastest growing *water purification and bottling sectors*. Natural springs have been harnessed and tapped for their content. Purification and bottling plants have been installed widely. Bottled water in supermarkets has attained departmental status, commanding staff and whole sections of its own. In offices, the exception now is to find one without a water dispenser.

All public functions, including weddings, funerals, fund raisings and public meetings, are graced with large consignments of water in disposable bottles. The same applies to all governmental functions as well, including ironically those of the ministries of water. In fact, the mineral water business has proved the easiest and fastest to establish in circumstances where other commercial ventures are practically non-existent or difficult to establish and sustain. For example in southern Sudan, long before any other type of business was set up, Aqua Fontana had been thriving for some time. In Somalia, despite a collapse of social order and security, the mineral water business is thriving. Two of the leading firms in this area are AFI and Saaxil.

Education

At the start of independence there was one teacher for 42 students in primary schools in Africa.[87] Every year thereafter the figures got worse, with swelling classrooms and a paucity of teachers graduating from teacher training colleges. Within three decades of independence Sub-Saharan Africa experienced a tripling of student numbers per teacher in primary education.[88] Education ministries used to supply text and exercise books, pencils and a host of teaching aids to each student free of charge. In a matter of 20 years these had disappeared and parents were being required to equip their own children fully with necessary educational materials and equipment.

School inspectorate departments, which actively oversaw the quality of education imparted to the students, gradually disappeared. Even classroom capacity stagnated while student enrolment was bursting at the seams. The result was that classrooms became too congested, teachers overwhelmed and overworked, and the

" Private primary schools in Sub-Saharan Africa started in the late 1970s and by the mid-1990s they had caught on. The pent up demand was so high that classrooms filled up faster than they could be constructed. "

ministries concerned had their heads buried in the sand while the products of the system continued declining in quality. Children left schools almost the way they came, semiliterate and without ambition.

It is against this backdrop that the liberalisation and privatisation of education and educational opportunities was born. Private primary schools in Sub-Saharan Africa started in the late 1970s and by the mid-1990s they had caught on. The pent up demand was so high that classrooms filled up faster than they could be constructed. Teachers who were disillusioned, overworked and underpaid were only too eager to take up employment in these private institutions where they could get market rates for their labours. Able parents were prepared to pay higher school fees as long as their children got an education worth the name.

Hence the model for education as a business was complete.[89] All the investors needed were funds to construct school blocks and administrative offices. The rest was almost assured with minimal marketing and business development costs. In very short order private schools raced to the top of the charts in national examination performance. Governments became so embarrassed that they started separate rankings for public and private schools. In Kenya, by 1994 private school student enrolment as a percentage of total school enrolment for secondary education stood at an average 30% for rural schools and 41% for urban schools.[90] Once again the private sector swung into action to save the children of Africa from systematic illiteracy.

Security

Lastly let's consider _security_, another paramount responsibility of government. African governments have never been able to guarantee the security of their populations. They only guarantee, by a double measure, the security of the political leaders and their family members. The police forces are small in proportion to the populations. For example, in Tanzania there is on average one policeman for every 1,298 people; Ghana has one for every 1,200 people, while Kenya has one for every 1,150 people.[91] In addition, they are ill-equipped to meet the various security needs of all the people across vast geographies and difficult terrains. The police officers are poorly compensated and scarcely motivated to perform at an optimal level. These factors predispose the forces to corruption and avarice. Transparency International annual corruption indices perennially return a dismal verdict on police forces across SSA. They are either the first or second most corrupt institutions in almost every African country surveyed.[92] Years of underinvestment in security apparatus, rising population numbers and widespread youth unemployment have combined to worsen the security situation in Africa.

Responses to the festering security question have been varied, both in mode and effect. At one extreme has been the rise of vigilante groups peopled by unemployed youths belonging to specific ethnic communities. They patrol their neighbourhoods and rid them of antisocial characters initially. Unfortunately, once they have success in restoring a semblance of security they often proceed to levy protection charges from the households under their purview. Their means are normally cruel and primitive. Some of these vigilante groups have mutated into militias and gangs which terrorise the same people they had assembled to protect in the first place. Their apparent success stems from the absence of law enforcement apparatus and from the unintended consequences of the neighbourhoods' total dependence on them for security in the first instance.

At the other extreme is the orderly privatisation of security. Private security firms have sprung up, initially only in big urban centres but with time the concept has been replicated in rural areas too, even in tiny trading centres without electricity connections. These have been largely brought into being by the overwhelming need for functional security by commercial businesses where government security forces have been non-existent.[93] Companies need to have their offices or other premises watched over during the day and night. Embassies and foreign agencies use security services to guard their offices and official residences. Some, like banks and security printers, need to have their cash and sensitive products escorted. In countries like Uganda and Rwanda, their personnel are issued with firearms.

A random comparative headcount in downtown Nairobi would result in more private security personnel than regular policemen. The merit of private security services is that they are able to directly link performance with remuneration. If a security firm does not deliver security under a preset arrangement it is dismissed and another one

" Private security firms have sprung up, initially only in big urban centres but with time the concept has been replicated in rural areas too. "

hired. This encourages competition between them and service enhancement. Commercialisation also puts a definite market price on security, which is a fundamental business driver in Africa. Commercial enterprises get the opportunity to evaluate and pay only for the security they need. It provides a backstop and actionable remedies in the event of security lapses. Most importantly it makes it possible to do business in Africa (again) in spite of a total collapse or absence of government security services.

Conclusion/marketplace implications

The foregoing is a characterisation of the resilience of the African societies and their ability to bounce back after numerous shocks to the normal structures of social architecture. Its business and entrepreneurial classes have a knack for carving out commercial opportunities from circumstances of disruption, and they have demonstrated agility in harnessing adversity to improvise, innovate and create durable business models which set new service delivery expectations.

This chapter records the commercialisation of basic services and the evolution and development of homegrown market-based solutions to ordinary but essential needs of society. It has shown how African societies and peoples were inducted into the ways of free markets.

DEREGULATION AND LIBERALISATION OF MANUFACTURING AND SERVICES

6

Background and perspective

In those states that gained independence in the 1960s, the new African governments quickly embraced industrialisation as a definite means towards self-sustenance and sustainable development. They founded state-owned corporations under policies of import substitutions, to develop local industries that produced goods which previously had been imported.[94] The government quickly became the chief businessman in town, with single or dual monopolies in every sector. It did not matter what it was that one needed; whether it was something as inconsequential as a tooth pick or something as substantial as a bag of cement, most items came from fully or partly state-owned industries.

Business, especially in industrial or manufactured products, was still alien to the local people who were only beginning to come out of simple, traditional systems of exchange; most of them rooted in barter trade or in primitive currencies like salt, cowry shells or beads. Limitation of the money economy and the complete nonexistence of private savings were the major factors behind state control of business.

The middle class was either completely absent or merely incipient. In countries like Kenya, Uganda, Ghana, Nigeria and Côte d'Ivoire there was a tiny private sector almost entirely within the hands of residual settlers who stayed on and also in the hands of the local Asian communities that had grown up as a result of British imperial division of labour. For instance, rail construction had been the preserve of British-India across the whole empire. In French West Africa it was the Lebanese immigrants imported by the French to work the west African agricultural boom who took over the reins of enterprise when the French settlers left. Even then, the private sector consisted mainly of tailor shops, *dukawallas* or corner candy shops, and delicatessens.

It was left to governments, therefore, to keep watch and administer the full enterprise of business through statutory monopolies or parastatal organisations, also known as crown corporations in Commonwealth countries. They often accounted for most industrial capacity and employment.[95] To say they were inefficiently run and managed is an understatement. Basically they were run as sinking funds.

In the intervening period between the 1960s and 1980s, consumer populations soared; tastes and preferences multiplied as more people were educated and advances in communication made interaction with other continents possible. Purchasing power heightened as more people found employment and the formal economy diffused beyond cities and urban centres. The demand for industrial or manufactured products surged as lifestyles changed and modern systems crept in.

Meanwhile the production capacity and technologies of government-owned businesses were frozen in time. They continued to operate with archaic technologies, producing products in low and declining volumes at exorbitant costs. They were unable to add capacity or to sustain what capacity they already had. They were constrained by high transportation costs, small unviable markets, limited skills and chronic foreign currency shortages. In time, and nudged by structural adjustment programmes (which required governments to rationalise budgets, restructure or privatise public enterprises), these government enterprises collapsed and left nothing in their wake.[96]

Against such a bleak background, deregulation and liberalisation were ushered into corporate Africa as saviours of the markets.

Driving forces

It is now pertinent to examine some of the driving forces of deregulation and liberalisation which swept over Africa in the late 1980s and the early 1990s.

Poor quality products and services from state-owned enterprise

Commercial enterprises owned and run by the state in African countries were never founded on good commercial sense; they were primarily intended to save economies' hard-earned foreign exchange by replacing imports.[97] As a result, they generally produced extremely low quality products or delivered mediocre services. They made no efforts to either diversify their product ranges or improve the existing products. Everything was drab, from the packaging, to the merchandising, to the product experience or utility. Products were priced extortionately and protected by constitutional monopolies. People were forced to consume them for lack of alternatives and, even, under duress of the law. They left a bitter taste in the mouth, and mounting resentment.

A silent resistance started, initially slow and insidious and later open and widespread. This resistance was manifest in the existence of deep and dynamic informal markets in contraband and smuggled products which relied on illegal border crossings and operated in dark alleys. The other form of protest was in the emergence of domestic private solutions and alternatives in cottage industries and informal operations. This formed part of the inspiration for the current vast informal sector and constituted the thrust of Africa's own self-sufficiency and economic resilience.[98]

Underinvestment in capacity

Decades of underinvestment in the state-owned commercial enterprises which formed the core manufacturing and processing capacity in SSA led to irresponsiveness to the demands of consumers and eventual industrial atrophy.[99] Investment decisions were generally governed by central government planning that ignored market realities.[100] Failure to add new capacity meant that demand, increasing annually with rising populations, was not met. Consequently no new products were introduced and shortages were experienced as more and more consumers competed for a fixed or declining volume of products. At the same time, failure to invest in sustaining capacity led to decline in plant efficiency, leading to substandard products which were often not available at all due to the increased frequency of unscheduled downtime at factories.

This naturally forced consumers to look for alternatives and stick with them permanently. By the time the wind of liberalisation began sweeping through Africa it only served to confirm a long overdue reality.

Inability to extend services countrywide

State-owned enterprises in Africa scarcely had fully national footprints. They operated mainly in large urban centres and along the ribbons of communication connecting major towns. They were lethargic and made no effort to push out to parts of the population that were not served. They failed to respond to the growing demands of the marketplace, instead prioritising non-commercial concerns like job protection at all costs.[101] In fact, rather than expand they systematically ground to a halt and scaled back services drastically, withdrawing from the rest of the country and recoiling into the dilapidated industrial areas of capital cities.

This created wide gulfs of services and product deficits, proving fertile soils first for the proliferation of illicit trade in smuggled goods and second for the emergence of the informal sector when structural adjustment programmes kicked in.[102] These events paved the way for continent-wide cross sector reform and liberalisation, particularly by encouraging the absorption of the sprawling informal markets into the mainstream.

Unnecessary budget costs through subventions were reduced

Another factor that promoted reform and liberalisation in Africa's (un)productive sectors was national budgets – or their erosion. Governments used to sustain ponderous, inefficient state corporations through subventions from national budgets. The dominant motive for this was to sustain large bureaucracies and systems of state control.

Keeping these state corporations alive amounted to throwing good money after bad. Every dollar put into the state-owned organisations (SOEs) was lost forever, never to be recovered again. In time African populations grew at astronomical rates, colonial-era infrastructure was collapsing, disease and ignorance had taken a stranglehold of vast swathes of Sub-Saharan Africa. On the other hand, world prices for African primary products had collapsed, agricultural production diminished due to neglect and soaring input costs rendered most of African agriculture unviable; floating exchange rates were the death knell to Africa's terms of trade.

At last it became difficult, if not impossible, to balance budgets in many African nations and, overnight, financial supports for SOEs became a luxury that threadbare African treasuries could ill afford.[103] Liberalisation and reform of public enterprises resulting in privatisation (trade sales, or liquidations) and the introduction of free enterprise through private sector participation and competition in erstwhile protected industries were the inevitable eventualities.

Pressure from donors to streamline budgets

In the 1980s and 1990s, donors, frustrated with African governments' utter irresponsibility and unaccountability with donor funds and tax revenues, saw an opportunity to help streamline government operations in Africa through budget capture. National treasuries had become too weak to survive without donor support. Donors used this desperation to exact certain conditions aimed at increasing the productivity of every dollar of foreign aid to Africa. These conditions came as a bitter pill to most African nations but they had to swallow in order to improve their economic health.

The infamous Structural Adjustments Programmes (SAPs) were followed shortly after by Enhanced SAPs and they spread across Africa with dual, antithetical effects. They were both at once loathed for the destabilising impact of wresting budget control from the whims of treasury mandarins and ruling parties' stalwarts, and loved for the corrective effects of identifying and remedying the flaws of state corporations and large bureaucracies.[104]

They introduced fiscal discipline and encouraged privatisation which in turn ushered competition through refreshing new products and services, and wider choice.[105]

New national policies for job creation through increased competition

For over three decades, governments in Africa had totally failed on their paramount mandate to install and sustain economic enablers to create employment. Instead, they resorted to the unbounded expansion of the state and its sprawling bureaucracy, which encompassed numerous needless parastatals and public enterprises as a means of ensuring job creation, without regard to productivity. This is popularly known in public policy circles as maintaining control of the commanding heights of the economy.[106] This created multiple shadow responsibilities; ghost workers who only appeared in the payrolls and massive diminution in productivity. It is these instances, for example, which led to Telkom Kenya (before privatisation to France Telkom) recording 15 fixed phone lines per employee, against a global average of 651 fixed lines per employee.

As budgets got squeezed and state corporations either died or downsized, there were long overdue jobs losses. Governments were stripped bare and exposed for what they hid in unwieldy, dysfunctional state corporations – revealing that they never really had any genuine programmes for job creation. They then presided over liberalisation of the major strategic sectors of the economies, including workforce retrenchment and downsizing of the state-run enterprises.[107] These had mixed results, but culminated in the eventual streamlining of government operations, refocusing them towards facilitation of private sector job creation through government divestitures, and promotion of competition and free enterprise. This progressively transformed the means of increasing government revenues by replacing the chase for elusive profits from SOEs with the taxation of high-performing private sector players.

Context for liberalisation and privatisation of public commercial enterprises

During the first two decades of independence African countries received a lot of foreign aid and official development assistance (ODA). They experienced modest economic growth on the back of high flows of inward investment and technical assistance. National budgets were financed largely from foreign grants and concessional ODA targeted principally at capacity building and extending the infrastructure of government.[108] The local economies were incipient, with private sectors and employed workforces too small and weak for governments to depend on for tax revenues that could sustain the economy.

> " Unbounded expansion of the state and its sprawling bureaucracy encompassed numerous needless parastatals and public enterprises popularly known as maintaining control of the commanding heights of the economy. "

The vital instruments of civilian production lay with governments. Governments not only had the means to produce for the consumers, they enforced price control regimes which did not particularly inspire private sector investments (where that was possible under the law). This structural arrangement quickly became so embedded in governments' policy thinking that for a long time it was wrongfully taken for granted that local manufacturing capacity was safest in the hands of the state. As long as monopolies were assured, and foreign aid kept flowing, the state was deemed to wield the highest, unassailable economic power of any entity within a nation.

Then aid was stopped and structural adjustments set in. Subventions proved unsustainable and many monopolies collapsed on themselves. Governments soon found that they could not rely on aid and SOEs for economic sustenance and had to find alternative sources of revenues. The idea of governments ceding economic power to citizens through liberalising industry, licensing free enterprises and privatising public commercial enterprise became fashionable. This was in keeping with the basic motivation for governments the world over to allow and facilitate liberalisation and privatisation. This enhanced government revenues initially through divestiture proceeds and thereafter through taxation of far more profitable, diffuse and commercially active private enterprises.

From capital investments, industrial inputs and finished products, governments discovered enhanced revenue sources. What is more, annual licensing fees, all rights of usage, marketing and advertising initiatives, etc., brought in more revenue for the government. Wage bills and corporations' net financial positions – especially when they were positive – also attracted the tax authorities. Thus, there was a new revenue stream for the tax authorities, in the form of statutory tax levied on the private sector.

Conclusion/marketplace implications

Liberalisation and privatisation programmes continue to bring multiple benefits to Sub-Saharan economies and in particular these helped in the development of the consumer markets. By opening up once-closed sectors and industries in most countries, healthy competition has been encouraged resulting in massive investments in new capacity and broadening of product ranges available to consumers. The effect is an increase in choice and exposure of consumer prices to market forces; in most instances leading to drastic lowering of real prices. At the same time, the competitive entrepreneurial spirit that unfailingly follows liberalisation across Sub-Saharan Africa results in a fast rate of job creation, coupled with its attendant effects on consumer buying power.

Finally, whether it is in financial services, telecoms, cement and construction, insurance, or any other sector, liberalisation has so far resulted in some of the largest and most successful sources of foreign direct investment (FDI) into African economies. African countries continue to need more FDI as a fundamental pillar for accelerated economic growth through massive-scale expansion, advanced technological and skills transfers, and global networking.

THE GROWTH OF CREDIT

7

Background and perspective

It is said that credit is the oxygenated blood of an economy and the financial system is the circulatory system that carries credit to every tissue in the body of the economy, keeping it alive and giving it ability to generate new tissues (expand). Africa's economies' total lack of domestic credit over the years and the apparent absence of credible financial systems denied them the performance efficiency of a full-blooded circulatory system.

The concept of credit has remained alien in most parts of SSA for a long time, even today. People contemplating purchases depended solely on their own income and savings, or sold property and other assets to be able to make the payments. In keeping with the Shakespearean exhortation *neither a borrower nor a lender be*, debt and its character were frowned upon in African societies as evidence of insufficiency and loss of personal independence. It was therefore a hard sell from a cultural point of view.

One of the other difficulties with credit arose from the conceptual conundrum of collateral and payback. That one needed to give up title or first claim to an asset momentarily to be able to

> **"** Credit is the oxygenated blood of an economy and the financial system is the circulatory system. **"**

access liquidity could not go down well among African societies. Land has remained communal for the better part of the past 40 years of independent Africa and individuals lay claim to few personal assets. For example, amongst agricultural communities individuals could lay claim to a hoe and possibly crop harvests; the cattle keepers laid claim to herds of cattle. Either way the emotional attachment left no room for dispassionate arms-length commercial transactions that involved pawning these assets for liquidity.

Paying back was the other part. It was difficult enough to receive credit, but it was impossible to pay it back. Lacking in regular income – and having no clear sense of interest as the cost of money – defaults and delinquency were always a distinct possibility. People could not feel obligated to return, especially where the instrument of exchange is something as intangible as paper and payback did not appear particularly enforceable.

Even where banking services were available, the attitude of bank management to local people was not good. Banking services in Africa for a very long time remained available only for merchants. Deposit products were purposely tailored out of the reach of the majority of the population

> " Liberalisation and privatisation of the African banking sector completed the first and most critical phase of putting in place a financial bloodline for African economies. "

by the inclusion of onerous requirements like high opening and maintenance balances, punitive withdrawal and ledger fees, and insultingly low deposit interest that was opaquely computed. Therefore only a small number of people could get access to credit. Most could not even apply for it. Collateral, as it was defined then, was unachievable; charging fees were disproportionately high and rates of interest extortionate. Default or any signs of it were severely punished.

A great deal of financial education was needed to allow people to understand credit and to bring them up to speed with how collateral works. Governments established national commercial banks whose primary charter was to take banking services closer to the people. They opened branches in rural Africa and penetrated deeper without a sound business case for doing so. People were encouraged to open accounts, to learn the discipline and motions of saving. Though these state banks hardly ever made any profits, they played an instrumental role in laying the foundations for national financial systems and inducting the greatest majority of people into the money economy.

Liberalisation and privatisation of the African banking sector completed the first and most critical phase of putting in place a financial bloodline for African economies – a process that is lengthy and as yet incomplete. The resultant proliferation of private banks and branches, the roll out of multiple alternative channels and the intensity of competition for customer deposits complemented the efforts of state banks to provide financial services to the African people.

It is against this backdrop of a slow but progressive construction of a network in Africa that the current megatrend of credit expansion has been made possible.

Driving forces

Liberalisation and privatisation

The wave of liberalisation which swept across Sub-Saharan Africa in the late 1980s and early 1990s started with the banking sector and national financial systems. Being the lifeline of the economies, these are fundamental to the economic health of nations. For economic reform to have the widest sweep of impact on large sections of an economy and to the greatest majority of its people, it would have to be implemented first in the financial sector. Besides, the same sector has proved the most responsive to economic policy changes.

A summary of the liberalising reform that took place in the financial sector is as follows: foreign exchange controls were repealed; capital accounts were liberalised; the licensing regime was overhauled to be criteria based; bank supervision was boosted to restore integrity and confidence in the system; regulatory and prudential

> **❝** Measures were intended to streamline the process of financial intermediation, mobilisation and efficient allocation of resources, and to support sustainable economic growth. **❞**

guidelines were overhauled and strictly enforced; caps on single client borrowings were put in place; risk assessment and loss crystallisation were standardised; ownership restrictions on foreign investments in the sector were overhauled; individual ownership ceilings were set; and interest pricing regimes were enacted. Basically, all of these measures were intended to streamline the process of financial intermediation, mobilisation and efficient allocation of resources, and to support sustainable economic growth.[109]

These reforms have not been uniformly implemented across SSA, for example, whereas the capital account has been long liberalised in most countries of SSA, some like Tanzania have consciously chosen to keep it closed for domestic economic reasons. Neither were these measures implemented at the same time. It has been a long and winding journey of reforms. Some countries like Kenya, Nigeria and Ghana are way ahead, while others like DR Congo, Burundi and South Sudan are still lagging behind, even though good progress is being made.

The end results of reforms have been varied, but mostly positive. The greatest impact is that it made possible a profitable model for private sector participation in the African banking sector. New private banks were incorporated and established, touching off a quick expansion of banking services, especially in major urban centres, and resulting in increased banking penetration for the urban populations of Africa (upwards of 60%).[110] The over-concentration of banking services in urban centres caused intense rivalry for deposits and put pressure on interest margins, making urban banking less glamorous from a mass banking perspective. It was this realisation that led to efforts to mobilise savings across whole countries, including rural areas, rather than have them concentrated in cities. This had the general effect of substantially reducing the cost of funds for banks.

As a consequence, democratisation of banking and financial services has been achieved by opening up access to banking services and credit to the great majority of the African population in a very short space of time.

Build up of domestic savings

The propensity to save in Sub-Saharan Africa has been quite commendable. From very little, if anything, at independence, most African states now boast considerable levels of domestic savings. Kenya for example had KShs1,228 billion ($15.35 billion) in deposits within the banking system by August 2010.[111] In 2005, deposits were KShs588 billion. This means deposits grew 108% in the five years to August 2010, equivalent to a compounded annual average growth rate of 53%. Taking Rwanda as another example, just ten years after the genocide the economy has been able to accumulate $739m in total bank deposits, representing a growth of 105% in dollar terms over the past four years, or 111% in local currency terms over the same period.[112]

> From very little, if anything, at independence, most African states now boast considerable levels of domestic savings.

Not all of these new deposits arose out of new savings. In fact most of it came from mobilisation from sections of the economies that had previously not used banks – the informal sector. Individuals who had previously not taken their revenues to the bank – perhaps instead trying to store value in physical assets like land, cattle or crop yields – were starting to convert these into cash and make deposits in new bank accounts. As well as this, a big portion of the deposits surge came from revenues generated from the expanding business and commercial activities across SSA. Economic liberalisation brought about a surge of fresh business in

> " Where equities markets are yet to be developed, active bond markets are already in existence. "

Africa, inspiring the establishment of numerous small businesses in the liberalised sectors, and a multitude of suppliers and distributors servicing the new business environment made possible by liberalisation and reforms. In addition, a considerable amount of these new deposits came from remittances of African diasporas and donor inflows.

Accumulated savings converted into long-term bank loans form the backbone of the funding for commerce and industry in SSA. Almost 100% of working capital requirements of all commercial enterprises in SSA, big and small, multinational or local, are met by local banks. Banking sector capacity has helped fund enterprise to such an extent that very large project financing is increasingly being accommodated locally by national or regional bank syndications.

One of the largest ever soft commodities trade finance syndications in the world was the Ghana Cocoa Board deal of 2008 which raised $1 billion. Though distributed internationally, the lead arranger was Standard Chartered bank, which used its local strengths to clinch the deal. Leading local banks committed staggering amounts, such as $75m from Stanbic Bank Ghana and $25m from Ghana Commercial Bank.[113] There was an even bigger Cocobod deal in 2010, for $1.5 billion, but the 2008 deal demonstrated the newly found ability of local banks to punch above their weight internationally.

African domestic savings have in the past decade achieved another important milestone. They have attained status as a viable base for domestic bond markets. In fact where equities markets are yet to be developed, active bond markets are already in existence. The Uganda bond market, which has only been in existence for around ten years, is $810m in size – from 32 listed treasury bonds and five corporate bonds by December 2010.[114] Rwanda, which only established a stock market in early 2008, has four bonds listed but already its bond market is $31m in size.[115]

In Zambia, the bond market had six listings by the end of 2010, with corresponding turnover of $116m in that year. In Nigeria, according to research by Vetiva Capital, 88 bond listings make for $15 billion in total bond market size, and a turnover of $98 billion in 2009 with domestic capacity taking up to 25% of this.[116] In Kenya, there are 92 total bonds listed, 74 treasuries and 18 corporate, with a combined size of $9 billion by December 2010. Annual turnover by December 2010 was $11 billion, against equities market turnover of $2 billion according to statistics from the Nairobi Stock Exchange. These commendable achievements have been made possible in the main part through domestic savings, which make up more than 50% of local bond participation in Kenya.[117]

Formalisation of the informal economy: banking for the un-banked

When colonial governments ruled SSA, formal economies were the exclusive preserve of settler communities. The African people were engaged in their traditional ways of life and exchanged goods and services by barter trade; they had little if any regard for the settlers' currencies. They operated their own shadow banking system that held cattle, sheep, goats, chicken and farm produce as a store of value and a means of exchange. They had scarce use for the modern banking system as erected by colonial administrations.

> **"** It suddenly became possible for banks to profitably push into rural Africa and take banking services to those that had not had them before. **"**

But then modern education and healthcare systems started to be introduced. Initially education was for a limited number with families being asked to nominate one or two children to attend school from groups of perhaps six to eight siblings. Healthcare started by inoculation and vaccination. At first this was paid for by governments. With time these services became more widespread. Eventually all children of a family were required to go to school, while healthcare needs extended beyond periodic visits by a mobile clinic. The necessary infrastructure started being laid down, the costs started stretching governments, and people were slowly introduced to paying for the services.

At the same time, lifestyle changes were happening at an ever increasing pace as a result of modernisation. Tribal communities which had their own cultural foodstuffs from local sources began expanding their tastes to include dishes from other communities and beyond. Where previously exchange was made by barter trade, price attribution was made faster and more efficient by money exchange. Mass markets for products were also being made possible by advances in transport infrastructure and penetration of retail services. The momentum for trade was sustained by improving producer prices which motivated more production for commercial purposes. In time, a cash economy was beginning to take shape in Africa's rural societies.

For a long time, banks either did not think there was cash to be mobilised in commercially viable quantities in rural communities or they had no means of knowing it. Besides, network extension in the days of manual operations was a logistical nightmare and a costly exercise. Justification hurdle rates were set very high, which left rural Africa without a banking system.

It was the advances of computing, technological innovations, such as VSAT (very small aperture terminal), real-time banking and the development of banking applications that brought down the costs of banking dramatically. It suddenly became possible for banks to profitably push into rural Africa and take banking services to those that had not had them before. Rural lending has proved one of the pillars of growth in African economics because financial discipline is high in rural areas and delinquencies are minimal. Aside from South Africa, Kenya leads Sub-Saharan Africa in terms of financial services inclusion, with only 34% of the population excluded – and this is thanks to the overwhelming uptake of the mobile deposit and remittances account solutions by mobile telecommunication providers.[118] The rest of Africa is speedily adopting it too and soon financial services penetration should breach all previously known barriers in Africa.

Emergence of MFIs

Africa is the poorest continent, with about 50% of its population living below the international poverty line on less than $2 a day per person.[119] For the majority of these poor people, financial services were just not conceivable in the way banks had traditionally packaged them. They live hand to mouth, half the time on nothing at all and the other half relying upon overnight credit from the local kiosks which must first be repaid, then renewed within 24 hours on a rolling basis. Whatever was done, no traditional bank business model could be executed for such a clientele.

Enter the micro-finance movement, building profitable business models on micro-savings. The concept of microfinance is organised within self-help groups (SHGs) for viability and sustainability. These groups inculcate a discipline for saving within their membership which then grows into an engrained culture. They build intangible collateral out of mutual trust and group guarantees or joint liability, which members use to borrow individually from micro-finance institutions (MFIs). Default is punished with authorised deductions from a member's contributions to the SHG and threats of dismissal from the group.

The level of institutional involvement is limited to oversight, education and coordination of the groups. All the rest – including the costs and effort of savings mobilisation, credit risk mitigation and default – is transferred to the groups themselves. This same model is what allows banks like Grameen Bank of Bangladesh to have 2,565 branches and 8.3m borrowers covering 97% of the villages in the country.

African societies were gregarious, and based on the dual principles of personal discipline and collective responsibility. They were also egalitarian. Social safety nets allowed individuals to slip without falling through, or to get back up again if they did. The system of microfinance was therefore not entirely alien to them. The modern concept of microfinance – better known as village banking – was introduced to Africa in 1999 by K-Rep Bank (Kenya) as an adaptation of the Grameen Bank model.[120] It has since caught on and spread widely across SSA. Vastly increasing numbers of villages in SSA now have several self-help groups under one or another microfinance institution. MFIs deposit accounts were reported to number more than 16.5m at the end of 2008, having grown 40% over the previous year in utter defiance of the global financial meltdown; MFI net borrowers stood at 6.5m at the same time.[121]

The successes have been so obvious within Africa and elsewhere that the sub-sector is beginning to become mainstream and is being brought under formal regulation and supervision by the monetary and financial authorities. Equity Bank of Kenya, which has only emerged from the ranks of MFIs in the early 2000s, has been winning awards regionally and internationally, including being recognised as Africa's most progressive and innovative bank for the year 2008.

Leading institutions like ACSI, DECSI, OMO and OCSSC of Ethiopia; MRFC and MUSCCO of Malawi; K-REP and KWFT of Kenya; CERUDEB, FINCA and UML (now owned by Equity Bank Kenya) of Uganda; CRG and Kafo Jiginew of Mali; FECECAM and PADMEC of Benin; WAGES and FUCEC of

Togo; Sinapi Aba Trust of Ghana; CMS of Senegal[122] and Micro Africa Group, which operates in five eastern African countries, are leading the push to bring economic and financial relevance to large numbers of people. This silent majority had long been ignored by traditional banks. The scale and breadth of credit generated as a consequence is profound and it is refreshing that it comes from local sources and that it is not fleeting.

Expansion in scale

When travelling across Africa by road, finding a bank was a difficult exercise as recently as a decade ago. Banks were concentrated in capital cities, industrial and mining towns, and in towns at waterfronts. Aside from these, Africa remained a vast, barren expanse as far as banking services were concerned. The main impediments to the extension of banking services were twofold. The first was the huge costs of putting up branches and coordinating their operations under 100% manual systems. The second was the apparent lack of compelling justification in most parts of Africa as little economic activity was happening.

Only within the last ten years (in the 2000s) has this bleak backdrop almost completely been pulled down. African city skylines are now defined by banks' skyscrapers, emblazoned with shiny emblems and logos. The names are mostly local and regional. Almost every town has representation of all the major commercial banks. The race is on to open new branches and the costs and time needed to do so have been reduced significantly as banks are concentrating on long-term leases and rental arrangements rather than constructing their own purpose built premises, which is clearly more expensive and time-consuming. In Kenya total commercial bank branches grew from 740 in 2007 to 996 in 2009,[123] representing a growth of 35% within two years.

Core banking systems in Africa have evolved very gradually, sometimes painfully slowly. But without doubt recent and ongoing investments in state-of-the-art, scalable, modular and integrated core banking platforms have allowed banks in Africa to make impressive advances in capacity expansion and service delivery. The ability to operate *branchless banking* with core banking systems – whereby a customer is offered the same services no matter which branch they visit – has aided the opening of new branches across extended networks, paving the way for deeper penetration into places otherwise difficult to reach, either because of geography or costs. As a result the assessment of creditworthiness and disbursement of credit among the

❝ Recent and ongoing investments in state-of-the-art, scalable, modular and integrated core banking platforms have allowed banks in Africa to make impressive advances in capacity expansion and service delivery. ❞

rural communities has become more straightforward.

The other factor behind the extension of banking services has been automated teller machines (ATMs). Banks have used ATMs to enhance their service delivery across Africa. The latest ATMs being installed can provide the same services as human cashiers. They dispense cash in local and foreign currencies; accept cash and cheque deposits; and give balances and mini statements. They can even be used to make mobile phone airtime top up and effect utility bills payments. Thus, ATMs have increased people's interaction with banking services in Africa by a large factor. Within two years total ATMs in Kenya increased by about 70% from 1,000 in 2007 to 1,700 in 2009.[124]

The advances of consumer finance

As recently as 2000 the concept of consumer finance was taboo within mainstream African banking. The average African labourer was considered to be earning far too little, having low job security, having no other revenue sources, living hand to mouth, lacking in financial flexibility and possessing neither financial discipline nor financial planning skills – in short, too much of a credit risk. Workers' earnings were also deemed not to be rising in line with increases in the cost of living and therefore were considered disproportionately susceptible to effects of inflation. In addition, these workers lacked the traditional collateral of land and physical assets demanded by banks in order to extend credit. As a result wage earners were not seen by banks to provide a business opportunity other than salary processing.

In the course of time banks accumulated short-term deposits – in the form of workers' wages that were paid into accounts by employers and then withdraw shortly after by the workers – which they could not find ways to deploy as fast and cost-effectively as they would have liked to. Renewed donor-engagement across Africa (following governance reforms, macro-economic stabilisation and public finance liberalisation) has been observed to increase governments' dependence on relatively cheap and longer-term external sources of programme funding. As a consequence, governments' domestic borrowing activities were reduced to funding short-term activities, such as recurrent expenses, managing price stability and refinancing or retiring short term borrowing instruments.

Productive sectors of the economies continued to struggle with the paucity of long-term deposits in the African banking sector to finance medium and long-term capital requirements, relying in large measure on private sources of equity funding or occasionally tapping debt capital markets through commercial paper or corporate bonds. What long-term deposits were available were too expensive and competitively sought after, and hence came at premium pricing for both deposit takers and borrowers alike. Banks found themselves stuck with liquidity far in excess of what it was prudent to hold. Besides, the high cost of funds mobilisation through newly established branches demanded that they generated revenues to at least match, if not exceed, the cost of funding.[125]

> **" Banks started experimenting with small amounts of very short-term lending – such as one to three months – against a pay-slip and an employer's letter confirming or assuring employment for the lending period. "**

Banks had hitherto only a large number of customers for one week in a month; when the working people came in to withdraw their earnings. On each occasion, the total of the short-term deposits – in the form of people's wages – that passed through the banks was huge in sum. Consequently, the banks needed a new plan – they developed credit risk assessment models that enabled them to lend against pay slips and tap into the temporary liquidity created by these wage payments.

Some banks started experimenting with small amounts of very short-term lending – such as one to three months – against a pay-slip and an employer's letter confirming or assuring employment for the lending period. The outcome was spectacular. The banks were encouraged by this success and rolled out the products across their entire networks. In Kenya this initiative was led by Barclays Bank, followed closely by Kenya Commercial Bank. Some preferred to wait in the wings until the trailblazers had generated a database of credit history on a wide cross-section of consumer borrowers, they then went ahead and tried to lure these borrowers into financing deals with top ups, refinancing programmes and even free promotional products, such as TV sets, DVDs and mobile phones.[126]

Consumer finance has now expanded to include mortgage finance, home improvement loans, car loans and credit card loans. It has been made available to everyone with a pay slip. Indeed, it is now being extended to the self-employed in the informal sector as long they can demonstrate consistent deposit histories. All retail banks push it as a standard product and it contributes immensely to their earnings.

This move has triggered an enthusiasm for taking finance among the African people and in five short years it has pushed through to the mainstream of banking assets. Amazingly, this category of loans has had low default rates. It has marked the genesis of consumer finance and birthed a culture of consumerism, fed by the banks' deep short-term liquidity. The expansion in credit that has resulted from the introduction and advances of consumer finance in SSA has made consistent consumers of a very large number of people within a very short time period.[127]

Conclusion/marketplace implications

Unrestricted access to reasonably-priced credit is perhaps the ultimate act of consumer liberation. Credit markets in Africa have expanded quickly, especially in the decade from 2000 to 2010, securing some important structural effects within the financial system; laying down the infrastructure and formalising the framework for consumer finance, and cementing gains that have been made in introducing the concept of credit into African culture over the years. The most fundamental contribution of credit and financial systems to African economies is their formalising effect; the democratising of access of bank accounts and the lowering of eligibility thresholds. Second, credit and its power of leverage has now been well received in most parts of emerging Africa with the effect of augmenting the potential to consume. At the same time, credit has contributed immensely to the collective work ethic by disciplining credit consumers to seek and stay in employment in order to service constantly rolling levels of credit owed.

Finally, small and medium size enterprises (SMEs) are the best proven system for the creation of new wealth in economies and they provide platforms for harnessing the imaginative, creative and entrepreneurial ambitions of society. As such, they badly need credit markets that function year-round. The current explosion of SMEs in Sub-Saharan Africa is a testament to the co-creational functions (where the fusion of SME finance with the entrepreneurial ideas behind SMEs create new industries) of domestic credit markets. SMEs are the vanguard in generating new employment opportunities and enabling a dynamic and bulging middle class in modern African societies.

DEVELOPMENT OF CAPITAL MARKETS

8

Background and perspective

As recently as 1990 there were only nine stock exchanges in the whole of Africa – in Botswana, Morocco, Egypt, Ghana, South Africa, Kenya, Nigeria, Tunisia and Swaziland. Now almost every country in SSA has a stock exchange; a total of 29 stock exchanges are fully operational, representing 38 nations.[128] It is within the economic policy of each SSA country to have a fully fledged financial market that includes a dynamic capital market. Between 2007 and 2009, over $10 billion was raised in equity offerings across 18 stock exchanges thanks to the listing of 170 new companies. The market capitalisation of the ten largest markets grew from $222 billion to over $700 billion between 2002 and 2008, a compound annual growth rate (CAGR) of 18%.[129]

As global financial markets expanded and cross-border private financial flows increased both in frequency and volume, the push for establishment of capital markets in parts of the world where they had been previously non-existent gained momentum. That said, the greatest agent for the establishment of capital markets in African states has consistently been the government. During the stressful days of donor-enforced austerity measures and structural adjustments, governments were under a lot of pressure to privatise state-owned enterprises. While non-performing bodies could be disposed of in fire sales, or private treaties, profitable enterprises in strategic commercial endeavour could not be sold off this way.

Multilateral partners, the IMF and World Bank especially, insisted that governments transfer these profitable enterprises, fully or partially, to their citizenry in the broadest possible way under a system of competent price discovery (an open, inclusive and participatory means of realising the fair values of companies through public capital markets) and that contained a mechanism for entry and exit thereafter with neither prejudice nor discrimination. Public capital markets emerged as the best option. As a result, therefore, 20 capital markets came into being in Africa in the wake of the reforms that followed structural adjustments.[130]

Capital markets in SSA play an increasing role in providing access to growth and development capital to businesses either through equity distribution or bond sales. This affords an alternative option to expensive bank borrowing, which is not always available. They are also proving to be a major link to the global financial and capital markets for African economies. As more foreign portfolio and private capital flows into African markets in search of investment opportunities with superior yield and risk profile diversification, more African economies become a part of the integrated global financial market.

More importantly, among African societies where the concept of asset ownership is only understood and confined to adult males whose parents had property to hand down, capital markets are providing the best route for the full and final liberation of the youth and women. Capital markets have created a basis for savings, capital and wealth formation for thousands of African youths who would otherwise never have imagined these things possible. Youths and women in African towns are now very much involved in applications for IPOs (initial public offerings – when businesses are listed on a stock exchange and their shares are sold publicly for the first time) and provide the bulk of new customers for investment banks and stock brokers.

Most of the new stock exchanges have taken a long time to break even and become self sustaining – this is because the processes of preparing companies for listing are still largely unknown in Africa. This is made worse by the lack of local advisory capacity, forcing governments to rely on expensive consultants from South Africa or London.

> " Capital markets have created a basis for savings, capital and wealth formation for thousands of African youths who would otherwise never have imagined these things possible. "

The fundamental constraint remains the lack of enough domestic savings and liquidity within African economies to absorb public equity distributions at such a rate so as to enable a reasonable pace of divestitures and public listings. However, this trend is changing as increasing numbers of listings come through and African populations get more involved and more accustomed to stock exchange investments – there is an emerging equity culture. Meanwhile, the World Bank, through the International Finance Corporation (IFC), has continued to play a critical role in the foundation of these institutions, acting as an incubator for capital market development across Africa. It has done this through its efficient market institution development programme (ESMID), which is active among eastern African stock markets, [131] and both its financial and institutional support for the formation of stock exchanges; an example being the Rwanda stock exchange.[132]

Driving forces

I have broken the driving forces in this area into two:

1. *Supply-side factors* – these pertain to the supply of investment instruments or securities – such as share listings and bonds – into the stock markets by all types of issuers, sponsors and vendors.

2. *Demand-side factors* – these pertain to the demand for the issued securities by all types of capital market investors.

1. Supply-side factors

Government privatisation programmes

Governments in Africa have been under pressure to get out of direct business by selling off commercial and business enterprises. Essentially government enterprises are owned and operated in trust on behalf of the citizens of their countries. So, naturally, at the point of exit, the handover should be to the same people in as direct a system as possible.

In special circumstances, where the business enterprises are not generating profits or positive cash flows, and require restructuring or massive injection of capital to operate again as going concerns, these become candidates for trade sales to strategic investors or for asset stripping to interested private players who find use for some of the assets in their businesses or to speculators in distress assets. Unfortunately, the latter has been the case for the majority of state-owned enterprises in Africa, which had been consistently run aground and methodically disembowelled under corrupt regimes and callous administrations.

Where there were profitable, progressive and well run businesses with good future prospects, attempts have been made to privatise them through public offerings with varying degrees of success. The necessities of public sector reform and government downsizing have led to the establishment of stock exchanges in countries across Sub-Saharan Africa. The Uganda Securities Exchange was established in 1997, with one of its principal mandates being to provide an avenue for government privatisation. Today, seven companies have been listed, all of them following government divestiture.[133] The same story obtains in Malawi, where from a total of 15 listed companies, apart from two private listings and one cross-listing, all the rest have been supplied by the government privatisation unit.[134] In Zambia, government divestiture supplied 12 out of a total of 20 primary listings.[135]

Multinationals seeking local acceptance

Another major source of equity supply has been multinationals operating in Africa. It is conventionally accepted that at independence in many African countries, the greatest force in business was the classic overlap between politics and business. This can be loosely referred as the *business-political complex* and it sought to replace colonial/settler commercial interests with local/native commercial interests under populist programmes of *Africanisation* or economic empowerment and business indigenisation. Many foreign-owned companies left Africa, others stayed on to fight it out. The ones which stayed were of two different kinds: the first being those that co-opted local political and special interest partners. These survived only to the extent that their political protectors stayed on in power. However, the other type, and the most enduring, were those that sold or gifted minority stakes to governments, which in turn have exited by transferring their stakes to local populations through stock exchange listings. During the public privatisation and divestitures induced by structural reform, these proved easy pickings for governments as they were already so well run and profitable under private sector management.

Across African stock exchanges, European names recur with frequency: Barclays Bank, Standard Chartered Bank, Cadbury, British American Tobacco, Guinness, Shell and Unilever are listed in economies with a British background. And in francophone Africa, including those parts of Africa where French influence was purposefully projected after independence, some French names are permanent fixtures in the stock exchanges. Such firms are Lafarge Cement, Total Oil and Société Générale. Some South African names have also become common fixtures in a number of African stock markets especially within the frontline states, such as Old Mutual, Illovo Sugar and Stanbic Bank.

Recapitalisations and exit or succession strategies

Local companies seeking growth and expansion capital are now able to find it by selling equity and equity hybrids through the markets. In the more developed markets like Zimbabwe, Kenya, Nigeria, Ghana and the BRVM (francophone west Africa), the depth and capacity of markets to absorb new stock exchange listings has already been tested more than a few times. Safaricom, Sub-Saharan Africa's largest listing in recent times, attracted $786m, four times the amount sought, while Dangote Flour Mills in Nigeria was over-subscribed six times.

Numerous private companies' IPOs and rights issues have been processed in Nigeria, Kenya and Ghana in the past ten years as growth has fuelled an insatiable demand for capital among enterprises. In Nigeria, the recapitalisation of the banking sector that happened between 2005 and 2008 grossed over $4 billion in new investment capital purely from local savings.[136] In 2008, Ecobank Transnational, a pan-African bank with the widest regional network – it is now in 30 countries – successfully raised $1.5 billion in the largest and the first simultaneous cross-border hybrid rights issue and new equity offering on the continent. This exercise was boldly undertaken against the bleak backdrop of global economic and financial crisis, and as a result it was distributed chiefly in Africa.[137] In Kenya, seven of the ten listed banks successfully tapped the local market for new capital in the five years to 2010 to finance growth and expansion into the region.

In recent years African capital markets have served as an excellent entry point for locally established businesses whose founders either were looking to bring on board other shareholders under broad succession planning strategies or, having done that already, were looking to broaden entry and exit opportunities for the new investors. Examples in Kenya include Scan Group, a conglomerate of advertising, marketing and public relations agencies; and Eveready Limited, a dry batteries and related accessories company.

Listing by introduction (the process of bringing non-listed companies which have already met the thresholds for public listed companies into local stock exchanges by registering them in the official lists) is another device that was used to find a mechanism for price discovery for those investors

“ Numerous private companies' IPOs and rights issues have been processed in Nigeria, Kenya and Ghana in the past ten years as growth has fuelled an insatiable demand for capital among enterprises. **”**

who were keen to buy stakes in these enterprises but who were wary of the inefficient pricing in over-the-counter markets. In Kenya, Equity Bank, Co-operative Bank and Trans-Century are good examples of this.

Government and corporate bond issues

❝ The reason bonds are easy to sell and distribute in these marketplaces where investing in intangible assets is alien to the greater majority is that government securities are relatively risk-free. ❞

Another major source of products to the African stock exchanges has been the addiction of governments to credit. National budgets in African nations never balance; they are always in deficit. Governments issue borrowing instruments in the form of bonds to the banks, pension funds, corporate investors and the investing public through local exchanges to raise funds to finance these deficits. In fact, at incipient stock exchanges bond listings precede equity listings. The Rwanda Stock Exchange, established in 2008, had four treasury bonds and one corporate bond listed without a single equity listing up to the end of 2010. Then its first IPO, of the national brewery Bralirwa, was completed.

The reason bonds are easy to sell and distribute in these marketplaces where investing in intangible assets is alien to the greater majority is that they entail capital preservation guarantees – government securities are relatively risk-free. Government bonds therefore provide the perfect meeting point between governments, which are hungry for credit and cannot always access it externally, and an inchoate investing community that is grappling to understand the features of financial instruments.

Corporate bonds, on the other hand, have had a different experience in African capital markets. By nature corporate bonds require independent credit risk assessment from established, independent and universally renowned credit rating agencies. These agencies have not traditionally been on the ground in Africa, making it very difficult for corporates to issue bonds. Since 1996, the African arm of the NYSE listed Duff & Phelps rating agency, Global Credit Rating (GCR), has established a rating system for banks amidst universal appeal.[138]

This has made it possible to compare banks' inherent risks across Africa using one set of criteria. It has also made it possible for banks to issue and list bonds on African stock exchanges. Lately, with the arrival of the big three international credit rating agencies in Africa – S&P, Moody's and Fitch – large corporates are now lining up to receive their own international ratings, which they hope will enable them to sell debt securities in local and international securities markets.

Cross/dual listings

The concept of cross listing is only just beginning to catch on in African capital markets. It happens where a company already listed on one stock market seeks a simultaneous listing on one or more other stock markets within the region or beyond. The rationale for cross listing is usually twofold. First, companies with operations beyond their country of incorporation often run into headwinds of cultural, political and regulatory natures in their endeavours to conduct business, especially in competition with local companies with local roots and protectors. They find that the best measure to counter these subtle, anti-competitive practices is to become local too, by making it possible for local investors to buy and sell their stocks through the domestic stock markets.

Second, where the entry into the new markets requires greater visibility and profile enhancement for an enduring business penetration, a stock market listing boosts the marketing efforts by guaranteeing the company a consistent mention in business media and financial news at no cost. Being listed on the stock market in a new region also of course gives the company hallowed status as one of the bell-wethers of the economy in the area.

The regulations and motions for cross listing are fairly light and the procedures few, making it possible to close a cross listing exercise in a very short time period – perhaps two to three months – whereas IPOs can take a full year or more in some cases.

More developed African stock markets like those in South Africa, Kenya and Nigeria have helped to prop up emergent stock markets in their localities by supplying cross listing entities. South Africa feeds Namibia, Botswana, Malawi and Zimbabwe; Kenya feeds Tanzania, Uganda and Rwanda; while Nigeria feeds Ghana. In Uganda, for example, cross listings from Kenya make up 46% of the total listing.[139] In Rwanda, there are only so far four equity listings, two primary and two cross listings from Kenya. Botswana has 11 dual listings from South Africa out of a total of 32 listings.[140]

2. Demand-side factors

Mediocre returns on bank savings

There used to be days in Africa when having a bank savings account was considered a very noble investment. Banks paid reasonable interests on deposits, enough to be considered a tidy expected rate of return. Nominal deposit rates would range between 10% and 55% per year and governments had not yet introduced taxation on financial returns.[141] Savings were practically non-existent across vast swathes of Africa, and banks were willing to pay handsomely to lure them through their doors where, once in, they stayed put and did not seek any alternative return elsewhere. Such was the attractiveness of bank deposit products in 1980s African banking that among employed and commercially active populations they were perceived as the ultimate investment opportunity. It was such a prestigious and enviable position to be in to have a bank account that the banked would flaunt their pocket-books with a sense of self-importance.

Then domestic savings built up, initially slowly but gathering momentum as time went by. Finally they exploded in the 2000s decade. Banks became choked by the expensive deposits and set out to do something about it. They started by developing wide ranges of savings and deposit products, targeted at all segments of society; to the men, the women, the youth, the self-employed, the old, the children, the rich, the poor, Co-operative Societies and corporations.

Then they took this further – they embarked on the expansion of service delivery channels, enabling them to hold on to the money for as long as possible. They encouraged their customers to carry ATM, charge and credit cards and call on their funds only at the point and time of consumption and in exact amounts consumed; thus money that was not required immediately stayed in the bank. Finally, they discovered a vast potential deposit base referred to as the *un-banked* and they hastily erected branch networks and electronic pipelines to deliver banking services to these areas of humanity. Obviously, the unspoken intention was to take in micro-deposits from far afield and use these to lend to those in the cities who sought credit.

The net effect has been an unprecedented level of savings in African banks. Deposit rates were reduced by banks in response to overwhelming new numbers of depositors and new, high deposit flows – ruling deposit rates obtainable across Africa now range from 1.5% to 3.5%.[142] Standards of customer service fell as banks experienced an upsurge of new customer numbers that they had not fully prepared for and became jaded by the surplus of deposits. Governments also discovered the revenue potential of taxing interest on deposits, thus further eroding net income to depositors.

Customers became unhappy about their flagging income from deposits, the treatment they received and penalties they sometimes incurred when taking their money to banks, and the extortionate withholding tax on their already dwindling savings returns. They started to look for alternative options. It was at this time that the capital markets burst onto the scene, finding a savings problem crying out for a solution. As a result it did not take long for capital markets in Africa to fill the void created by mediocre savings yields across the continent. Thus a basis for rapid stock market growth in Africa was created.[143]

> **" It did not take long for capital markets in Africa to fill the void created by mediocre savings yields across the continent. "**

Emergence of pension funds, asset management and investment companies

As more people engaged in gainful employment in African society the seed for the viability of pension funds was sown. This started with national pension and old age security arrangements, popularly known in many African countries as National Social Security Funds (NSSF). They are state-run and statutory monthly contributions are made by individuals and their employers. Over the years, these pension funds have been able to accumulate vast investable resources.

The Kenya NSSF boasted an asset base of KShs80 billion ($1 billion) at the end of 2009, having grown 51% in five years to that point. Of this, 40% is invested in the equities markets (up from 30% in 2004) and a further 21% in government securities (up from 8% in the same period).[144] Its Ugandan counterpart is almost as well endowed, with $726m of assets under management, and is the largest single investor in the local stock market.[145] NSSFs hold large liquid assets and act as stabilisers, or if you like buy-side central banks for African stock markets.

Independent asset management as a business has taken a fairly long time to come of age in Africa. Excepting the pan-African names like The Old Mutual Society, Robert Fleming, Investec, Genesis and AIG (now trading as Pine Bridge), the scene remained inactive for quite some time. Big corporates had pension funds but they managed them in-house with asset allocation being overweight in property and real estate. However, the situation changed when new legislation required them to outsource fund management to professional asset managers under regulated asset allocation criteria which gave greater emphasis to marketable securities. These measures set the stage for the broad expansion of local buy-side capital markets in African securities.

Investment groups and investment companies, either government owned, quasi-government or privately owned, have also had a major role to play in buttressing African capital markets. They take long-term investment views, therefore acting as market makers, supplying the necessary liquidity and market support. In Malawi, Press Corporation and National Investment Limited are the lifelines of the Malawi Stock Exchange.

Another major factor for the growth in the pension and investment groups in Sub-Saharan Africa is the proliferation of professional management capacity and capability. Young African graduates are becoming more sophisticated and better qualified to research, identify and analyse investment opportunities. The rate of CFA and ACCA enrolment and qualification in the African capital markets is increasing and will continue to accelerate into the future. African returnees from Wall Street and the City of London, casualties of the 2008-9 global financial crisis, are also increasingly plugging their well-honed asset allocation and management skills into African stock markets with good effect.

Liberalisation of national capital accounts

Until the 1990s full exchange controls ruled in African currency exchange regimes. Decades of deteriorating terms of trade that diminished export proceeds, and declining or non-existent domestic manufacturing capacity which necessitated the importation of finished goods, led to poor foreign exchange balances for African economies, tipping them into deficit for a very long time. This forced African governments to regress into exchange controls, making it cumbersome, if not impossible, to buy foreign exchange from the banks. All foreign exchange transactions had to be referred to central banks for authorisation and the banks were under instruction to decline more than they authorised.

These constraining macro-economic circumstances made it unattractive for foreign investment of any form to come to Africa, least of all foreign private portfolio inflows into private equity investments or public listed equities. These kinds of investments demand viable exits for the investors. As long as repatriation of investment proceeds, dividends, or any other outflows were subjected to lengthy approvals which were not guaranteed from monetary authorities, foreign investment into African capital markets was virtually minimal.

> **❝ In most of Africa where savings were low and financial assets incomprehensible, liberalisation of the national capital accounts to give access to foreign private portfolio flows gave more viability to local stock markets. ❞**

So it was that, as African economies started slowly to come back to life towards the end of the 1990s and the beginning of the 2000s, the critical need for new investment to re-invigorate economies was acknowledged. Access to external investments was deemed as the fastest and most assured way to kick-start economies which had long ground to a halt, and which lacked sufficient domestic savings to thrive on their own. As a consequence exchange controls were repealed, capital and trading accounts liberalised, and comprehensive and concessional investment codes written to give incentive to foreign investments to come to Africa.[146]

In most of Africa where savings were low and financial assets were simply incomprehensible, it was the liberalisation of the national capital accounts to give access to foreign private portfolio flows that gave more viability to local stock markets than any other factor. Whether these portfolio flows actually arrived in the magnitude expected was another matter altogether. The potential that they could gave impetus and confidence to national governments and the development partners to establish and sustain stock markets in SSA where there were none before.

Innovative products that aggregate micro-savings into unitised investments

One of the major challenges that faced stock market practitioners in Africa was how to make markets meaningful and accessible to the widest possible majority of African populations. In economies where the upper and middle classes make up not more than 5% of the population, it is easy to leave stock markets as a preserve of the elite. For a long time the Kenyan, Zimbabwean and Nigerian stock markets were the preserve of a very small group of people who had access to information and sizeable discretionary resources. The opaque system of operation, plus the high entry points for substantial and sustainable investments, made these markets inaccessible for ordinary members of the public.

The late Prof. C.K. Prahalad, in his seminal book *The Fortune At The Bottom Of The Pyramid,* proved that micro-savings are possible as long as they are organised to create a critical size and channelled into mainstream investment opportunities. The concept of unitised investments under collective investment schemes draws immensely from this principle. In African stock markets, one of the most revolutionary and progressive initiatives of the past decade has been the establishment of unit investment trusts.[147] The drive for this has come from two major underlying forces.

> **The proliferation of collective investment schemes and unitised products in African stock markets over the last ten years has enabled participation of more ordinary folks.**

The first of these forces is *regulation*. Stock market transaction and brokerage fees regimes are graded in a way that gives cost advantages to bigger, single transactions over smaller, multiple ones. Guidelines and regulations to govern the establishment, operation and management of collective investment schemes were promulgated and entrenched in the relevant laws. Simultaneously, tax incentives in the form of tax relief given for payroll deductions were dedicated to long-term focused investments under collective investment schemes. These steps allied together promote collective investments rather than inefficient, small or partial individual investments.

The second is *market forces*. Priority in terms of the amount of allocation of shares to investors, especially in primary offers, increasingly favours collectivised investments organised under qualified institutional investors' categories. Liberalisation of transaction brokerage fees has also ensured that institutional investors can drive down the transaction fees they pay because of their aggregated ticket sizes and the regularity of their transactions. Regulated collective investment schemes are expected to push back the savings they make to their customers. An upsurge in local professional management, investment analysis skills and portfolio-management experience has also enhanced the formation and acceptance of unitised investment products among the African public.

These developments have led to unit trusts lowering the threshold substantially while raising the bar in democratising stock market investments. The proliferation of collective investment schemes and unitised products in African stock markets over the last ten years has enabled participation of more ordinary folks, with the highest rate of new subscribers coming during the most recent stock market boom of 2003 to 2007. In Kenya, from a base of nothing in 2003, a total of 43 unit trusts/funds managed by 11 administrators have been registered since.[148] Between September 2009 and September 2010, the only period for which statistics are available, total aggregate collective investment scheme portfolio values have grown by 79% from $172.8m to $310m. The growth rate is much higher in local currency terms, at 93%.[149]

Increase in the profile of African markets abroad

The term *frontier markets* is synonymous with African markets; it has connotations of the furthest limits and conjures the image of an untapped marketplace. It was coined by IFC's Farida Khambata in 1992 but has only made it into the international lexicon since 2007 when S&P launched its Select Frontier Index.[150] The same is true of African capital markets. As an asset class, they have only gained global recognition since the beginning of the last world economic boom in 2003-4; they are the last to be considered by international investors. They present unprecedented potential though.

The profile of African capital markets has been boosted abroad lately. Several factors are responsible for this. The greatest appeal of these markets has been sustainably high nominal and real returns, where developed world markets consistently produce poor nominal returns and even worse real returns. The other major factor came to the forefront only following the 2008-9 global financial crisis – namely the rewriting of global risk perceptions. Where hitherto developed Western economies were considered risk-free or having minimal, fully diversifiable risk and developing economies were perceived to be laden with excessive, irreducible risk, even toxic in the case of Africa, the financial crisis upended this theory. Risk was once and for all unified across the entire world; venturesome investors were emboldened and began to look beyond familiar frontiers.

It was in the clearing of this fog of stereotypical profiling that African markets came within the sights of major international institutional investors. Africa-focused frontier market funds based either in London, Luxembourg or the Channel Islands sprung up. Their capacity to raise funds abroad and invest them across Sub-Saharan Africa – though these funds are still in their early stages – has led to a phenomenal preliminary impact. Their ticket sizes surpass anything that has been seen so far, injecting unparalleled liquidity to African markets. Their demand for investment research and superior market intelligence has engendered widespread efforts towards modernisation of these markets and the professionals operating within them.

These days, seminars and conference circuits on African markets are being held across the world to familiarise people with the rising African economies and markets. *Africa Investor*, a prolific magazine rich in content about African businesses, markets and entrepreneurs, has been holding annual award ceremonies for African companies, stock exchanges and investment funds since 2004. Now in collaboration with the New York Stock Exchange and Euronext, *Africa Investor* launched an annual Ai index summit series for global investors in 2008. The series facilitates one-on-one meetings between issuers and investors to enable international institutional investors to meet African companies, discuss latest trends in corporate governance, high-growth opportunities and the next wave of African securities and IPOs. Marcus Evans, an international business events organising firm, in 2008 and 2010 ran two conferences on investing in frontier markets which saw a sizeable turnout and brought together international investors with a focus on frontier/African markets on the one hand and investment bankers and stock brokers from African capital markets on the other.

> " Seminars and conference circuits on African markets are being held across the world to familiarise people with the rising African economies and markets. "

Conclusion/marketplace implications

Why are capital markets vitally important to the growth and development of African economies?

Firstly, they provide the best means, so far, for the greatest proportion of the population to participate in the economic growth of their economies and share in the wealth and value chains generated. They achieve this by channelling, pooling and harnessing individual savings and deploying them into productive sectors of the economies, further contributing to GDP growth.

Secondly, the introduction and wide distribution of marketable financial assets with better liquidity and efficient price discovery, are features that aid asset growth and capital formation and build into a collective wealth-effect among modern African societies. This acts as as an incentive to spend and consume.

Thirdly, they act as traps for global private investment capital flows, with the twin effects of bringing down the cost of capital for African economies and deepening liquidity, which is necessary for long-term asset price stability and appreciation.

LAYING DOWN THE ENABLERS

II

Introduction

There are two parts to *opportunity*. The first is confirming that it is there, or being able to describe and present it in terms of what brings it about or makes it possible. The second part is pointing to the means or tools by which it can be appropriated, or being able to describe and present it in terms of what makes it practical. To put it another way, opportunity can be broken into two equal parts:

1. finding a 30-foot tall palm tree with ripe coconuts, and

2. finding the ladder to climb to the top of the tree and bring down the coconuts.

Part I of this book has taken care of the first part or parts. Part II of this book moves on to address the second aspect of opportunity of business and investment in SSA. It surveys, reviews and analyses all the means assembled by which Africa's economic propositions have become or continue to become viable. It presents the fundamental and deliberate interventions which have been put in place especially in the past decade to enable the operation of profitable business and investments within and across African economies.

INFRASTRUCTURE IMPERATIVE

9

For a very long time *infrastructure* and *Africa* would not have been found in the same sentence, unless in a negative sense. Now probably the leading and most dominant developmental trend in Africa is infrastructure; there is a rich story in between these two extremes. Colonial era transport infrastructure was laid down upon two broad connected themes. The first was to ship Africa's raw materials from the mines and agricultural production from the plantations to sea ports and onwards to European industries. Where raw materials were bulky and uneconomic to ship, infrastructure connected first-level processing plants to the main arterial one-way traffic grids ferrying Africa's raw wealth to Europe. Railway lines to such remote places as Magadi in Kenya, Kasese in Uganda and Ndola in Zambia were testaments to colonial infrastructural design and layout. The second theme involved finding means for ferrying European capital goods and finished products to African countries, thereby expanding markets for European goods.[151]

A quick glimpse at the history of power generation reveals the same experience. For example, before the last decade neither Tanzania nor Uganda have added any meaningful long-term generation capacity since the Union Flag was lowered in Dar and Kampala. Uganda's installed generation capacity has remained frozen in time at 300MW from the Owen Falls hydropower plants. Likewise, Tanzania failed to invest in new generation capacity for a long time on the back of the failed public policies of *Ujamaa* because it was hamstrung by the resources limitations in the face of having far too many things to do to play catch up. Its current capacity is 773MW, 70% of which is hydro-based from the dams on the Great Ruaha and Pangani rivers.

Malawi has three hydro-power stations (Nkula, Tedzani and Kapichira) generating a total of 282MW, and this is in a country with vast coal deposits. Rwanda has only 69MW of installed capacity – largely from thermal sources and Burundi has 38MW of installed capacity. In Nigeria every factory, office property and home has a standby generator which runs more than it stands-by. In DR Congo only 1,170MW of the 2,446MW[152] installed capacity is available, despite there being enough hydro potential in this country to light all of Africa and southern Europe.

In Ghana, the sense of triumphalism that followed the heroic completion of the (mighty) Akosombo Dam (912MW) in 1965 was not seen again – in spite of the growing needs for more generation capacity – until 1981 when the Kpong Dam was built downstream. Underinvestment in electric power and the absence of considerable industrial capacity in Africa became a proverbial chicken and egg situation; industrial investments stayed away because power was unavailable and power generation capacity stalled because there was no effective industrial demand to utilise any new power generated.

> **African infrastructure currently reigns as the most-talked about topic in development policy circles and also among corporate and institutional investors in Africa and beyond.**

For water, one peculiar aspect underscored years and years of under-investment in its delivery in Africa; nature. Natural drainage systems in non-arid regions delivered water into close proximity of just about every homestead, and householders also located dwellings next to rivers, streams and lakes. The corollary is that without laying down as much as a meter of piping, people still got running water. Therefore, for a long time, piped water remained the preserve of factories, urban centres and critical public institutions like hospitals. Even for schools and prisons, water was viewed as a luxury. Even though in 1990 SSA countries lived with only an average of 49% of their population having access to piped water – a figure that had improved to 56% by 2006, there has been no major crisis – yet.[153]

Clearly, infrastructure development in Africa was abandoned between 1980 and 2000, and has only gained momentum in the last decade. In most of SSA, infrastructure has only become mainstream as recently as 2005 and thereafter. Undoubtedly, African infrastructure currently reigns as the most-talked about topic in development policy circles and also among corporate and institutional investors in Africa and beyond. How it pans out in the near future will affect Africa's readiness to conduct business on the global scene and its competitiveness in doing so.

Driving forces

The need to interconnect cities and countries and extend arteries of commerce

The greatest infrastructural challenge in Sub-Saharan Africa is to link Africa to itself (interconnect countries) and states to themselves (networking within individual states). In most countries only a few major cities have road connections and where they do exist the pattern is a centripetal one – single spokes connecting the rest of the country to the capital city (the hub). Other large, important towns are unlinked and when travelling from one to another, one first has to travel to the capital city to obtain bearings from there. Large parts of countries have not been served by road, posing challenges of viability to numerous upcoming entrepreneurial activities in rural Africa.

It is out of this deficit and realisation of the critical role of transport infrastructure that ongoing ambitious efforts to lay down a network of roads in Africa have been embarked upon. Almost every SSA country is currently undergoing unprecedented road construction, expansion or extension. National budgets are suddenly bulging with high levels of development expenditure, which is being enhanced immensely by international grants, bilateral funding and multilateral facilities. Many countries are directly tapping capital markets – both local and international – for ring-fenced infrastructure finance by selling bonds. Seven SSA countries – South Africa, Seychelles, Senegal, Ivory Coast, Gabon, Republic of the Congo and Ghana – have sovereign bonds. All of them, aside from South Africa, have entered the market since 2007.

Nigeria, Kenya, Angola and Zambia were expected to tap the market for international capital by starting to sell Eurobonds from 2011.[154] All these were suspended, however, due to the resurgence of the global economic crisis in 2011. The government of Kenya only restarted infrastructural development in 2004. From zero in

" The greatest infrastructural challenge in Sub-Saharan Africa is to link Africa to itself (interconnect countries) and states to themselves (networking within individual states). "

2002, Kenya's annual infrastructure budget had increased to $2.25 billion (KShs140 billion) by 2010.[155] Major trunk roads have been re-laid, others have been expanded to increase haulage and vehicular carrying capacity, and new roads are being constructed where there were none before. In the five years to 2011, 830km of brand new tarmac roads have been built in Kenya (from Emali to Loitokitok; and from Isiolo to Moyale) while 1,400km of existing roads that had been in disrepair have been fully rehabilitated.[156] Liberia is currently implementing a co-ordinated road reconstruction programme at a cost of $175m; while in DR Congo, China has entered into a $3 billion *infrastructure for minerals* deal, most of which is concentrated around the rehabilitation of major trunk roads. Rwanda has just spent $44.5m to redevelop its paved road network to some of the best conditions available in SSA.[157]

At a policy and regulatory reform level various measures have been implemented in the past decade by African countries to put in place well devised frameworks or framework options for the speedy delivery of modern infrastructure to African economies. At the same time they are trying to ensure the optimal use and management of infrastructural networks in a sustainable way. These measures include, but are not limited to, the following: establishment of second generation road funds in most countries, financed by fuel levies imposed and collected at fuel pumps (most countries already have these funds and those without are developing them); creation of autonomous road agencies or authorities with express oversight responsibilities; and management of the development, use and maintenance of national road networks. In some countries, specialist maintenance management agencies have been established over and above the roads agencies to look after continuous road maintenance and in others new forms of contract-based maintenance have been introduced using private sector providers.

China is at the vanguard of this African infrastructural onslaught with its model of aid-for-trade. To quote from a McKinsey & Company article 'Making The Most of Chinese Aid to Africa':

> *"From 2002 to 2007 China offered over $33 billion of government sponsored aid and development, over half for infrastructure projects, to African countries. Today the continent is dotted with Chinese sponsored projects from railways to agricultural centres, to clinics, to stadiums."*

African governments recognise the importance of inter-country connectivity in making commerce possible between them and in supporting the export-import industries of landlocked countries. There are 15 landlocked countries in Africa which rely on the transport access of transit countries to be able to reach international trade partners. According to 'African Infrastructure: A time for Transformation', a co-publication of Agence Française de Développement (AFD) and the World Bank (2010), trans-African transport corridors include no more than 10,000km of road and carry about $200 billion of trade a year.

Efforts to revive and improve management of old earmarked international transport corridors across SSA are informed by the imperative for a fully networked, efficiently managed, multimodal, pan-continental transport and logistics system. This is vitally important in making the continent ready, open and enabled for global business, plugging it into the global supply chain. Between 60,000km and 100,000km of road will be required to provide full intra-continental connectivity.

For a list of the major transport corridors in Africa see the appendix.

Expansion of finance for infrastructure development

According to the article 'Infrastructure: A long road ahead' by McKinsey & Company consultants Rod Cloete, Felix Faulhaber and Markus Zils, between 1998 and 2007 spending on African infrastructure rose at a compound annual rate of 17% from $3 billion in 1998 to $12 billion in 2008, significantly outstripping the growth of global infrastructure investment.[158] The article added that this growth has been driven largely by increased financing from non-OECD (Organisation for Economic Co-operation and Development) governments – particularly China, which provided 77% of the finance in 2007.

Another source of infrastructure finance for African countries that has notably expanded has been the Arab funds co-ordination group (incorporating the Abu Dhabi fund for development, Arab Fund for Economic and Social Development, Arab Bank for Economic Development in Africa, Islamic Development Bank, Kuwait Fund for Arab Economic Development, OPEC Fund for International Development and the Saudi Fund for Development) though most of this is still concentrated in north Africa.

Difficulties faced in African transport systems development

The endemic problem with African transport systems is capacity constraints. These include unnecessary delays caused by crippling bureaucracy, dysfunctional customs services, customs and procedures that are not harmonised, and chronic corruption. To streamline the functions of these crucial arteries of commerce, transit corridor management authorities have been established in the past five to seven years.

The general objectives of these authorities are to: promote the increased utilisation of the corridors for surface transport of goods between the respective countries and sea ports; take measures to accelerate movement of traffic and avoid delays in the movement of goods; minimise evasion of customs duties and taxes; simplify and harmonise documentation and procedures relating to the movement of goods in transit; promote improvement of surface infrastructure and capacity enhancement; ensure the corridor is efficient and cost effective; and to engage in marketing activities, focusing on business development and attracting maritime business from traditional routes.

The make up of these agencies is increasingly taking into account private sector stakeholders' inputs, contributions and strategic importance. The Walvis Bay Corridor Group, regarded as a model transport corridor in Africa, is purely a Public Private Partnership (PPP), with full participation by private players at all levels. Others, for instance the Northern Corridor Transit Transport Coordination Authority, have a stakeholders' committee designed and run as a PPP with inputs, ideas and resolutions cascading to the executive board and the authority.

Dominant themes and major projects

The dominant themes cutting across infrastructural development in Africa today are the connecting of missing links for the existing corridors, or restoring and rehabilitating collapsed sections. Table 9.1 shows some of the flagship regional road and railway infrastructure projects either under development since 2009-10 or just about to begin, with funds having been provided by the various multilateral and co-investing financiers.

Table 9.1 – a selection of the major road and rail projects in Africa

Project	Region	Financial estimate ($m)	Finance commitments secured ($m)
Mombasa – Nairobi – Addis corridor extension	East Africa	530	338
Kenya Northern Corridor rehabilitation	East Africa	N/A	253
CEMAC Transport Transit Facilitation (CAR & Cameroon)	Central Africa	N/A	217
Route Ketta – Djoum (Ouesso-Sangmelima/Dousalla-Dolisie)	Central Africa	336	195
Nacala Road Corridor	Southern Africa	319	186
Abidjan – Lagos Transport & Transit Facilitation project	West Africa	445	N/A
Douala – N'Djamena Corridor	Central Africa	43.2	N/A
Northern Corridor (Mabarara – Gatuna) Uganda – Rwanda	East Africa	292	N/A
Beira corridor project	Southern Africa	263	N/A
WAEMU Road programme 1 (Burkina Faso, Ghana, Mali	West Africa	305	N/A

Source: ICA annual report 2009. N/A: Not available

Demands for industrial and power capacity

All over Africa today, power generation is an important trend. That is alongside the trends in transport and logistical infrastructure. Almost every country has a growing pipeline of power projects to be commissioned and delivered in quick succession between 2013 and 2020. In fact, a new power race has begun in Africa; the

> **❝** Almost every country has a growing pipeline of power projects to be commissioned and delivered in quick succession between 2013 and 2020. In fact, a new power race has begun in Africa. **❞**

yawning power deficit has become too critical to ignore. The fast pace of real estate development and capacity expansion in industries to cater to the ever-growing needs of a constantly bulging population have put overbearing pressure on available power generation capacity across Africa.

African governments are now beginning to awaken to the fundamental role of power generation capacity for industrialisation and economic growth. Accordingly, the ongoing expansion of power generation capacity at projects all over Africa has a twin focus: to meet immediate unmet demand accumulated over decades of underinvestment; and to prepare for the anticipated explosion of future demand on the back of the accelerating momentum of real estate development, urbanisation, and the industrial and consumer demands of an expanding and modernising African population. With this comes the need to create an enabling environment for additional private investments.

Energy projects ongoing in Africa

Some of the largest and most ambitious hydropower plant projects completed in the past five years or nearing completion include: the 4,300MW Inga III hydropower project on the River Congo in DR Congo; the 1,478MW Gibe III Dam on River Omo in Ethiopia; the 1,300MW Mphanda Nkuwa hydropower plant on the Zambezi in Mozambique; the 850MW capacity extension project on the Cahora Bassa dam of Mozambique; the capacity extensions on Capanda and Cambambe hydropower plants in Angola to increase their generation capacity to 520MW and 700MW respectively; the 560MW Karuma Falls hydropower project on the river Nile, Uganda; the

256MW Bujagali hydropower plant on the river Nile in Uganda; the 50MW Bumbuna hydropower project in Sierra Leone; the 143MW Ruzizi III regional hydropower project on River Ruzizi at the borders of DR Congo, Burundi and Rwanda; and the 120MW Itezhi-Tezhi hydropower project on Kafue River, Zambia.

There are currently some other renewable, alternative energy initiatives in the continent of Africa that have gained attention for their economic and trailblazing significance. In Botswana the Mmamabula energy project is a 1,200MW coal-fired power plant intended to supply South Africa's energy needs. The Lake Turkana Wind Power project in northern Kenya (with installed potential of 300MW) is set to be the biggest wind energy project in Africa. In Lake Kivu, on the border of Rwanda and DR Congo, 700MW of power potential is being developed separately. Kivuwatt, a subsidiary of US energy company Contour Global, has the major stake while Rwanda Energy Company, owned by a local investment concern Rwanda Investment Group (RIG), and Industrial Promotion Services of the Aga Khan Foundation for Economic Development, are developing the rest.

In Kenya, geothermal potential is estimated to be anywhere between 4,500 and 7,000MW. The government has established a geothermal exploration and steam field development company to shoulder the upfront risks and costs of exploration drilling. This arrangement instantly assures the viability of power plant investments based on geothermal energy by state and private power players. The state power generation company, Kengen, is at the advanced stage of bringing a total of 280MW on stream by the year 2013. Private players, including international names, are lining up for a piece of the show in this emerging energy bonanza. Power experts have billed it the long-term, lowest cost power development option for Kenya.

The show stopper for the pan-African power supply solution will be the Grand Inga project. With a power generation potential of between 39,000MW and 45,000MW, it has the potential to supply southern, eastern and central Africa. It is being designed to feed two separate transmission grids and existing power pools: the eastern transmission corridor to stretch from DR Congo through Zambia and Mozambique to the eastern African countries, including South Sudan; and the western corridor power inter-connector of the southern African power pool, taking power to Angola, Botswana, Namibia and South Africa. The most significant aspect of the Grand Inga power project is that it will offer possibly the cheapest power supply to the broadest expanse of the African continent, freeing national resources to be diverted to opportunities that meet their own competitive advantage in an environment of assured and secure power supply.

Improving transmission grids

Another important variable of Africa's power development equation is fixing inadequate national transmission grids. The irony of Africa's power solution is that almost all newly surveyed and proven vast energy resources are in remote places; far removed from centres of existing development and often hundreds of miles away from existing power transmission and evacuation grids. In order that the power plants come on-stream quickly, grid extensions have become essential.

This phenomenon has added to the feasibility of numerous otherwise unrealisable, albeit vast, renewable resources. For these, new incentives such as negotiated commercial wheeling tariffs and capacity charges have added new grid procurement possibilities through various PPP development and operating options. For example, a 400km grid extension is being erected as a Build Operate Transfer (BOT) PPP option to evacuate the Lake Turkana wind power to the city of Nairobi and its environs.

Regional energy markets

Efforts to create regional energy markets are being pursued through establishment of regional power pools – the Southern African Power Pool, the East African Power Pool and the West African Power Pool. These pools link countries with surplus generated power or installed capacity with countries with energy deficits. The principal aim is to ensure uniform availability and access to power in countries within one economic and trading bloc, as well as to standardise the cost of power within one regional bloc to reduce or eliminate undue economic advantage for some countries on account of greater access to, or lower cost of, energy.

A major positive consequence of regionally integrated power transmission and distribution systems is the contribution to the viability of single blockbuster energy development projects, for example the Grand Inga Hydro or nuclear power plants, which are by nature high capacity and which would otherwise fail feasibility tests on the basis of meagre potential of national economies. The Southern African Power Pool is up and running, while the western and eastern pools are still being connected. Inter-country interconnector projects are currently ongoing in both these regions. Other countries that will have a surplus in the foreseeable future include Uganda, DR Congo, Mozambique and Ethiopia.

Table 9.2 summarises some of the big ticket power development projects for which financing has been arranged between 2008 and 2010, and which are either already in progress or just about to commence in Sub-Saharan Africa.

Table 9.2 – a summary of major power development projects

Project	Project type	Region	Financial estimate ($m)
Gibe III Hydropower	Hydro plants	Ethiopia, East Africa	2,018
Rift Valley Geothermal power	Hydro plants	Kenya, East Africa	1,810
Itezhi Tezhi Hydropower	Hydro plants	Zambia, Southern Africa	418
Ruzizi III Hydropower	Hydro plants	DR Congo, Burundi, Rwanda	487
Rusumo Falls Hydro project	Hydro plants	Rwanda,Tanzania (E. Africa)	190
Mmabula Energy project	Coal plant	Botswana, Southern Africa	6,000
Lake Turkana Wind Power	Alternative	Kenya , East Africa	635
Senegal Wind power	Alternative	Senegal, West Africa	150
Ethiopia-Kenya-Uganda Interconnector	Grid	East Africa	1,176
Caprivi Regional power market – Interconnector	Grid	Southern Africa	700
Kenya – Uganda interconnector	Grid	East Africa	400
Zambia-Tanzania-Kenya Interconnector	Grid	SADC-EAC	860
Burkina Faso – Ghana – Mali Interconnector	Grid	West Africa	350
CLSG Interconnector	Grid	West Africa	402
Inter-zonal transmission hub	Grid	West Africa	147
Ghana – Côte d'Ivoire interconnector	Grid	West Africa	80
OMV-Sambangalou et Kaleta Interconnector	Grid	Senegal-Gambia (West Africa)	696

Source: ICA annual report 2009.

New transport corridors

Africa has undergone various geographical and political changes over the course of the past decade. Some of these have been landmark shifts like the birth of a new country (South Sudan); the end of long, bloody and debilitating civil wars (Liberia, Angola); and the discovery and consequent exploitation of new mineral wealth in hitherto remote and inaccessible geographical areas. Either independently or in combination, these three factors have acted as the major driving forces in the current push into virgin territories across Africa, inspiring the conceptualisation of brand new transport and transit corridors, or the restoration of erstwhile abandoned ones, long overgrown by forest and vegetation cover. Either way, transport and transit infrastructure is now arriving in parts of Africa where it was inconceivable before.

The aspect of the African transport architecture that has had the biggest impact is the development of new transport corridors, created to serve parts of the continent that were hitherto unreachable. The need for access to newly discovered resources and vast, newly established farmlands, or newly politically feasible markets, is the major driving factor for this new push into parts of Africa that were previously untapped.

The Lamu-Juba/Addis Ababa corridor is a multimodal transit corridor designed to link a second deep sea port to be built on the east coast of Kenya at Lamu to the landlocked states of South Sudan, Ethiopia, Northern Uganda, and hopefully into the north-east of DR

❝ Transport and transit infrastructure is now arriving in parts of Africa where it was inconceivable before. ❞

Congo and Chad. The key infrastructure envisaged is an ultra-modern high capacity deep sea port at Manda Bay in Lamu, Kenya, to be served by a complex of communication and transit infrastructure as follows: a trans-continental superhighway linking the capitals of Juba, South Sudan, and Addis Ababa, Ethiopia, to the port at Lamu through the city of Isiolo in Kenya; a standard gauge railway line running parallel to the highway; a high-speed fibre optic cable, also to run parallel; a 1,500km pipeline from Juba to Lamu; a refinery to be integrated with an oil export terminal; a high voltage power grid; and international airports in Lamu, Isiolo and Lokichoggio in Kenya, which are being redesigned as concept resort cities under Kenya's Vision 2030 development blueprint.[159]

Another not so new, but until 2006 fully collapsed, corridor is the Lobito corridor that terminates at the port of Lobito in Angola. This once served the resource-rich countries of the south-west of Africa including Angola, DR Congo, Zambia and Botswana, but has been out of operation since the mid-1970s due to the Angolan civil war. The government of Angola, together with regional governments' initiatives under SADC and NEPAD (New Partnership for Africa's Development), have been restoring this corridor since 2007 through refurbishment and capacity enhancement of the Lobito port, rehabilitation, upgrade and extension of the 2,149km Benguela railway line within contemporary conventions, and the construction of an oil refinery at the port. The roads system that feeds and complements the railway line is also in a state of serious disrepair and needs to be restored to enable the railway to operate optimally. This transit corridor is uniquely placed to service the mineral rich Katanga province of DR Congo and the Zambian copper belt. These, like most other transit corridor modernisation and enhancement projects going on in the continent of Africa, are taking place under the prevailing international frameworks of concessioning, co-investment and PPP in construction and operation.[160]

In Tanzania, the Mtwara Development Corridor is another brand new trans-African infrastructure system. The port of Mtwara, located very close to the southern border with Mozambique, is being upgraded to a full service trans-shipment port. It is intended to relieve the port of Dar es Salaam, which is over-burdened by servicing two massive corridors – the central corridor serving Rwanda, Burundi and DR Congo, and the Dar es Salaam corridor serving Malawi and Zambia. It is therefore designed to open the rich natural resources base, relatively undeveloped, emerging mining and agricultural belt of southern Tanzania, northern Mozambique, Lake Malawi, Malawi, and eastern and north-eastern Zambia.

The area is well endowed with mineral, agricultural, forestry, gas and tourism assets. The main infrastructure is, or will be, a 400MW coal-fired power station at Mchuchuma, Tanzania; a 950km power grid from Mchuchuma to Mtwara; and the upgrade of Mtwara port to handle, among other things, vast coal exports to Australia and Asia. The other major projects within this corridor include the upgrade of the ports of Mbamba Bay and Manda on the shores of Lake Malawi, and the construction and upgrades of the road and rail links, especially the road from Mtwara to Mbamba which is expected to provide the corridor with a transport backbone.[161]

The place of deep sea ports in international trade

In the last decade (the 2000s), both general and container cargo passing through African public ports has trebled. Persistent capacity constraints in terms of port equipment, trans-shipment infrastructure, terminal storage, dredging capability and operational challenges, have continued to be the hallmark of Africa's public ports; hampering trade flows and precluding further expansion in maritime trade. Current capacity of most Sub-Saharan African ports does not allow them to handle vessels above 2,200 TEUs (20 foot equivalent) containers. For this reason, none have direct transit connections with the major world ports of Rotterdam in Europe, Baltimore on the eastern seaboard of America and Shanghai in China, leaving major trans-shipment for Africa-bound freight to be done outside of the region, in Algericas (Spain) and Tangier (Morocco) for west African countries and in Dubai or Salalah (Oman) for east African countries.

Privatisation of ports and port operations

Various measures have been put in place across SSA to address these challenges and others are still being considered. African ports are increasingly moving to the landlord port system, where the state owns and operates major port infrastructure, but allows the private sector to provide basic services. Since 2000, several major container terminals have been concessioned to private operators. "The clear leader so far is Bolloré Africa Logistics, a division of Bolloré Group, a French industrial conglomerate", said *The Economist* magazine.[162] It added, "as a port operator, stevedore, warehouser and freight forwarder, Bolloré handles 80% of west Africa's exports (excluding oil), 25% of east Africa's – in short, nearly all of Africa's cotton and cocoa, as well as much of its coffee, rubber and timber."

Bolloré operates private container terminals in the following African ports: Abidjan, Côte d'Ivoire; Tema, Ghana; Douala, Cameroon; Cotonou, Benin; Libreville and Owendo, Gabon; Pointe Noire, Republic of Congo; Lomé, Togo; Mombasa, Kenya and Pointe de Galets, La Reunion.[163] The port of Dar es Salaam is now operated by Hutchison Port Holdings, a division of Hutchison Whampoa of Hong Kong; Djibouti port has been taken over by DP World, a division of Dubai World; and the ports of Maputo and Matola in Mozambique have also been concessioned to Maputo Port Development Company, a joint venture between Grindrod and DP World.

> **❝** Eleven African countries, dominated by Nigeria and Angola, supply 12% of world demand and 19% of US demand for oil. **❞**

Where full port operation privatisation has not yet been achieved, specific terminal operations have; for example the Grain Bulk terminal at Mombasa which is privately owned and run by Grain Bulk Handling Limited. In Port Harcourt, Nigeria, two terminals of the port of Onne have been concessioned to Intels. Liquid bulk terminals – principally oil terminals – of most western African ports have attracted mainly Chinese and US investments on the main oil export platforms, with generally high international standards. Eleven African countries, dominated by Nigeria and Angola, supply 12% of world demand, and 19% of US demand for oil.

Increasing capacity and improving efficiency

Being located in major urban areas limits the capacity of most ports to expand, with terminal storage remaining an ever chronic problem. In response to this, most port agencies have established inland container ports to which containers are transported under bond and storage. Trans-shipment is then done there where land is not a constraining factor.

Maintenance and dredging to increase capacity is also ongoing in most ports so that bigger ships can be handled; with the ultimate objective of making some African ports Panamax compliant (meaning they are able to handle vessels with capacity of 4,500 TEUs and above). This thereby would attract major shipping lines which have hitherto neglected Africa because of its shallow ports, meagre container storage capacity and lack of cargo to carry on the return trip.

Djibouti port, since being taken over by DP World, is expected to take over trans-shipment business for cargo destined for east Africa, from the ports of Salalah in Oman and Dubai in United Arab Emirates (UAE). DP World is scheduled to bring on-stream a special facility in Doraleh, Djibouti, with specialised high capacity trans-shipment infrastructure for east Africa and the Indian Ocean islands. For the main southern African trans-shipment port of Durban, South Africa, plans to tackle endemic congestion and delays are advancing through scheduled commissioning of major new capacity on the new Pier One Scheme.

According to the article 'Ports and Shipping: Landlords Needed', most landlocked countries now have alternative outlets to the sea.[164] The five landlocked states in west Africa have 15 transit possibilities. Zambia alone has five competing corridors. The total cost, including border and port delays, determines the choices of shippers. More competition among corridors could lower the administrative blockages to free flows of goods on the corridors and shipping lines have introduced *congestion charges*. Intense rivalry for trans-shipment business among neighbouring ports, such as Mombasa and Dar es Salaam, is emerging as a very welcome positive agent for service enhancement, limitations of delays, rationalisation of handling costs, integrated port, customs and inland transport arrangements, and equipment upgrades. In this regard Mombasa has been converted into a 24-hour service.

According to the same report, trade corridors are shifting and changes in direction of maritime trade are expected to soon positively impact African sea trade. Some Asian liners are reported to be considering services to the east coast of Latin America and the Caribbean through the southern tip of Africa. This is thanks in no small part to the Somali pirates, but also to the steady

❝ Dredging to increase capacity is also ongoing in most ports so that bigger ships can be handled, with the ultimate objective of making some African ports Panamax compliant. ❞

improvements and reliability of the port of Durban as a fully-fledged trans-shipment facility which shortens distance covered and costs incurred. This is anticipated to strategically favour ports on the eastern seaboard of Africa as they will stand on a major maritime corridor. As major traders attract the global operators, they may also develop a niche market in African feeder services thereby re-establishing African-owned shipping companies. For example, the re-establishment of Togo's Ecomarine in the west African feeder market in 2003 is deemed as a preliminary move in the expected repositioning of Africa's sea trade.

Evolutions in deep sea shipping markets that are directly affecting the African shipping market will necessitate location change as space for manoeuvre, storage and expansion becomes a constant problem in hub ports. This fact informs the decision by South Africa to build a brand new port at Richards Bay, which has deep water and adequate space as opposed to Durban, which is congested, and Cape Town, which is too distant.

Plans have been initiated for the phased development of a mega port, including a container terminal. The same logic supplies the merit for the second port on the Kenyan coast, in Lamu. In Nigeria, a new deep sea port, Lekki Port, is coming up with dedicated terminals for containers, dry bulk and liquid cargoes. Intended to complement the three congested ports in Lagos, it is touted to be the first port in west Africa to accommodate Suezmax ships.[165]

Demands of urbanisation on infrastructure

Another major series of events taking place in African infrastructure has to do with urban systems. Almost every major city in Africa is experiencing gentrification and modernisation. Ambitious new plans have been drawn for almost every capital city in Sub-Saharan Africa, containing not only short-term and immediate remedial responses to the effects of years of neglect and decay, but also medium-term developmental and capacity extension initiatives within current budgets, and ultimately plans for the long-term vision of world class international cities. Some countries, for example Kenya, have established full government ministries with the specific remit of overseeing the metropolitan development of their capital cities.

In the short term, streets are being re-laid and lanes remarked, downtown grids have been redesigned to allow a one-way only feeder concept, and street lighting is being repaired and extended to all parts of the cities under concessioning to private sector players. Drainage systems are being unclogged and extended; buildings are being freshly painted. City walks, bus stops, road divides and parks have been replanted with flowers, and fitted with benches and water fountains.

> **Almost every major city in Africa is experiencing gentrification and modernisation.**

In the medium term, more changes are to be introduced. Community lighting programmes are being deployed in all public areas, residential estates and city suburbs to enhance security; as yet unfinished access roads, exits and slip roads are being completed; major grid roads are being dualised or broadened with additional lanes; and by-passes and beltways are being constructed to decongest city centres and redirect traffic away from the cities.

Long-term development plans for major cities

For the long term, visions vary according to the size and shape of the ambition for the economy. Generally the plan is to bring major African cities to the standards and character of leading international cities. For Nairobi, Abuja, Addis Ababa, Accra, Kigali and Lusaka the concepts are not too dissimilar. The idea revolves around giant metropolises designed deliberately for functionality and aesthetics. This involves bringing neighbouring districts and municipalities that have open spaces and land at reasonable costs under the authority and management of the cities.

The grand plans envision systematic planning with the intention to cluster specific commercial and municipal functions in specified locations within the metropolises and link them with modern, world-class multimodal infrastructure. For example, in Nairobi, a world class ICT city named Konza City is being designed on the eastern outskirts, numerous interconnected private residential cities are coming up to the north of the city and a vast logistical hub is clustering around the Jomo Kenyatta International Airport. Two major traffic bypasses have been completed and a third is under construction to keep unnecessary traffic out of the city centre.

Plans are advanced to outfit the city of Nairobi with a rapid metro train service intended to reduce vehicular traffic on the main grid road connecting the city with the airport. "The Project will provide a link to the Jomo Kenyatta International Airport, to enable smooth and rapid transit between the airport and the Nairobi Central Business District, further cementing Nairobi's reputation as the commercial hub of East Africa" – so runs a description of the project by InfraCo Africa, a partner in the development of this project with the Kenya Railways Corporation.[166]

Under the Kigali City priority infrastructure projects of the 'Kigali City Master Plan', which commenced in 2007, expedited upgrade of infrastructure is paramount: complete the paving of the 84% unpaved city roads, development of both an inner and outer ring road and the completion of the drainage system (which was previously only 6% complete) were initially envisaged for 2011.[167] These have been delayed by funding challenges arising from the global economic crisis of 2011, especially affecting the key source markets for capital: North America, Europe and Asia. In 2011 the government conducted investor road shows abroad to interest international investors in the projects being procured under a PPP framework.

In Abuja, an upgrade of two formerly six-lane highways to ten lane highways – the first to the Nnamdi Azikiwe International airport and its industrial and residential environs, and the second to the city of Kaduna – has begun to reduce congested vehicular traffic along these routes.[168] Under the Integrated Transport Project for Botswana, the third component is an ambitious urban roads infrastructure investment for the greater Gaborone city. "The investment aims to solve the urgent urban congestions along the major city roads/streets and intersections introducing modem and advanced planning, design and implementation techniques."[169]

Expanding aerial connections and airline networks

Four factors driving sustainable growth in African aviation

Sustainable growth in African civil aviation business has been, and continues to be, driven by four important factors, which are discussed below.

1. The world coming to Africa

Africa is opening up and the rest of the world is increasingly fascinated with it. This has been helped a great deal by collective silencing of guns and artillery (though sporadic reports ricochet from time to time); adoption of Western modernity, including democracy or semblances of it; and the world's insatiable appetite for the wealth buried deep under the soils of Africa; or just to take in Africa's endlessly diverse beauty and range of attractions. Tourists and business travellers from the rest of the world are therefore coming to Africa in increasing numbers.

2. Africa reaching out to the world

Africa's willingness to consume what is made outside of Africa lays bare its woeful manufacturing capacity and variety deficit, as well as the punitively high-cost manufacturing base. Africa just cannot have enough of what Asia, North America and Europe, and even South Africa, produce.

3. Africa trading with itself

Before 2000 there were scarce economic or social links between most African countries. Trade within African countries was non-existent, as most of them were producers of raw materials and primary resources supplying European or Asian manufacturing and processing systems. Since 2000, trade between African nations has been rising; regional manufacturing capacity growing;

political and social interaction increasing, the numbers of diplomatic and business conferences rising. There is also a distinct revival in regional or inter-country cultural activities.

For these reasons travel needs within Africa are escalating. Kenya Airways in 2011 operated 35 spokes terminating in African cities and ten direct international connections, all from its hub in Nairobi. Ethiopian Airlines operated 33 African routes and 17 international links from its hub in Addis Ababa, while South African Airways had 33 direct connections with African cities and countries and 16 direct international destinations. Daily frequencies can range between one (as is the case with most of the routes) to eight (i.e. Nairobi to Entebbe). Convenient and reliable air travel within Africa has at last become a pleasant reality.[170]

4. Network carriers originating from Africa

There are only three full service carriers with continent-wide networks in Africa and with substantial intercontinental reach; these are Ethiopian Airlines, Kenya Airways and South African Airways. These three have done a fine job of networking African countries and joining them by air using the hubs in Johannesburg, Nairobi and Addis Ababa. These hubs have been connected with the rest of the world by direct flights to and from virtually every major city in Europe, Asia, North America, South America and Australasia. Where they do not reach directly, they are able to transfer traffic to a plane belonging to an alliance member that can then carry it on to any destination in the world. Thus, these network carriers have succeeded in connecting Africa by air to other countries – facilitating communication, travel and trade with the entire world.

Airlines meeting the new demand

To meet these growing network requirements within and outside of Africa, African carriers have in recent times either completed or embarked on substantial fleet modernisation and expansion – preferring the city jets such as the sky workhorse Boeing 737, Airbus A319/320, Embraer 170/190 and Canadair Regional Jet (CRJ 100/200) for domestic and regional travels, and larger, wide-body, extended-range carriers like Boeing 767/777 or Airbus A330/A340 for the crucial intercontinental linkages.

Ethiopian Airlines and Kenya Airways have placed orders for the new Boeing 787 *Dreamliner*, while South African Airways has placed orders for the biggest jet in the world, the Airbus A380. Both planes continue to suffer delays in completion and postponements in delivery schedules for a number of different reasons, forcing these three African carriers to review their equipment needs and leasing sources.

Development of airport infrastructure

The other critical aspect of air transport infrastructure and aerial networking for Africa is the availability of a sufficient number of fully functional international airports with adequate capacity to handle the biggest passenger and cargo carriers in the world – Airbus A380 and Boeing 747-400 – and terminal capacity to process millions of passengers and travellers per year, as well as the air traffic control and navigation facilities to match the best obtainable anywhere in the world.

In this regard Sub-Saharan African countries have not fared well. Only airports in South Africa have had that capacity. To make up for this deficit and prepare the continent for the anticipated massive future growth in travels and cargo airlift within and outside of the continent, almost every SSA nation has entered a phase of airport modernisation, capacity extension, facilities upgrades and navigation system enhancements. Some have also established pilot training and aircraft maintenance centres. A few examples below illustrate the scale and extent of this drive towards superior aerial connectivity for SSA states.

According to information compiled from Airport Technology:[171]

- Ethiopian authorities have constructed a second runway at Bole International Airport to handle any size of aircraft from Boeing 747 to Airbus A340, and a new international terminal building to process a total of 3,000 people per hour once completed. The airport is now enjoying a 12-fold increase in capacity to handle 6m to 7m passengers annually from its previous capacity of 500,000 passengers.

- Jomo Kenyatta International Airport in Nairobi is being expanded with increased taxiways, a new terminal building to separate departures and arrivals, increase of cargo handling capacity and putting in place more aircraft parking stands (up to 43 from the current 23). The authorities are also considering a second runway.

- At Nnamdi Azikiwe International Airport in Abuja, Nigeria, a new runway is being constructed, plus two new terminal buildings and state-of-the-art radar navigation system.

- In Swaziland, a brand new airport has been under construction since 2003 to serve as the country's only international airport hub. Known as Sikhuphe International, it will have the capacity to handle Boeing 747s and serve as a tourism gateway to the Kruger, Maputo, KwaZulu-Natal, Victoria Falls and Swaziland game parks. It will replace the current Matsapha Airport as the hub for origination of inter-continental flights. A new automated cargo terminal has been added to the Mauritius Airport and the air traffic management system has been upgraded.

- A new passenger terminal is under construction at the Gaborone airport, Botswana, with runway extension and parallel taxiway additions.

- The government in Rwanda is developing a new international airport at Bugesera near Kigali to serve as a gateway to Rwanda and the great lakes region.

At the same time a new trend of airport management concessioning under PPPs is gaining traction in Africa. Abuja airport was handed to a PPP operator, Abuja Gateway Consortium, led by Airline Services Limited in 2006, and Bi-Courtney Consortium built and operates a cargo terminal at Murtala Muhammed airport in Lagos. Mauritius Airport management has been transferred to British Airports Authority (BAA) and in Senegal, Fraport, a German PPP airports operator, leads a consortium which in 2009 won a 25-year contract for the construction and operation of a planned new airport in Dakar – Aeroport Internationale de Blaize Diagne.

“ To prepare the continent for the anticipated massive future growth in travels and cargo airlift within and outside of the continent, almost every SSA nation has entered a phase of airport modernisation. **”**

In Côte d'Ivoire, Houphouët-Boigny International Airport is under management by AERIA, a French-led consortium. Likewise Sofreavia, which is part of Egis Avia, now operates the Libreville airport in Gabon as well as the newly rehabilitated Maya-Maya airport in Brazzaville, the Republic of the Congo. At the same time, French private airports operator Suez has also taken control of the international airports in Madagascar, through Aéroports de Madagascar, and in Cameroon through Aéroports de Cameroon.[172]

TECHNOLOGICAL NETWORKING

10

The penetration of mobile telephony in Africa

For many years it was the role of government-owned telecom incumbents to bring telecommunication services to the people. They failed spectacularly, creating an ever-expanding lacuna in African telecommunications. The hallmarks of the service were parlous networks, chronic call dropping, new connections backlogs (that ran back over three and a half years according to International Telecommunication Union – ITU), expensive calls, opaque billing, indifferent customer service and an absence of network extension plans. These challenges also provided the perfect backdrop for the entry of private sector mobile telephone operators.

As recently as 1995, as mobile phones were being introduced into Africa, average Sub-Saharan tele-density was 0.52 lines per 100 people,[173] but currently it stands at a penetration rate of 42%.[174] Over 98% of the new connections come from mobile penetration. Physical wire connections – which are expensive and difficult to deploy – are now unnecessary so mobile providers have taken telephone services to rural Africa in a short time.

The African mobile telecommunication industry has featured the fastest rate of growth of any region in the world in the last decade (the 2000s) – attaining 43% annual growth in the period.[175] According to a working paper of the Centre for Global Development, "by 2008, an area of 11.2 million square kilometres had mobile phone services – equivalent to the United States and Argentina combined.[176] By 2012, most villages will have coverage, with only a handful of countries – Guinea Bissau, Ethiopia, Mali and Somalia – relatively unconnected". And in terms of universal subscriber numbers, about 453m mobile lines are now functioning in the countries of Sub-Saharan Africa, closely rivalling China Mobile, the world's single largest mobile network (580m subscribers – December 2010).[177]

" Physical wire connections – which are expensive and difficult to deploy – are now unnecessary, so mobile providers have taken telephone services to rural Africa in a short time. "

Three strategic approaches at the root of the telecommunication revolution

The telecommunication revolution has been achieved, in the main part, on the back of three fundamental strategic approaches designed to increase uptake and permanence.

1. Active total cost of ownership (TCO) reductions

Mobile operators realised that unless they did something to assist in putting mobile phones in the hands of people, their businesses would never get anywhere despite ambitious roll out programmes and marketing initiatives. They therefore put some resources behind bulk purchases under robustly negotiated contract pricing and arranged shipping of these handsets to their vast network of agents and distributors.

Some also lobbied governments to zero-rate mobile handset devices, and have gone forward to bring into being extensive supply chains of spare parts and charging systems as diverse as solar, wind, and car-battery based, besides electricity, which comes in handy in a continent with barely 23% average electrification. Licensing of new players, liberalisation of competition and introduction of independent regulators as guarantors of fair play and consumer rights, has seen the average calling cost trend down sustainably over the past decade, helping to bring into the networks vast segments of African societies which hitherto were cut out on account of affordability.

2. Ease of connection and activation

Where the large telecom incumbents had in place long, arduous and cumbersome registration and activation processes with prohibitive fees and needless inconveniences, the smaller mobile operators compete to connect people by pushing starter kits through agents and distributors, which in turn hand them down to networks of retailers.

The industriousness of Africa's streetwise enterprise has since kicked in. Starter kits are now being hawked anywhere: in traffic jams, at college and university graduation ceremonies, along crowded pedestrian city pavements, at sporting events, and even door to door. The kits have been made self-activating upon execution of a maximum of only three simple steps by anyone, even the illiterate and technologically challenged. The current rate of new connections and activations has attained viral levels.

3. Airtime sales in micro-denominations

The African mobile operators, which have had to come to terms with the fact that they are catering to economies with GDP per capita of $500 and below, and more than 50% of the population living under the universal poverty borderline of $2 per day, are thriving under these circumstances. The logic has been sustainable *bottom of the pyramid* business strategies.

Single-use or micro-denominated airtime sales are by all arguments easily the single most important driver for mobile penetration to rural Africa. Packaging it in scratch cards with near-or-full currency status, i.e. exchangeable directly for the face value in local currency, and fully fungible with full bearer rights, has made airtime sales in Africa the most effective consumer driven, least costly system of distribution ever created.

To further enhance distribution, cutting out the middleman and therefore reducing distribution costs, operators have implemented electronic top-up conventions that allow subscribers to buy airtime using their bank's mobile banking, or their electronic cash accounts with mobile services, such as M-Pesa, the money remittance service of Safaricom (Kenya's leading mobile service provider). This same platform allows people to send airtime to others, as well as access an airtime advance to be repaid on the next cash or electronic top-up.

***

It is therefore without a doubt singularly on the back of mobile telephony that SSA has suddenly become a viable business proposition from a telecommunication standpoint.

The ICT revolution

Every nation of Africa is now connected to the rest of the world by undersea cables and connectivity within Africa by terrestrial cables is very well advanced. This makes delivery of high speed, broadband internet and its commercial and technological capabilities a reality in Africa.

The first and main international undersea fibre optic cable is the South Atlantic/West Africa submarine cable, known as SAT-3/WASC. It links Europe and Asia through South Africa, forming part of the SAT-3/WASC/SAFE cable system where the SAFE cable links South Africa to Asia. This cable runs down the entire western seaboard of Africa, with landings in each African country that has a sea frontage on the Atlantic

Ocean, from Morocco to South Africa, thereby connecting west, central and southern Africa to the rest of the world through Europe.

SAT-3/WASC has landings in Dakar, Abidjan, Accra, Cotonou, Lagos, Douala, Libreville, Cacuaco, and Melkbosstrand, South Africa, from where it proceeds to Asia. It also serves the two landlocked central African countries of Chad and Central Africa Republic (CAR) through the landing in Douala, Cameroon.[178] A new cable, Main One cable system, with capacity of 1.92Tbs (more than five times the capacity of SAT-3) was completed mid-2010 with landings in Senegal, Côte d'Ivoire, Ghana and Nigeria, linking West African countries to the rest of the world through Portugal and the United Kingdom.[179]

> " Every nation of Africa is now connected to the rest of the world by undersea cables and connectivity within Africa by terrestrial cables is very well advanced. "

The east of Africa was the last region in Africa to connect to worldwide international cable networks and to build an intra-African network of terrestrial cable connections. The region instead relied for a long time on expensive satellite communications, with some of the highest data costs in the world (of up to $5000 per megabit of bandwidth).[180] In the span of three years, multiple and competing investments in undersea fibre optic cables have resulted in three international cables landing on the east African coastline, with the capacity to rival the best connectivity anywhere in the world.

The East African Marine System (TEAMS), an initiative of the government of Kenya and Emirates Telecommunication Establishment (Etisalat) of the UAE, was the first to make landing on the port city of Mombasa, Kenya. With a capacity of 1.2Tbs, it links Kenya, Tanzania, Uganda, Rwanda, Burundi, Ethiopia and South Sudan to the rest of the world through Fujaira in the UAE.[181] Second was SEACOM, a private sector initiative over three-quarters African-owned, with a capacity of 1.28Tbs. Originating from Mumbai, India, it interconnects Kenya, Tanzania, Mozambique and South Africa in addition to express fibre pairs for linking Kenya to South Africa, Kenya to Tanzania, Kenya to France and Tanzania to India.

Last was the Eastern Africa Submarine Cable System (EASSy), a regional initiative by governments of southern and eastern African countries and their national telecommunication companies. Owned and operated by 16

African and international telecom operators and service providers, it has capacity of 3.84Tbs, the highest in Africa. It has rolled out landing stations in nine African countries and provides high-speed terrestrial connectivity to around a dozen landlocked nations. It links South Africa with Sudan via landing points in Mozambique, Madagascar, the Comoros, Tanzania, Kenya, Somalia and Djibouti. It is connected to both the southern African and east African terrestrial loops at Maputot to Mozambique and Mombasa to Kenya respectively.[182]

Terrestrial mapping of the east Africa region with a nexus of fibre optic networks had been going on in preparation for the undersea cable. Some countries have national coverage programmes, but most have been or are being implemented under regional initiatives to complement and integrate with the undersea cables approaching the continent from all directions with pre-determined national or regional landing sites. For example, the Economic Community of West African States (ECOWAS) broadband connectivity programme has successfully bridged the connectivity gaps by addressing the missing links in regional broadband connectivity.

The Central African Backbone Project (CAB) is doing the same for Chad and the Central Africa Republic through the SAT-3/WASC landing at Douala, Cameroon. Southern Africa's regional communication infrastructure programme is a terrestrial loop connecting all the countries of south-eastern Africa – Mozambique, Swaziland, Lesotho, Botswana, Zimbabwe, Zambia, Malawi and the east of South Africa – to the EASSy undersea fibre optic cable. In east Africa, although there are numerous players with national terrestrial backbone networks, Altech Stream East Africa (KDN) has the only truly regional carrier footprint having laid down extensive high-speed data carrier networks in Kenya, Uganda, Rwanda and DR Congo. Next will be Tanzania and Burundi. It provides interconnections between cities and between countries.[183]

The cables are reported to reduce costs substantially to below $500 per megabit (from $5,000), purely due to the technology switch. With the expected competition between them induced by excess capacity and regulatory pressure to rationalise internet costs further, $200 is deemed as an appropriate point of equilibrium by various ICT experts.[184] Sub-Saharan African internet users have soared from 3m in 2000 (less than 1% of the population) to 53m in 2008 (7% of the population).[185]

A summary of the advantages of undersea cable for SSA countries is as follows:

- It brings the power of high-speed, high-bandwidth connectivity to Africa.

- It enables new services and products that were previously not possible due to bandwidth restrictions.

- It contributes towards the macro socio-economic development of the region.

- It improves high capacity optic connectivity within Africa and the rest of the world.

- The unit costs (capital and operational) for global connectivity are reduced, leading to increased profits, and lower tariffs and charges for the end users.

- The out-payments to foreign telecommunications (satellite) facility providers are reduced.

- Direct routes through countries' own infrastructure are provided, obviating the need for transit through third parties. This again reduces out-payments.

- It provides more profitability for telecom entities, enhancing the chance of successful privatisation.

- It meets the telecommunication needs of high bandwidth users such as ISPs (internet service providers) and mobile operators.

- An expansion in intra-Africa trade is facilitated by better communication in the region.

HUMAN RESOURCES DEVELOPMENT

11

This chapter looks at the African human development improvements from two perspectives. Firstly, as a progressively enlightened, educated and sophisticated consumer base. Secondly, as a constantly deepening human capital reservoir. It surveys the concerted efforts currently underway to attain these twin objectives.

Some of these efforts are geared towards reducing the deficits of the first 40 years of independence – such as addressing the quantitative obligations of education for every child (and adult). Others are focused on the qualitative ideals of providing skilled human resources to the growing demands of corporate Africa – such as addressing the labour productivity and overall structural competitiveness of rising African economies.

Universal, free and compulsory primary education – a foundation for an enlightened society

Most African countries today have put in place structures for easily accessible, free and compulsory primary education. Almost every village now has its own primary school and new schools are being constructed at a faster pace than before. Primary education has been elevated to a basic human right for every child and efforts to universalise it have earned international status through the UN Millennium Development Goals (MDGs).

Under the initiatives of the MDG programmes, African states have received enormous foreign and international support in their quest to extend basic education to their populations. A large amount of funds have been accessed for the construction of physical infrastructure for schools including building classrooms, boarding facilities, school libraries,

" In the spirit of self-help and community mobilisation a great number of primary schools have been, and continue to be, built and opened up all over rural Africa. "

teachers' housing facilities and common utilities. Funds have also been accessed for buying books and teaching aids, as well as for paying teachers and educational officers under the ministries of education.

National budgets in most African countries depict the greater emphasis that African governments are now placing on education. With very few exceptions, votes for education ministries are by far the highest for any government ministry. The bulk of these funds go towards paying teachers' salaries and providing teacher training, as well as equipping school libraries and providing stationery. In countries which have implemented devolution of public finances, the district and constituency committees charged with administering these funds have tended to give priority to the construction of basic educational infrastructure, like school buildings.

In addition, in the spirit of self-help and community mobilisation a great number of primary schools have been, and continue to be, built and opened up all over rural Africa. This same spirit has even been stretched in some circumstances to hiring of temporary teachers in deepest rural Africa where governments are not in a position to send enough teachers or where community-established schools have not been handed over to the relevant ministries or departments of education.

Teacher training

Another factor driving education expansion is the establishment of teacher training and preparation colleges. The urgent need for more and better trained teachers for basic education in Sub-Saharan Africa was at critical levels already. This need was further exacerbated by the rapid, unplanned introduction of universal primary education in many countries without the necessary investments in teacher training facilities and in adequate teaching capacity.

A buffer to the implementation constraints was provided by a large reservoir of trained but unemployed teachers who had graduated from teacher training colleges in the years prior to the introduction of universal primary education in the majority of these countries. This was a one-off, quick win resulting from several years of down time when governments could no longer find the funds to employ new teachers.

Once this backlog of teaching capacity was fully exhausted, governments were forced to increase the number of teacher colleges and teacher training opportunities in order to reduce teacher-student ratios, as well as boost the quality of preparation that students received in public schools in SSA.

Increase in enrolment numbers

Every country has now established laws making it compulsory to send to school every child of school age; this is enforced through the provincial administrations. The advances made here are manifested by the figures for Sub-Saharan Africa's Gross Intake Rate (GIR), which registers the number of new entrants regardless of age; it recorded the biggest increase in the world between 1999 and 2006, at 20%.[186]

The objective of the Millennium Development Goal 2 is to ensure that, by 2015, children everywhere will be able to complete a full course of primary school. The most recent UN MDG Report 2010 indicates that though SSA may not be fully on target to achieving this goal by 2015, commendable progress has been recorded to date.

In SSA, the adjusted net enrolment ratio in primary education has improved from 58% in 1999 to 76% in 2008. Though this belies the fact that SSA (and southern Asia) are the regions where the largest numbers of children are out of school, the number has reduced in Africa between 2000 and 2008 by some 14m children, from 45m to 31m. The abolition of primary school fees in Burundi resulted in a threefold increase in primary school enrolment since 1999, reaching 99% in 2008. Similarly, Tanzania doubled its enrolment ratio over the same period and Zambia broke through the 90% threshold.

***

There is still a fairly long way to go in order to bring public schools in Africa to the educational standards and quality levels of the developed world, but the journey has now begun. The investments going into the eventual realisation of full access to quality, universal, basic education for every child anywhere in Africa might take some generations for full effect, but it lays a firm foundation for an enlightened and worldly conscious society with the mental development and preparation to engage and take on the demands of a dynamic and global workplace.

Privatisation of educational services has enhanced capacity and improved quality

Ever since education laws were reformed in African countries to allow for private sector investment and participation in public education, hope was restored that future generations of Africans would be able either to access education where public education is non-existent (as with *harambee* schools in Kenya and community junior-high schools in Botswana)[187] or quality education where the public system is currently substandard.[188]

The pace started rather slowly, but it accelerated with time and now the momentum is unstoppable. Initially it was the premise that public schools ran high-volume, low-quality academic models which inspired the search for alternatives by parents who were willing to pay a premium for their children to get quality education. To meet this demand, a small number of highly exclusive private academies were established in the 1980s in leafy, upmarket sections of major cities. These had steep fee models and enrolment criteria to keep inquiries as few and as serious as possible.

Before long these academies rode to the top of the charts in national school examination rankings continent-wide. As reforms in the educational sector evolved and opened up avenues for systems diversification, these academies introduced exotic curricula more attuned to the development of mental faculties and talent promotion rather than the examination-focused public schools rote systems. In due course middle class parents were swiftly coming to terms with paying high fees for quality and for the durable competitive advantage that early childhood development gives. The two factors fed off each other and were mutually reinforcing – good grades motivated parents to pay high fees and the high fees received in turn enabled standards to be set high and improved.

These private schools distinguished themselves so remarkably in SSA that they became the undisputed bywords for a quality, must-have education, whilst public schools occupied the dubious distinction of quantity, mass-produced academic products. As demand for quality became imperative, parents increasingly looked to the private sector for answers – engendering a steady increase in private school enrolment capacities.

As scale was added, pricing for the products started to be rationalised as unit costs came down. The upshot is that private education has now become easily reachable and attainable for many more parents in the African employed classes.

According to statistics from UNESCO there is sufficient evidence that private education in both primary and secondary school levels is catching on quickly in Africa.[189] The series of Tables 11.1 to 11.4 show figures for the countries that have the fastest national enrolment for primary and secondary schools in Africa.

Table 11.1 – private primary schools highest percentage (2009)

Country	Private primary school enrolment (%)
Equatorial Guinea	47
Mali	40
Mauritius	27
Cameroon	23

Table 11.2 – private secondary schools highest percentage (2009)

Country	Private secondary school enrolment (%)
Mauritius	56
Burkina Faso	42
Madagascar	40
Mali	32

Table 11.3 – biggest gains in private primary schools, as a percentage of all school enrolments (between 2000 and 2009)

Country	2000 primary school enrolment (%)	2009 primary school enrolment (%)	Gain (%)
Guinea	16	27	11
Gambia	14	20	6
Mali	37	40	3

Table 11.4 – biggest gains in private secondary schools, as a percentage of all school enrolments (between 2000 and 2009)

Country	2000 secondary school enrolment (%)	2009 secondary school enrolment (%)	Gain (%)
Benin	16	25	11
Niger	11	20	9
Burkina Faso	34	42	8
Mali	26	32	6

Private schools have proliferated not only in numbers but also in geographical reach all over SSA. They remain the schools of choice for the majority of parents who are conscious about the quality of education and preparation for life that their children get. They have played a role in filling the gaps in quality and capacity left by the public school systems in many SSA countries and they have collectively upgraded the quality and standard of life of African societies. With very few exceptions, they have consciously remained custodians of quality and they are responsible for advances in workforce preparation and standard of life that African societies are making, and must make, in order to catch up with the rest of the world.

Increase in opportunities at universities and other tertiary colleges

Zain Africa, a pan-African mobile services provider, taken-over by Bharti Airtel of India in 2010, ran a televised inter-university academic challenge for three years (2007-9) bringing together universities from the 15 African countries where it had a presence. The show produced numerous surprises about the African youth in their sophistication and readiness to engage with the world.

Expansion of university coverage and capacity

One of the biggest surprises the university challenge brought to the fore was the sheer depth of penetration of universities and university education into the length and breadth of SSA. From 1995, universities have sprung up across SSA at a rapid pace, aided by multiple efforts both public and private. In this period university capacity has increased immensely.

Where previously public universities were only to be found in or very close to capital cities and a few major towns, they have now been diffused to provinces and taken as close as possible to the rural populations of Africa. This has largely been achieved through the conversion of some public polytechnics, technical institutes, farmers' training institutes and teacher colleges into constituent colleges of major public universities. This move has occasioned the fastest and least expensive means of capacity addition for public universities ever witnessed in Africa. In Kenya, for example, annual university admission has increased from about 8,500 in 1995[190] to more than 24,300 places in 2010.[191]

Parallel degree programmes

Another major contributor to expansion of university opportunities in African countries has been the inclusion of parallel degrees and certification programmes in the public universities. The main obstacles to public university growth in African countries have generally been twofold – the limitations of boarding and residential facilities and the limitations of higher education budgets committed to university subsidies or student loans. Parallel degree programmes have provided the perfect answer to this conundrum. Students do not have to be housed on campus and pay full commercial fees for the education without the benefit of subsidies from public finances.

Part of the logic for this was also towards maximising the utilisation of public university system physical infrastructure in ways that would bring badly needed revenues to the university treasuries by starting evening and weekend classes. Through these innovations, many public universities are now handling, preparing and graduating larger numbers of students than would have been possible through public funding dependent programmes. What is more, most of the universities with these programmes are now self-sustaining in their funding of most of the administrative, research and business development programmes, and for some even in hiring and retaining faculty.

These parallel/Module II or dual-track programmes were introduced in public universities in east Africa between 1992 and 1996, and the response has been phenomenal. In Makerere University, Uganda, thanks principally to dual track programmes, enrolment dramatically increased from 5,000 to 30,000 over a single decade from 1992 to 2002. Among all public university students in Kenya, within a short five-year period from 1998 to 2003, parallel or dual track enrolment made up about 40% of the total.

University finances were improved by these programmes, drastically curtailing their dependence on state allocations. At the University of Nairobi, Kenya, in the academic year 2002-3 alone parallel programmes contributed close to 40% of the total university income, while government allocation dropped from 70% (1996) to 49% (2003). At Makerere, privately generated funding has grown from 17% to 53% in the seven years from 1996 to 2003.[192]

Faith-based universities

A third major source of new university opportunities in African countries has been the proliferation of faith-based universities. Churches in Africa have continued to play an unchallenged role in provision of education opportunities in many countries, at least in areas neglected by governments.

Traditionally churches kept their interventions within basic and secondary education but within the past two decades they have expanded their frontiers to include university education as well. They established campuses initially to train and instruct on faith-based subjects and curricula only, but they have since opened up to arts, business and commercial courses. Some even have science, technical and research faculties.[193]

Their combined addition to the expansion of Africa's university opportunities and quality education has been tremendous and the trend is accelerating. Those mainstream denominations without universities of their own are working to establish them, while the existing ones are expanding by opening new campuses.

These faith-based universities are also adding to the provision of metropolitan evening classes which was started by the public university parallel programmes.

Private university opportunities

Another notable source of university opportunities is through private commercial universities. The desire for university education among the youth and working class in Africa could now be described as being at fever pitch. Every working or commercially engaged family wants its children to obtain college education.

According to a paper, *Private Higher Education in Africa* by N.V. Varghese:

> "The 1990s saw the emergence of private sector institutions in Africa. It can be argued that the deregulation policies under the structural adjustment programmes, the fiscal incapacity of public universities to respond immediately to household demand for certain market-friendly courses, led to a movement towards increasing social demand for private higher education. The globalisation process further reinforced the need to go beyond the public institutions of higher learning. Private higher education institutions in many countries operate in collaboration with foreign universities and institutions

located in Europe, the United States of America and Australia. This marks a definite shift in the conceptualisation of development of higher education from a national public entity to a market-based service to be offered on demand and for a price, and traded with other countries if necessary."[194]

For a long time, the manifestation of the demand of Africans for university education was seen in the numbers of students who travelled abroad in search of higher education. The demand was not only sustained in the intervening period, but in fact continued to grow. Obviously cost remained a constant issue for many parents who either lacked access to foreign exchange or the full resources to meet increasingly tough visa application criteria.

It was for this reason that some international universities designed business models to bring international education to African people in their own countries. The United States International University-Africa (USIU) in Nairobi, Kenya, a campus of the San Diego based USIU, was established to meet this need; so was the African Virtual University, also in Nairobi, Kenya. Another example is the Igbidion University Okada in Nigeria.

> **❝ By 2003, SSA countries had more than 100 private, market-based universities and more than half of these were established between 1990 and 1999. ❞**

By 2003, SSA countries had more than 100 private, market-based universities and more than half of these were established between 1990 and 1999. At that time Senegal led SSA with the highest number of private universities, with 48, followed by Ghana with 28 and Benin with 27.[195]

These universities have not only made considerable net additions to the growth of university opportunities in SSA, they also bring African youths together to collaborate in intellectual and academic adventures, leading to knowledge and experience sharing across the continent.

Establishing highly specialised and advanced training facilities

Finding the right human resources for the emerging technical businesses arriving in Africa – in ICT, telecoms, biotechnology and other areas – has been a challenge. Finding the appropriate engineers, technicians and suitably trained personnel initially presented difficulties and threatened the growth of these businesses. But these challenges have created new and exciting opportunities in academia and technical training. The ready market for technical skills has inspired the development of advanced technical educational and training institutions in various SSA countries. This development has followed three broad themes, namely:

1. Introduction of technical departments at state institutions.

2. Creation of specialised skills-specific universities.

3. Fulfilment of the needs of multinational institutions.

1. Introduction of technical departments at state institutions

Technical departments have been introduced at state institutions, including polytechnics or universities, and existing courses have been revamped and re-oriented to cater to the needs of the labour market.

In countries where parallel (commercial) degree programmes have been made available in state universities alongside the regular (sponsored) programmes, these courses have grown because of an increase in demand and the promise of lucrative prospects for graduates upon completion. Nokia, the mobile handset and telecommunication accessories manufacturing company of Finland, has increased engagement with learning institutions in Kenya to equip instructors with knowledge regarding mobile applications development techniques. According to an article carried by *Ratio Magazine*:

> *"These engagements will involve trainers, established and upcoming mobile application developers who will then be expected to rollout the same training at their own institutions and colleges enabling knowledge sharing to a wide audience."*[196]

2. Creation of specialised skills-specific universities

The appearance of specialised skills-specific universities, now dotted all over Africa, is another theme that has been playing out. These have arisen predominantly to plug holes in skills supply chains. Chronic skills shortages and the inability of governments to move fast enough to fill the yawning demand gaps have motivated specialised institutions to found technical universities of their own – principally to train and ensure a regular number of trained personnel for their own needs, and then to supply national and regional demands as a subsidiary role.

❝ The ready market for technical skills has inspired the development of advanced technical educational and training institutions in various SSA countries. ❞

These institutions have so far been either government owned under direct technical and financial support from donor countries, or private institutions raised to cater to technical skills deficiencies in related industries or social services. In a short span of time this trend has caught on across Africa and is expanding technical skills supply and human resources development opportunities at a fast rate.

Jomo Kenyatta University of Science and Technology in Kenya was established with the assistance of the Japanese government to lead the vanguard in training, research and innovation development in the region. Hubert Kairuki Memorial University in Tanzania is allied to Hubert Kairuki Hospital, offering programmes in health sciences only, and is an excellent example of a private sector initiative as part of this trend.

3. Fulfilment of the needs of multinational institutions

A third and final theme playing out in the area of specialised training facilities is the fulfilment of the needs of newly arrived multinational institutions, which when established in SSA are affected by the shortage of technical human resources. Huawei, the Chinese multinational telecommunication network equipment company, now operates technical training institutions in six African countries, namely South Africa, Nigeria, Kenya, Egypt, Tunisia and Angola. The objective is to supply technically trained people to work with wireless Wimax and fourth-generation networks, thus overcoming the lack of technical staff and engineers in Sub-Saharan Africa. Huawei has future plans to convert some or all of these institutions into telecommunication universities.[197]

The principal business of both Nokia and Huawei are that they make, sell and maintain sophisticated network equipment and mobile handsets and other interface devices, as well as providing IT consulting. They have continental operations with a presence in almost every country in SSA. For these they need large numbers of installation personnel, technical support and training forces, for the present and also an assured future supply.

The quality of these services is core to their businesses; this explains the sensitivity of training and preparation of personnel, leading them to start their own advanced training facilities. The inevitable externalities created by these facilities will benefit African economies and help lower entry thresholds for other global players making their adventures into Africa.

Table 11.5 shows the percentage of tertiary-level students in training in science, engineering, manufacturing and construction disciplines in a range of SSA countries. These figures show that the pursuit of science and related courses is already fairly popular in African nations and the basic training infrastructure exists.

Table 11.5 – percentage of tertiary students in science, engineering, manufacturing and construction in some SSA countries

Country	Enrolment (%)
Kenya	29
Mauritius	26
Ghana	26
Mozambique	24
Tanzania	24
South Africa	20
Ethiopia	19
Botswana	17

Source: Higher Education in Africa: The International Dimension – Damtewa Teffera and Jane Knight, 2007

Obviously the quality and appropriateness of technology imparted may be another matter but no doubt opportunities for improvements through collaborations with lateral (advanced training institutions) or vertical (highly specialised technology firms) continue to accelerate the quality of Africa's workforce.

International airlift – the dividend of global Africa

Perhaps one of the biggest gripes that international businesses have that militates against setting up in Africa is the perceived scarcity of adequate management and technical skills among the African people to run businesses and formulate strategy on an international scale.

It has been argued that African universities lacked the resources, curricula and faculties to prepare and empower would-be business managers, and that African companies in turn lacked the scale, vision and environment to nurture talent and ingrain the experiences necessary to equip managers for international appointments and participation on the world stage.

These may all be moot points, but to argue with the owners and allocators of capital would only lead to even more adverse consideration. So it should come as a relief to note that there is an African answer to this problem, which is a rich and diverse, foreign-trained and globally-experienced African diaspora eager to return to Africa.

African students have travelled to the West in search of higher education since independence. The flow began slowly and intermittently, depending much on the availability of foreign scholarships and the ability of families to meet the cost of flights. But from the 1980s a greater number of African students have had the opportunity to acquire good education in overseas universities.

The top universities of the world – at least those in the US, Canada, Australia and western Europe – opened up to international students, even allocating fixed quotas of their annual enrolment to students from aboard. Most have been able to back that either with full scholarships or partial academic grants, whilst at the same time making it easy for those students who pass the mark and are able to pay to obtain admission without much hassle. Many African students have been beneficiaries of these developments – which oversaw the large numbers of students from African nations moving to study at Western universities – and this trend continues today.

Upon graduation the majority of students have proceeded to take up jobs in the host countries; a few taking the opportunity to work in the top firms of business and industry, with a great majority of others going into employment with technical orientations and acquiring world-class experience in engineering, medicine, research, law, ICT and consultancy, among other areas.

❝ With the global financial and economic crisis of 2007-8, as a result of which many people lost their jobs in Western countries, Africa received back the highest number, compared to previous periods, of its best educated, highly trained and urbane crop of careerists and technocrats within a span of one year – this was the dividend of global Africa. ❞

Over time some of these African students who studied abroad have returned to their respective home countries to take up senior leadership and management positions in public or corporate sectors, or in academia and research. Some have established businesses of their own that have become landmarks in corporate Africa; for example, Africa-online, a pan-African ISP. Admittedly, the flow of graduates back into African countries was slow, with periodic surges being witnessed for countries which have either installed popular democratic governments (as in Zambia and Kenya), embarked on economic growth inspired by public sector reform or commodities boom (such as Mozambique and Angola), or a combination of the two of these (for example, Nigeria and Ghana).

However, with the global financial and economic crisis of 2007-8, as a result of which many people lost their jobs in Western countries, Africa received back the highest number yet of its best educated, highly trained and urbane crop of careerists and technocrats within a span of one year. This was the dividend of global Africa.

These returning graduates are rejoining corporate Africa with a significant effect already. In an interview in May 2009 with *TradeInvest Africa*, Mr Ade Adutola, managing director of **www.wazobiajobs.com**, a recruitment firm working to bring West African professionals back home, said:

> "What we have seen over the past few years is a gradual increase in the number of Nigerian and Ghanaian professionals based abroad returning home to work. The West African economy is growing fast and consequently there are abundant opportunities opening up that many of these returnees are taking advantage of. Companies operating in the region are embracing them because they bring international best practices that local resources may not have been exposed to."[198]

For those who worry about the current and future availability of competent and dependable management and technical skills, a sizeable and growing body of highly trained section of African diaspora is returning to the continent.

There are consultancies and placement agents established already in some Western capitals with the express remit of connecting African nationals working abroad with emerging and exciting opportunities back in Africa. From time to time they run recruitment and networking workshops and conferences to highlight the developments and bring together prospective employers and employees.

A good example is Global Career Company, which is "an international recruitment consultancy that specialises in recruiting internationally based candidates from Africa (and other emerging markets) back into jobs within their home countries".[199]

REFORM OF THE BUSINESS ENVIRONMENT

12

In discussions and debates about business in Africa – which are held more and more at conferences, summits and at academic institutions – a common thread of conversation is that the business environment generally continues to be a big hindrance to the establishing and running of business in most African countries. The business environment in African countries is still very often contrasted negatively with the environment in Western countries.

It is true that African countries still have quite some way to go in developing environments that are conducive to business but there are two important factors to emphasise about the environment for doing business now obtaining in Africa: these are that the environment is nascent, but improving, and this is because of hard work and reforms by governments and other groups in Africa.

Nurturing the incipient business environment

Contrary to a widely held view that the business environment in Africa is obstructive, reactionary and anti-business, it is instead embryonic and incipient in many African countries.

Before the 1990s, for most of Africa there was no business environment to speak of, basically because there was hardly any business taking place there. Governments were commonly dictatorial, totalitarian and patronage-powered; they were not wired to do business, so they did not feel the need to foster environments conducive to conducting business. A large number of African countries have only recently (within the last two decades) come out of periods of conflict, civil strife or outright wars, but a transition towards new and inclusive constitutions under democratically elected governments is now in progress in the majority of these countries.

It was after democratically elected and progressively inclined governments were established that African nations realised the urgent need to establish regulatory frameworks within which competitive free enterprise could thrive. Since African states awakened to the necessity of providing an environment that promotes and nurtures business in order that enterprises can be formed and investment is attracted, they have worked hard at doing just that; introducing reconstruction and reform programmes. There is evidence that shows this to be the case.

For a country like Burundi, this opportunity emerged in 2007 (when civilian rule returned through a negotiated peace deal) and since then it has worked

❝ After democratically elected and progressively inclined governments were established, African nations realised the urgent need to establish regulatory frameworks within which competitive free enterprise could thrive. **❞**

hard to improve the environment for business. For Kenya, it has been eight years since the regime change of 2003. For Liberia, the elections that saw Madam Ellen Johnson Sirleaf take power in 2005 were an important turning point.

Business reforms as measured by the World Bank

In recent years' reports (2007-10) by the World Bank's *Doing Business*, African countries have featured prominently in the list of the world's ten top reforming nations: in 2008 Ghana came third in the world with five substantive reforms, while Kenya was eighth with four substantive reforms. In 2009 Senegal was fifth with three substantive reforms, Burkina Faso sixth with four substantive reforms, while Botswana was seventh with three substantive reforms. In 2010 Rwanda led the world with seven substantive reforms and Liberia came tenth with three substantive reforms. In 2011 Rwanda was second with three substantive reforms, Cape Verde was fifth, also with three substantive reforms, and Zambia came seventh, again with three substantive reforms.

As an example of the quantum leaps African countries are making in improvements to their business environments, in 2010 Rwanda became the 'best reforming nation' in the world, having vaulted 76 places from number 143 in 2009 to number 67 in 2010.[200] Liberia also featured in the list of top ten reformers in the world, having jumped ten places to finish at number 149 in 2010 from number 159 in 2009, and with three reforms to its credit. *Doing Business 2010* proceeded to report that low and lower-middle income economies accounted for two-thirds of reforms recorded in 2008-9, continuing a trend that started during the preceding three years.

Co-operation and competition of trading blocs

A common thread connecting regulatory reform in African economies is that every nation is a member of a regional trading and economic bloc. As the status of a trading bloc moves from just being a community, to a customs union, to a common market and finally to a monetary union, economic integration tightens and competition between economies intensifies, necessitating accelerated business and regulatory reforms. Those countries that are coming out of periods of civil disruption have the most catching up to do within their economic and trading blocs, where they sit alongside countries which have been in the reform agenda longer. It is little wonder therefore that Rwanda and Liberia lead Africa, and indeed the world, in speed and substance of regulatory reform.

Doing Business 2010 reports that the East African Community (EAC) has been expanding co-operation among member states, which have intensified efforts to co-operate and learn from each other. They have worked to harmonise legislation relating to the EAC customs union and common market protocols while establishing such links as the network of reformers based on similar models in the OECD and the EU, which is expected to help establish benchmarks. For EAC countries, *Doing Business* has recorded a total of 46 major reforms since 2004.

Longer-term measures

Doing Business has also introduced a longer-term, five-year measure of how business regulations have changed in the 174 countries that it assesses. This is used to illustrate how the business environment has changed within economies over time – between *Doing Business* reports 2006 and 2011.

Again, predictably, among the ten economies that have seen the greatest improvements in making their regulatory environments more favourable to business were three SSA countries – Rwanda (second), Burkina Faso (fourth) and Ghana (eighth). The cumulative improvement over the past five years shows that change has been occurring over a period of time and that the improvements made have been substantial. In the period under review Rwanda in particular introduced a total of 22 reforms.

To ensure co-ordination of efforts across relevant implementing agencies, some countries around the world have formed regulatory reform committees reporting directly to their presidents. These use *Doing Business* indicators as one input to inform their programmes for improving the business environment. In Africa these countries include Rwanda, Sierra Leone, Kenya, Liberia, Malawi and Zambia.

Summary of reforms in African countries within individual categories

Looking at the ten major areas of reforms that *Doing Business* focuses on, African economies have made giant strides over the past seven years towards promoting environments that are more business-friendly.

Among economies deemed to have reformed the most in each of the *Doing Business 2011* areas, DR Congo topped the world in 'dealing with construction permits' reforms; Swaziland improved the most in 'protecting investors' reforms; Ghana led in 'getting credit' reforms; while Malawi was the best reformer in 'enforcing contracts' reforms.

About half of all trade facilitation reforms in 2009-0 took place in Sub-Saharan Africa with a total of nine reforms. Overall, 27 of 46 Sub-Saharan African countries implemented substantive reforms in their business environments, a total of 49 reforms in all. Several were motivated by regional integration, for instance in east Africa single border controls speeded up crossing between Rwanda and Uganda.[201]

Following is a summary of the business reforms in African countries.

Starting a business

Reforms that have been crystallised in the area of starting a business across Africa are encouraging. According to *Doing Business 2010,* creating or improving a one-stop shop has been the most popular reform feature since 2004. This involves bringing company registration, tax registration and town planners into one central place.

In 2006, Uganda created a new, independent registration agency; in 2009 Rwanda consolidated procedures for name search, registration fees payment, tax and company registrations. A total of 15 other SSA countries had one or several similar reforms in this area. For example, Central Africa Republic and Zambia established one-stop shops with representatives from all agencies involved in business registration, merging four procedures into one. Madagascar has streamlined requirements at its one-stop shop and introduced flat registration fees; Sierra Leone too has operationalised its one-stop shop; so has Togo, streamlining the business registration process by eliminating six procedures. In Ethiopia the company registry now automatically forwards information electronically to its licensing authority.

Standardisation of documentation follows and in this area progress is equally impressive. Kenya in 2006 eliminated the need for a trading license separate from a business permit. Tanzania in the same year simplified its system of licensee categories, resulting in a reduction in the number of different licensed activities from 15 to four. Rwanda has introduced a standard memorandum of association and in Mauritius, which had also standardised business registration documents, the rejection rate for new business registration has come down to 8%.

Another major reform area has been in making services electronic or putting them on the internet. This not only mitigates certain risk, such as total loss in the event of fire, but it also facilitates information sharing and transparency. Rwanda is now posting publications online such as applications for permits or licences, and so are Burkina Faso, Cape Verde and Guinea Bissau.

Dealing with construction permits

In the category of construction permits, SSA countries accounted for the second highest number of reforms in 2009-10 – 23 reforms in total – with the overall effect of reducing permit delays by 16 days (although costs are still generally high at an average of 1,631% of income per capita). Owing to a regulatory reform programme which streamlined construction permits in the country, reducing the time to deal with construction permits from 248 days to 128 days, and the average cost from $6,908 to $4,307, the world's best reformer in this category in *Doing Business 2011* was DR Congo.

The leading reform agenda has been identifying areas of overlap among agencies – dealing with construction permits involves multiple agencies and levels of approval. To obtain all construction-related approvals and connect to utilities, builders around the world deal with nine different agencies on average. Understanding how these agencies interact with one another and identifying areas of overlap is often the first step toward hastening approvals while maintaining quality control. Rwanda has consolidated two processes (obtaining a location contract and a building permit), lessening time taken by two weeks. Burundi has reduced interactions from between eight agencies to only three. Through automation Benin, Burkina Faso, DR Congo, Rwanda and Sierra Leone have all also reduced the time needed for processing permit applications.

" The leading reform agenda has been identifying areas of overlap among agencies – dealing with construction permits involves multiple agencies and levels of approval. "

Another item is streamlining project clearance. One-stop shops are being designed to integrate services through a single point of contact between building authorities and entrepreneurs. Kenya's rapid results initiative, introduced in 2008, moved permit approvals from an overburdened city council to a new technical committee that meets every two weeks. It also uses a risk-based building approval convention. Burkina Faso has also implemented a one-stop shop window. Côte d'Ivoire and Mali have streamlined procedures too, with Mali introducing a risk-based approvals system designed to simplify environmental impact assessment, cutting time by 9% and costs by 33%.

More progress comes from rationalising inspection and moderating requirements for technical studies. Eliminating redundant procedures has been proved to increase transactions and fees to governments. For example, Kenya reported an increase in revenue of 33% after replacing dozens of local permits with a single construction permit. Burkina Faso, DR Congo and Rwanda have reduced fees substantially.

Another reform area is the setting of targets and measurement of progress. It involves taking a broad view of what needs to be reformed and what is feasible, then committing to a target reduction in the administrative costs of licensing and related requirements, and setting up measurement systems to ensure that the target is achieved. Kenya again is on course to implement these comprehensive reforms under an approved building code.

Registering property

According to *Doing Business 2011*, SSA was the best reforming region in the world under the property registration reform category in the 2009-10 period with a total of 42 reforms. Among the top ten leading reforming economies were two SSA nations – Cape Verde (third) and Malawi (sixth). Among the leading reform areas, simplifying and reducing fees was foremost. This included either charging fixed fees independent of property value to avoid under-reporting and diminish incentives for paying bribes – Cape Verde, DR Congo, Mali, Rwanda were compliant with this. Another is lowering the fees payable as a percentage of property value – in the past six years SSA countries have reduced taxes and fees by an average of 3% of the property value.[202]

Another area is ease of access to the registry. This helps reduce time spent on due diligence to verify ownership, encumbrances and other required documentation. Angola, Ethiopia and Rwanda all decentralised their land registries in 2008-9 to eliminate bottlenecks. Burkina Faso increased administrative efficiency at the registry to reduce delays for entrepreneurs in 2008-9 by introducing time limits. Angola computerised its registry resulting in reduction of time to transfer property in Luanda from 334 to 184 days. Malawi and Sierra Leone increased administrative efficiency by removing restrictions on private land transfer. Botswana and Madagascar achieved greater efficiency by hiring more staff, bringing in more computers and opening more branches. Mali and Niger boosted efficiency by reassigning work loads and enhancing supervision.

Getting credit

Sub-Saharan Africa was the second most reforming region under the 'getting credit' category in *Doing Business 2011*, with 26 reforms implemented among various economies. Ghana was the most improved in the areas of credit information and legal rights – it created a unified collateral registry for movable property. Another country which implemented this was Uganda.

One aspect of this is the reform of secured transaction law to allow businesses to use their assets – including movable assets such as machinery and accounts receivables – as security for credit borrowing. Rwanda was the top reformer in the world in this category with its new secured transaction law which enables SMEs to obtain credit with a wider range of assets as collateral. Sierra Leone has also put in place a new company act that broadens the range of assets that can be used as collateral.

Efforts to develop much needed credit information systems started picking up in 2008 – Zambia, Kenya, Mauritius, Nigeria, Ghana, Uganda, Rwanda and Cape Verde have either established or put in place processes

> **❝ The reform of secured transaction law allowed businesses to use their assets – including movable assets such as machinery and accounts receivables – as security for credit borrowing. ❞**

" Capital market growth and the entry of private equity houses is providing a growing base of non-controlling investors (minority investors) in both listed and unlisted enterprises. "

for new laws on credit reference bureaus that provide frameworks for regulated and reliable systems of sharing credit information, making it mandatory for all banks to share negative information. Kenya is already distributing credit and other financial information from retailers, trade creditors, utilities and the higher education loans board.

A major effort is underway in the 16 member countries of the Organisation for the Harmonization of Business Law in Africa (OHADA) to amend the uniform act organising securities in the member states which was first implemented in 1998. The objective is to allow a more general description of encumbered assets and give priority to secured assets.

Protecting investors

Minority interest and its protection is gaining prominence in many African countries where capital market growth and the entry of private equity houses is providing a growing base of non-controlling investors (minority investors) in both listed and unlisted enterprises. Reforms aimed at increasing market transparency have focused on internal and external disclosure requirements. Internal reforms – related party transactions – call for notification of company boards and shareholders, while external reforms call for notification of stock exchanges or market regulators and disclosures in company accounts and public announcements.

The main focus of reform in this area is on increasing the level and detail of disclosures (especially of related party transactions), extending directors' responsibilities and liabilities, encouraging more shareholder rather than director approvals, and making it easy for minority shareholders to bring suits against management and directors by improving their access to internal information.

These issues have already been addressed and laid to rest in most African countries. In April 2010 Swaziland enacted a new company's act which strengthened investor protection by requiring approval of the board of directors for related party transactions. Rwanda in 2008-9 put in place sweeping reforms that addressed each of the issues above in one fell swoop. Sierra Leone has also adopted a new law addressing disclosure requirements for related party transactions and directors' liabilities if such transactions pose a risk to the company.

Mali has put in place a new civil procedure code to strengthen investor protection by increasing shareholders' ability to access internal corporate information during a trial to establish directors' liabilities. Tanzania's new company's act of 2006 provides greater protection to minority shareholders by clarifying duties of directors and increasing directors' liabilities. For instance it prohibits tax free loans to directors, and introduces statutory procedures for the removal of directors. Mozambique now allows shareholders access to any internal documents except corporate and trade secrets.

Burundi, Kenya, Malawi and Uganda are developing new commercial laws to improve corporate governance programmes. According to *Doing Business 2011*, most research suggests a positive relationship between sound corporate governance systems and firms' performance as measured by valuation, operating performance and stock returns.

Paying tax

In the period 2009-10 SSA was the second best reformed region in the tax area, with 40 tax reforms. It was represented in the top ten most improved economies in the world in tax reform by Cape Verde (second) and Sao Tome & Principe (third). The most widespread reform has been to reduce profit tax, which came down an average 3% across SSA in the 2009-10 period. Rwanda reduced corporate tax from 35% to 30% in 2006 and allowed faster tax depreciation for certain fixed assets. Benin, Cape Verde, Sudan and Togo reduced profit tax by an average of 9%.[203] Other countries which followed suit in 2009-10 were Burkina Faso, Republic of Congo, Madagascar, Niger, Seychelles, Sao Tome & Principe and Zimbabwe.

Additional tax reform measures included broadening of the tax base, and making compliance easier so as to reduce costs for firms and encourage business investments and job creation. In the past five years, seven economies – Burkina Faso, Cameroon, Cape Verde, Ghana, Madagascar and Sudan – reduced the number of payments by eliminating, merging or reducing the frequency of filings and payments.

❝ The major challenge affecting cross-border trade in Africa is not the lack of the right laws and protocols to facilitate trade, it is normally that these regulations lack uniform interpretation across the region. **❞**

In 2010 Sierra Leone introduced administrative reforms at the tax authority and replaced four different sales taxes with a single VAT tax. Angola and Sierra Leone have simplified tax paying processes. Sierra Leone and Sudan both revised tax codes and reduced capital gains tax. Benin reduced labour tax or mandatory contribution rates. Cameroon suspended business licenses for two years for new businesses. Many countries are implementing electronic tax filing systems.

Another raft of measures were as follows: Cape Verde eliminated all stamp duties; Sierra Leone and Zimbabwe simplified tax compliance processes; Sao Tome and Principe introduced new tax laws; and Burundi and Sierra Leone introduced VAT in place of transaction taxes.

Trading across borders

The major challenge affecting cross-border trade in Africa is not the lack of the right laws and protocols to facilitate trade, it is normally that these regulations lack uniform interpretation across the region. An example is varying interpretation of customs procedures concerning rules of origin and valuation with no effective mechanism for dispute resolution; this limits the potential for intra-regional trade in the East African Community, for example. Reforms that have been undertaken in this space have centred on the following themes.

- *Improved coordination among customs authorities* – Most countries have automated their customs systems. In 2009-10 Ethiopia and Mali improved customs administration. Joint inspections by customs authorities between Kenya and Uganda have enhanced border co-operation.

- *Automation of customs procedures and electronic data interchange systems* – Both Tanzania and Kenya in 2005 modernised customs clearance to allow traders, inspection agencies and shippers to submit their customs declarations electronically and pay duties directly. In 2009 Rwanda increased declaration acceptance points and introduced automation of clearance of goods and services at select border points. However, the pervasive challenge at the regional levels is that national customs systems are not integrated to enable information sharing. Both Zambia and Swaziland introduced electronic data interchange systems at their borders during 2009-10.

- *Developing a single window which brings together relevant public agencies at a single facility* – Senegal has put together 15 agencies under one roof; in Ghana, Madagascar and Mauritius electronic document messaging is helping reduce paper documentation.

- *Streamlined transit procedures* – EAC countries are working on implementing a region-wide cargo tracking system which would eliminate the need for road blocks on transit routes and save time for truckers. Kenya already cut transit roadblocks between the port of Mombasa and the border with Uganda from 14 to five in 2009. In the same year Uganda introduced a system of seals for transit goods placed at the point of entry and removed at the point of exit, reducing the need for inspection at different stages of transit and therefore saving time and money. Rwanda and Uganda, and Zambia and Zimbabwe, have already implemented border co-operation agreements.

- Much of the marked drop in time for exporting and importing among some SSA countries has also been achieved by simply *extending office hours at ports or border points* – this has been done already in Kenya, Rwanda and Senegal.

Enforcing contracts

Enforcing contracts is another area where African nations have led the world by the pace of reform and substance of the changes that have taken place. Botswana was the top reformer globally in 2008-9. New rules for its high court reduced the average time to resolve a commercial dispute by 30%, with introduction of pre-trial conferences leading to faster resolution. It also installed a sophisticated new computerised case management system which has made it easier to monitor compliance with deadlines by court personnel and litigants. Zambia too has introduced an electronic case management system.

Ethiopia in 2008-9 also reduced the average time to resolve a commercial dispute by 10%. This was achieved by implementing a backlog reduction programme that involved devoting the traditional summer recess to dispensing with backlog cases. It also computerised case management systems and this has sustained court improvements. Burkina Faso, Malawi, Mauritius and Uganda have also increased procedural efficiencies at the main trial courts.

A landmark reform cutting across many African nations has been the establishment of commercial courts or specialised commercial sections of high courts to deal specifically and more professionally with business disputes. Burkina Faso, Guinea Bissau, Uganda, Nigeria, Rwanda and Tanzania are the most recent adopters of this practice. Another major area of reform has been in making legal information public in recognition of the fact that readily available information on the law and on the courts' interpretation of the law benefits the general public and the courts, which in turn makes the law more predictable. A majority of SSA countries now make legal texts and recent court judgments available to the general public through publication in the press, legal journals and on public law websites.

Another substantive reform in this area is the now popular assignment of a single judge to a case rather three judges, which frees up judicial resources to be spread over wider case loads. Forwarding cases to obligatory conciliation committees and allowing parties to use arbitration is helping reduce cases that go to court, which ensures that only serious, actionable cases are taken to court. Rwanda adopted these practices in 2008-9. In 2004 Burundi adopted a new code of civil procedures summarising procedures for uncontested claims.

According to *Doing Business 2011* Botswana, Mali and Rwanda have reduced the time to file and try a case by 40 days on average.

Closing a business

The stigma of bankruptcy continues to be among the major reasons why debtors in many economies including SSA do not readily resort to insolvency procedures. SSA as a region has the largest share of economies with little or no insolvency practice of anywhere in the world.[204] However, encouraging reforms are beginning to be seen in the region. In 2008-9 Rwanda improved its process of dealing with distressed companies through a new law intended to streamline reorganisation procedures and allow viable distressed firms to continue operating. It sets clear time limits on insolvency procedures and regulates the profession of bankruptcy administrators.

In 2007 Burundi adopted its first bankruptcy law since independence. In Malawi, in 2008-9, a new companies regulation was adopted which has set a cap on liquidators' fees at 5% of value of estate, and caused the overall cost of insolvency procedures to fall from 30% to 25%, as well as making the system of payment of liquidators more transparent. Mauritius in 2009 simultaneously passed a new insolvency act and established a rehabilitation procedure for companies as an alternative to winding up. Sierra Leone also passed a new company act that makes reorganisation procedures available to companies.

> **❝ A landmark reform cutting across many African nations has been the establishment of commercial courts or specialised commercial sections of high courts to deal specifically and more professionally with business disputes. ❞**

Finally, the 16 member countries of OHADA are discussing amendments to the uniform act on insolvency.

Conclusion

It is one thing to have potential. It is quite another to have realisable potential. The first was Africa before the 2000s decade. The second is Africa now and beyond. And the difference is the enablers of business. African governments and private sectors have made conscious attempts to make possible and improve the viability of business endeavours in their economies.

It may still be a work in progress, but the simultaneous, concerted, multi-modal and continent-wide infrastructural developments currently underway in Africa speak to a consensus to outfit the continent with modern and efficient arteries of commerce.

Human capital is by far the greatest trans-generational resource any economy or society can boast. Africa is now in the throes of a demographic dividend, like Asia experienced between 1980 and 2000 (and which is now coming to an end). In order to be better prepared to benefit fully from its largest ever workforce (ages 24-60 as a percentage of total population) African nations certainly seem keen to equip it with better skills and a modern and progressive worldview essential in appropriating the imminent global business and commercial shifts.

Finally, the welter of business reforms already concluded and those still in the pipeline in virtually each and every African nation point to a society acutely aware of the business and commercial issues that need development and what it needs to do to make them possible.

To put it metaphorically, the decade of the 2000s was a wave of house-keeping in African economies. Suffice it to say that Africa is now officially open for business. In the third and last part of this book, we look at the major opportunities ready to be grabbed.

OPPORTUNITIES

Introduction

Assembling the themes and framework

The first part of this book showed the basic underpinnings for Sub-Saharan Africa's gradual economic rise over the past five decades, with the pace accelerating in the most recent decade as Africa encountered and breached certain thresholds. Put together, the advances amount to a critical mass for irrepressible economic take off.

The second part described the deliberate efforts and initiatives already in place, or those that are being considered, to complete a web of multi and inter-modal infrastructural linkages; investment in the human complement as well as improving the environment for business. Basically all that is necessary to enable Africa's emergence into the global economic and commercial community as a region that can vie for global investment and worldwide consumers.

The third and last part of this book begins with a summary of the broad and dynamic themes that are expected to influence business and commercial decisions in Sub-Saharan Africa going forward. It then proceeds to identify and develop the individual opportunities in seven sectors which hold the keys to the African consumer market bonanza.

Summary of themes that influence African business now and in the future

It is useful to begin Part Three with a summary of the themes that will influence African business in the future. The information here has been drawn largely from McKinsey & Company articles 'Lions on the Move: the Progress and Potential of Africa's Economies' and 'What is Driving Africa's Growth?'

Population growth

Africa's long-term growth will be aided by internal social and demographic trends, particularly Africa's growing labour force, urbanisation and the related rise of middle class consumers. Africa currently has the world's fastest population growth rate of 2.5% (Asia is growing at 2%, while the world in entirety is growing at 1.2%). By 2025, or the next 14 years a net of

364m people will be added to the SSA population. And by 2050, a total of 966m new people will have been added – more than doubling the current SSA population of 864m people within the next 40 years.

Diversified economic growth

It is important to recognise that the commodity boom of the decade from 2000 to 2010 explains only part of Africa's growth story; natural resources directly accounted for just 24% of Africa's GDP from 2000 through to 2008. The rest came from other sectors – including wholesale and retail, trade, transportation, telecommunications and manufacturing. In fact between 2000 and 2008 GDP grew at similar rates in African countries with and without significant resources exports.

Urbanisation

Africa's long-term growth will increasingly reflect interrelated social and demographic trends that are creating new engines of domestic growth. Chief among these is urbanisation. In 1980, 28% of Africans lived in cities, today this has risen to about 40%. As more Africans move from rural to urban jobs, their incomes are rising.

Between 2000 and 2008 the rate of urbanisation in SSA was more than double the world average.[205] The UN projects that the proportion of SSA people living in urban areas will nearly double between 2005 and 2050 from 35%, or 300m people, to more than 55% of the total population, or 820m people. The density of these urban concentrations (with an average of 8,000 people per square km)[206] will allow easy access to consumers and excellent distribution opportunities.

Capital flows

The annual flow of foreign direct investment (FDI) into Africa increased from $9 billion in 2000 to $62 billion in 2008 – relative to GDP, this is almost as large as the flows into China. Between 1990 and 2007, the World Bank has made cumulative fiscal lending to SSA of $57 billion, as opposed to only $3 billion for the Middle East and north Africa. Private flows into Africa have grown from only $17 billion in 1999 to $57 billion in 2007, while annual remittances from Africans abroad doubled from $6 billion to $12 billion between 2003 and 2007.[207]

Expanding labour force and improving productivity

By 2040, Africa's labour force is projected to reach one billion, overtaking China and India. The World Bank estimates that by 2020 almost 20% of the world's population will live in Africa, up from only 7% in the 1950s, and that by 2050 young people (in the 15 to 25 age group) will account for one-in-five in SSA.

Labour productivity has been rising in Africa by a robust 3% annually since 2000. As long as Africa can provide its young with the education and skills they need, this large workforce could account for a significant share of global production and consumption in the future. Since the 1990s, 75% of Africa's increased GDP per capita came from an expanding labour force, the remaining 25% from higher productivity.

Growing GDP per capita/rising incomes

Sub-Saharan Africa's GDP per capita should continue on its trajectory of 5% compound annual growth rate until 2015. This implies a more than 35% increase in the spending power of individuals from 2010 to 2015. Combined with a strong population growth rate of 3% annually and continued urbanisation, this increase leads to estimates that 221m basic-needs consumers will enter the market by 2015. It is therefore projected that "the number of attractive or highly attractive national markets – with more than 10m consumers and gross national income exceeding $10 billion a year – will increase from 19 in 2008 to 24 in 2014".[208]

A rising middle class with greater discretionary income

As reported in a paper by the African Development Bank (AfDB), "the African middle class has increased in size and purchasing power as strong economic growth in the past two decades has helped reduce poverty significantly and lift poor households in the middle class".[209] It added that by 2010 the total middle class (including the floating class – those who spend between $2 to $4 a day) had risen to 34% of the population or nearly 313m people, up from about 111m or 26% of the population in 1980.

In 2008, roughly 85m African households earned $5,000 or more – the level above which they start spending roughly half their income on items other than food (discretionary spending).[210] The UN projects the number of households with discretionary income to rise by 50% over the next ten years, reaching 128m by 2030. The continent's top 18 cities could have a combined spending power of $1.3 trillion.

Africa's five largest consumer markets in 2020 – Alexandria, Cairo, Lagos, Johannesburg and Cape Town – will each have more than $25 billion a year in household spending, and be comparable in size to Mumbai and New Delhi. More than a dozen other African cities – Dakar, Nairobi, Ibadan, Kano, Rabat, Kinshasa, Addis Ababa, Khartoum, Kampala, Accra, Harare, Windhoek and Luanda – will each develop consumer markets worth more than $10 billion a year by 2020.

Consumerism

The result of the 2005 International Comparison Programme managed by the AfDB shows that per capita expenditure among Africa's middle class has increased almost twofold in the previous ten years, compared to more marginal increases in all other regional economies in developed countries.

In 2008 an article in the *Washington Post* highlighted the growing trend of consumerism in Africa.[211] It estimated that 300m people, representing one-third of the African population, comprise the *Africa 2* – these are people "who are neither obnoxiously rich nor desperately poor. These pre-conscious Africa 2s are expected to increase in number and to remain a key stimulant in the demand for global low-priced manufactured goods".[212] 'Africa's Path to Growth' records that between 2005 and 2008 consumer spending across the continent increased at a compound annual rate of 16%, more than twice the GDP growth.

Technological leap frog

During the Y2K scare at the turn of the last century, Africa was sitting pretty while around the world many other countries were concerned. This was because parts of Africa had no computers at all and those parts that did have computers had the machines installed only shortly before so the software and programming had taken care of the millennium handover.

This is indicative of Africa's position as technology neutral – the continent has not had much chance to become accustomed to the legacy of old technology systems which tend to hobble the West's ease of adoption and embrace of new innovations. This phenomenon is responsible for African consumers' exceptional flexibility in accepting advanced technology readily. They are more willing to adopt because they have nothing to forget or give up. This has informed, among other things, the success of the penetration of wireless telephony in Africa in a very short time.

Location

Africa is cut into two almost equal parts by the equator and it is the only continent that has both the equator and the prime meridian cutting through it. Indeed, the geographical centre of the world is Accra, the capital of Ghana. In terms of geo-position relative to other parts of the world, Africa is the only continent close to every continent without compromising its distance to any. It basically sits in the middle of the world.

This is important because the world we currently live in and the one we are evolving into is going to be location-sensitive. The whole world is moving from an industry-driven economy to a service driven one. Parts of the developed world have already completed that transformation – for example the United States, Britain, Singapore, Hong Kong, Ireland and Dubai are all service economies. India is becoming one, as is South Africa, and so is the Philippines.

Outsourcing and global sourcing is already the next big thing in global business. To effectively service global consumers, round the clock or *follow-the-sun* operations will be the mainstream service models. In this regard Africa's enviable geo-location – matters of world class infrastructure and human resources capabilities aside – positions it uniquely as the ideal seat of global service industries.

Africa today and Africa tomorrow[213]

The data in Tables 12.1 and 12.2 provide a means of comparison between the Africa of today and the Africa of the future.

Table 12.1 – Africa today

$1.6 trillion	Africa's collective GDP in 2008, roughly equal to Brazil's or Russia's
$160 million	Africa's combined consumer spending in 2008
316 million	The number of new mobile phone subscribers signed up in Africa since 2000
60%	Africa's share of the world's total amount of uncultivated, arable land
52	The number of African cities with more than one million people each
20	The number of African companies with revenues of at least $3 billion

Table 12.2 – Africa tomorrow – projected figures for the future

$2.6 trillion	Africa's collective GDP in 2020
$1.4 billion	Africa's combined consumer spending in 2020
1.1 billion	The number of Africans of working age in 2040
128 million	The number of African households with discretionary income in 2020
50%	The proportion of Africans living in cities by 2030

OPPORTUNITIES IN AGRICULTURE

Context

Before delving into the broad themes expected to underpin investments in African agriculture in the coming decades, it is necessary to provide some basic context:

- Africa is claimed to have 12% of the world's arable land

- 80% of Africa's arable land is uncultivated

- Africa has 60% of the world's uncultivated arable land

- Only 7% of Africa's arable land is under irrigation (Asia has 40% under irrigation)

The following are the broad themes that will influence demand and consumption of agricultural products across Africa, as well as the world's demand for African agricultural commodities, now and in the future.

Themes underpinning Africa's agricultural appeal

Population increase

It has been recorded before that Africa currently has the fastest population growth rate in the world, and that this growth rate is projected to be sustained into the very long term. It has also been observed that going forward Africa will not only be looked upon to feed and fully nourish its own but the rest of the world, owing to the enormous untapped agricultural potential to be aided by biotechnological advances.

Population increase therefore leaves African agriculture with a difficult quandary: the population is increasing and more need to be fed on a daily basis. There will be 340m more mouths to be fed between 2010 and 2025, and another 620m between 2025 and 2050, which means that African agriculture has to swing into action and fast. This supplies the basis for bringing large tracts of hitherto uncultivated arable land under cultivation in the shortest time possible.

The challenges this state of affairs poses to agriculture are various:

- How to bring vast uncultivated land under cultivation without major population dislocation and injury to the environment

- How to reduce crop cycles and increase harvest times per year/period

Pressure on high-potential agricultural land

As population continues to increase in African countries, pressure on land and conflicts over land use in very high potential areas will continue to intensify. Due to earlier primitive modes of agriculture, some of the most agriculturally productive parts of Africa are also the most densely settled.

Sustained population growth, especially in rural Africa, continues to result in more high potential land falling casualty to new settlements as people move out of their parents' homes to get married and establish their own homes at designated flat locations on the family land – this is land that would otherwise be ideal for farming. The resulting subdivision of land lots that are already too small and uneconomic poses the danger of rendering large parts of African arable land with highest agricultural potential inaccessible.

The Kisii highlands of Kenya are some of the most agriculturally productive parts of eastern Africa. The situation there is already critical and in a matter of very few years, possibly a decade or two, the region will succumb fully to built-up settlement with its agricultural productivity neutered. The same thing goes for the republics of Rwanda and Burundi, most of Uganda, the western province of Kenya, and vast sections of the Ethiopian highlands. This poses the following challenges:

- How to produce more food with less land

- How to reclaim land for agricultural use by managed resettlement efforts

Urbanisation

There are two broad waves of urbanisation in Africa, each with distinct effects on agriculture. The first is the classic *rural-urban drift*, where the young and energetic move from rural areas to urban areas in search of a better life. This has the effect of taking away the more vibrant labour force from agricultural activities and re-allocating it to commercial, industrial, manufacturing and other economic activities usually found in urban centres.

Another effect has to do with the fact that urban jobs are better paid, so the people who get them are able to afford more food and in more variety. It therefore has the net effect of reversing the roles of most rural youth from agricultural producers to paying consumers. As urbanisation intensifies, demand for agricultural produce tends to increase; this is already playing out in African countries.

The other wave of urbanisation taking root is that of the *urbanisation of rural Africa*. With time urban systems that develop in the countryside eat up agricultural land and draw

> 66 As urbanisation intensifies, demand for agricultural produce tends to increase; this is already playing out in African countries. 99

rural people, the youth especially, into commercial activities and away from agriculture. Some of the fastest growing urban centres in the world are to be found in Africa and the ensuing urban sprawl is resulting in a great deal of agricultural land being reclassified or rezoned, to cater for ever-growing residential needs of these centres.

The implications of urbanisation on agriculture are various. These are the main points:

- More urbanisation comes with better-paying jobs and a greater ability to afford food. Food consumption levels are therefore set to increase in Africa in tandem with the increasing rate of urbanisation.

- Urban dwellers tend to take more balanced diets than rural folks. Demand for beef and other meat products is set to increase as more African people become urbanised.

- Uptake of processed and packaged foods is a direct impact of urbanisation.

Climate change

Climate change has had adverse effects on world agriculture already, but this is most severe in Africa. Environmentalists and climate scientists posit that going forward climate change will have the most damaging effects on Africa because of its position straddling the equator and the tropics. Therefore, any strategy for commercial agriculture in Africa has to take account of the effects of climate change on rainfall patterns, soil degradation and seed germination.

There are many ambitious, large-scale agricultural projects in Africa that have been started to great fanfare with realistic forecasts and expectations, but which invariably run foul of the random variations of unseasonable weather. Either crop yields turn out far too mediocre to be reported, or there is outright crop failure due to a lack of rain or too much of it.

In 2011 Monsanto, a US-based agricultural giant, launched its first drought tolerant products. Between 2008 and 2010, the firm has started to play a leading role in a collective effort to create a green revolution in Africa. To this effect it has, "donated all its intellectual property, seed and know-how for developing drought tolerant genes to Water Efficient Maize for Africa (WEMA) a public-private partnership that has received grants from Bill & Melinda Gates Foundation and the foundation of Howard Buffett, an Illinois farmer (and son of Warren Buffett)".[214]

Due to climate change, minds are becoming more focused on the complexities of innovations in large-scale agriculture. As a consequence, 21st century agriculture in Africa will have to work to develop:

- More weather-proof agriculture – agricultural practices that are not dependent on natural seasons for watering the crops

- Drought resistant seeds and water-clogging resistant crops

- Soil quality improvement initiatives

Infrastructure

It is reported that large-scale commercial agriculture was not possible in the Western world before the advent of national and intercontinental networks of transport infrastructure – the railroads made mass markets possible because they offered assurance that if land was cleared and crops were grown on it, there was access to deep, organized markets for the goods.

The lack of access to markets, both national and international, was one of the single most serious impediments to agricultural enterprise in Africa. Now there are countless anecdotes of places which had been quiet, barren areas but turned into agricultural miracles by the putting in place of a road giving access to neighbouring town centres. Recent dairy and horticultural farming breakthroughs owe their successes more to infrastructural connections than anything else. A good example is western Uganda.

As African countries get more interconnected with road and rail transport infrastructure, the broader the prospects for intra-African trade in agriculture become, adding viability to more large-scale crop production. By the same token, the establishment of more bulk handling terminals in sea ports of Africa, and additional capacity enhancement for existing ports, increases the viability of African agriculture's linkage with the global food supply equation.

The airlift of African horticultural produce is becoming a more common practice. Increased air freighting capacity and specialised speedy handling of highly perishable produce – such

❝ As African countries get more interconnected with road and rail transport infrastructure, the broader the prospects for intra-African trade in agriculture become. **❞**

as horticultural goods and dairy products – is bringing Africa's perishable agriculture to within reach of new markets in the Middle East and Asia.

Going forward, modern and dependable transport infrastructure will be expected to positively impact Africa's agriculture in the following ways:

- Scalability of erstwhile smaller operations

- Providing national, regional and global viability, where previously this was not possible

- Market/consumer-driven agriculture, such as contract farming or global outsourcing

Technological breakthroughs

Technological development is difficult to predict but there is one fact that always remains accurate; technology is constantly changing and very quickly. It is the game-changing technological innovations that really matter in terms of determining the future of business landscapes. Agriculture has had its fair share of technological breakthroughs in recent times, not necessarily in Africa but some of these can be easily replicated in the continent to boost productivity.

According to an article in *The Economist*, Embrapa, Brazil's agricultural research corporation, achieved the greatest agricultural feat of modern times by turning the Cerrado (Brazil's vast savanna) green. It achieved this by adding industrial quantities of lime to the highly acidic soils and then introducing a bacterium that helps fix nitrogen within legumes, therefore reducing the need for fertilisers. Today, the Cerrado, which in 1990 was a hopeless wasteland, accounts for 70% of Brazil's farming output.[215]

Embrapa then patiently crossbred Africa's brachiaria grass to create a new variety called braquiarinha with three-times the pasture yields of the original

❝ Being on the lookout for other transformational technological or research finds should serve to put African agriculture in good stead for contention for world-class status. ❞

African grass. Where before it took four years to raise a bull for slaughter, it now takes 18 to 20 months. By the stroke of this singular breakthrough, Brazil now boasts the second largest national herd in the world after India, but leads the world in beef exports.

Embrapa also domesticated soya beans, which are otherwise a temperate crop, to the tropics and sped up the growing period, cutting about ten weeks off the usual life cycle. This made it possible to grow two crops a year, revolutionising the operation of farms.

The miracle of the Cerrado is exportable to Africa in the main part because Brazilian soils are much like those in Africa – they are tropical and nutrient-poor. Rolling out the techniques used in the Cerrado, and other approaches used in Brazil, should be a priority for African agriculture into the foreseeable future.

Importantly, being on the lookout for other transformational technological or research finds should serve to put African agriculture in good stead for contention for world-class status. Technology generally should make the following possible for agriculture in SSA:

- Reclamation of wastelands

- Yields and breeding improvements

- Crop cycle reduction and ratcheting up productivity

World food market scares and national food security policies

Since 2007 world food price increases have spiralled out of control. Between 2007 and 2008, *The Economist* food-price index rose 78%. In both 2010 and 2011 world food prices were up 50%, of which 26% happened in 2011 alone.[216] This phenomenon was caused initially by a slump in global food stocks, but was later painfully aggravated by unprecedented and completely unexpected world food export bans by the major cereal growing and exporting giants – principally Russia, India, Argentina and Ukraine – to keep the prices of food low at home.[217]

These measures caught the resource-rich Middle Eastern countries unawares – they had the money to buy food but were prevented from doing so. This raised fears that one day food importers might not be able to secure enough food supplies at any price – rendering world food markets ineffective and dysfunctional. This led food importers to the conclusion that they could no longer rely on world food markets for basic supplies.

This has since touched off a large and co-ordinated land-grab and the target has predominantly been Africa's arable land. In total, the International Food Policy Research Institute (IFRI) says that between 15m and 20m hectares of farmland in poor countries, most of them in Africa, have been subject to transactions involving foreigners since 2006. This is an area the size of France's agricultural land and equal to a fifth of all the farmland in the European Union.

These projects are expected to result in massive crop yields; estimates put the figure at 30-40m tons of cereals per year. It is expected that this will side-step world food markets and go directly to secure the food security of client countries. The dynamics of these unique arrangements and their impacts on African agriculture would be expected to result in strides forward on commercial agriculture infrastructure in the continent. China has already set up 11 research stations in Africa to boost yields on staple foods.

Other impacts may be as follows:

- Support for rural infrastructure
- New and better seeds
- The impetus for the search for food security at home
- Competition for arable land

World Trade Organisation (WTO)

Were it not for the deliberate and systematic trade distorting agricultural practices of the EU under the Common Agricultural Policy (CPA) and the United States farm policies that limit direct access and impose tariffs on Africa's agricultural products to European and American markets, the profile of Africa's commercial agriculture would be different.

It is the universal mandate of the WTO to remove barriers to international trade and put the whole world on a uniform rules-based system of trade practices and policies. Progress is slow and sometimes reversals or stagnation are the order of the day rather than the exception. However, African, Latin American and Asian nations are fighting under a common front of the Group of 77 (G77) – a caucus organisation which helps developing states pursue common goals and develop leverage in United Nations deliberations[218] – to force the EU and the US to remove the obstructionist policies.

The Doha round of trade negotiations continue to give relevance to the advocacy of this inevitable overhaul of the architecture of world agricultural markets. To the extent that the G77 continues to achieve concessions and gain territory while the EU/US yield ground, prospects for African commercial agriculture will continue to improve. The final collapse of these restrictive practices will unleash the natural competitive and comparative advantage of Africa's agriculture, being situated with good proximity to the EU. As the WTO and G77 work towards a level playing field, this will impact agriculture in SSA in various ways:

- Cost competitiveness and weather neutrality (climate-controlled or greenhouse agriculture) will be unleashed

- Marketing and distribution networks will be opened up

- Transport and freight opportunities will be opened up

- New crops will be added to Africa's product portfolio

Summary of the opportunities in agriculture

Land

The most pertinent statistic for this investment opportunity is that Africa has 60% of the world's uncultivated arable land. The emphasis here is on *uncultivated* – this establishes Africa's distinction as the undisputed last frontier. The patterns of claiming land that were earlier seen in North America as people moved west and then in Eastern Europe after the collapse of communism are being seen again in Africa today. The logic is simple – in order to conduct large-scale agriculture on a long-term basis the land has to be secured first.

A surge of investments focused on Africa's agricultural land is only just beginning. Special funds are being registered and money raised as early adapters and pattern identifiers start taking strategic positions to benefit from the next major global agricultural play. For example, African Agricultural Land Fund (Agriland), established by London-based hedge fund Emergent Asset Management and the South African agricultural trader Grainvest, now grosses €3 billion in funds raised.[219] It plans to buy up agricultural land throughout Africa with the aim of increasing production yields through the introduction of progressive farming techniques, large-scale mechanisation and centralisation across the value chain.

Chayton Capital, a UK private equity firm, has also embarked on building an agricultural company in Africa that it hopes will become one of the largest on the continent. It plans to acquire and develop up to 10,000 hectares, which is equal to 120,000 tones of wheat, maize and soybeans. It will buy farms which are under-managed, under-capitalised or in receivership and increase capacity through better techniques and modernisation.[220]

> **" A surge of investments focused on Africa's agricultural land is only just beginning. Special funds are being registered and money raised as early adapters and pattern identifiers start taking strategic positions to benefit from the next major global agricultural play. "**

Commodity traders are also moving into Africa. Armajaro, one of the world's largest cocoa trading firms, is planning a private equity fund to acquire land, storage and transport infrastructure. Starbucks Coffee has also made reconnaissance visits to Africa with a view to obtaining long-term supply contracts with major coffee growers and exporters. It is also likely that other similar deals and contracts are happening off the radar and many more are in the pipeline.[221]

The opportunities to develop and commercialise Africa's abundant agricultural land offer a range of hugely compelling economic opportunities for Africa as well as for international investors.

Water

The next investment opportunity is in water and water resources.

Numerous estimates put the amount of global water withdrawal by agriculture at between 70% and 75%. Many countries in the world are facing a growing gap between the amount of water they can supply reliably to their economies and the amount needed. In an article, 'The Business Opportunities in Water Conservation', McKinsey estimates that by 2030 only 60% of global demand will be met by available water supplies.[222]

African nations have the greatest challenge of any; currently some nations struggle to meet even 50% of their need and the story is about to get even more grim in the face of explosive population growth, rapid urbanisation and imminent industrialisation, even without considering the food needs and sanitation demands of these future African societies. Companies in engineering, mining, beverages, utilities, oil, pulp and paper, and others, are already influenced by water considerations in their strategic decisions about where to locate operations. The CEO of Monsanto, Hugh Grant, has suggested that "arguments over water will dwarf the discussion that has taken place so far over food".[223]

In the developed world, water is no longer a *use-all-you-can* resource. Pricing mechanisms have been developed and scarcity is raising prices and increasing the level of regulation and competition among stakeholders for access to water. Climate change is expected to worsen the problem. In the most advanced water markets a concept known as *usufructuary rights*, which enables trading in rights to use water more than a fixed quota of entitlement, is already being implemented. The result of this trading is a market that has done what markets do – allocate resources to more productive use.

African municipal authorities are under increasing pressure to develop and extend access to water, and also to charge a market rate for water use – be it for commercial, industrial, residential or agricultural purposes. This is expected to create clearer scope for a market in water for vast industrial and agricultural use. To achieve year-round production in agriculture, access to or ownership of deep reservoirs of fresh water is going to be a source of competitive advantage going forward.

Selling water to industrial and green house farming concerns is also expected to create fresh business opportunities. Mining companies with fully exhausted deep extraction pits will enjoy inexpensive storage advantage if they use recent techniques of rain water capture and ground storage. Municipal and urban water supply by private water utilities is a good opportunity made ever greater by the spectacular failings of local authorities to sustain constant water supply and exacerbated by the population growth and urbanisation in Africa.

Of all continents, Africa is the least irrigated and electrified, and it has been referred to as *undammed* because of the lack of river-water reservoirs that are in place. However, Africa uses only 3% of its renewable water, against 52% in South

> **❝** Access to an inexpensive year-round water supply is going to be a major factor for competitive agricultural production in Africa in the coming decades. **❞**

Asia, so there is plenty of scope for an African dam-building boom.[224] With ever-longer dry spells and falling water tables, prospects for year-round agriculture seem to lie increasingly with extensive rain water capture projects – access to an inexpensive year-round water supply is going to be a major factor for competitive agricultural production in Africa in the coming decades. Both public and private initiatives to harness and store vast quantities of rainwater are emerging.

Soil quality

The story of the miracle of the Brazilian *Cerrado* mentioned earlier is compelling in showing what might be achieved in Africa by addressing soil quality – an agricultural miracle cannot be realised without efforts to vastly improve and maintain soil qualities. This will make the difference between Africa growing enough to feed itself with spare to sell to the rest of the world, or continuing in subsistence mode. The good news is that there is evidence that measures to improve soil quality can be successful in Africa – in Malawi use of fertiliser to improve soil quality resulted in a bumper national harvest in 2008 that was four times the size of normal crop yields.[225]

Fertiliser production in Sub-Saharan Africa so far makes up only 3% of Africa's total. The constraints have been scale, political will and deficiencies in raw materials.[226] However, now with the new demand anticipated there is an urgent need for establishment of fertiliser factories and other facilities in Africa. The infrastructural improvements happening speedily to make industrial investments viable – such as power availability and connecting markets – should help this need to be met. Common market protocols now obtaining across Africa have aided in removing the constraints of scale that hitherto hindered investments in large-scale fertiliser production in African economies.

Scientific farming

As arable as most of Africa is reputed to be, it still relies upon the basic combination of good soil conditions and reliable rainfall to grow crops and harvest good yields. Rain-fed agriculture remains the dominant means of achieving agricultural productivity in many an African village and indeed for most commercial farming. The pattern of deteriorating rainfall across most of SSA has posed so far the greatest challenge to the system of crop husbandry and increasingly the highland model of agriculture (or rain-fed agriculture) seems to suffer a consistent pattern of threats to its viability as a first-choice option for large-scale commercial farming.

Even parts of Africa where certain crops were perceived as almost indigenous due to the near perfect natural conditions – such as maize production in southern Africa – are now beginning to lose their advantage and increasingly require deliberate interventions to boost soils and new crop varieties to sustain yields or just to maintain production levels.[227] There are vast swathes of territory where the cultivation of wheat and beans – some of the staple foods in most of Africa – was a natural choice just a decade ago, but where now such land use has virtually ceased. The reason for this is due to crop failure – which has become more and more common – and the main cause of this situation is *climate change*.

Governments are resorting to unbudgeted and economically unsustainable food imports at usurious rates to feed their populations. This used to happen about once every eight to ten years; it is now down to once in every two to three years. It not only redirects resources badly needed for development programmes, it also depletes meagre foreign reserves. Basic food security was something that Africa used to be sure of and proud of but it seems to be on its way to losing this.

This situation cries out for answers, which can only be found in sustainable commercial agriculture. The opportunities in scientific farming on a very large scale are yearning to be filled. There are numerous concepts or combinations of known systems capable of large-scale commercialisation, but none so manifestly persuasive as *irrigated agriculture* (for the large scale) and *greenhouse farming* (for the small scale).

Irrigated agriculture

As an illustrative example of irrigated agriculture, Mumias Sugar Company, the leading sugar milling and marketing company in Kenya, has a project planned to grow sugar cane under irrigation on 20,000 hectares on the Tana River basin. It claims it will be able to grow a fast-maturing cane variety that will yield a crop in 10 to 12 months as opposed to the 18 months it takes on the western Kenyan sugar belt, with vastly improved yields of 120-150 tons of cane per hectare (TCH) compared to the 70-100 TCH from rain fed farms. It will employ a regime of water control which can boost sucrose content in the irrigated sugar cane to 15% against an average of 13.5% from rain fed sugar cane.[228] This means that it will be able to increase sugar production by more than two and half times due to the compounding effect of these three fundamental adjustments – irrigated land, fast-maturing cane and water control. The system of irrigation to be deployed is reported to withdraw only 30% of reservoir capacity in a year with up to about 45% to 50% flow back in a system of channels and drainage networks.

Greenhouse farming

At another level, greenhouse farming is useful in the cultivation of horticulture and floriculture. Statistics obtained from the Kenya Horticulture Development Programme (KHDP) indicate that tomato farming using greenhouses yields huge quantities on a very small piece of land under continuous harvesting.[229] For example, a greenhouse gives an average of eight months a year of crop harvesting as opposed to three months for open farming. This is due to control of water supply and temperatures. The harvest cycle per plant is also reduced to two months from the three months that it would be under open farming.

> **❝ Scientific agriculture is emerging as the most feasible option for producing larger crops with fewer natural resources (the most important being water). ❞**

Yields per plant improve from harvest to harvest, normally starting with average 15kg at first harvest and growing to even 60kg by completion of the first cycle of a year. Effectively therefore the minimum plot of land (smallest size of greenhouse) can yield up to 25,000 tons of tomatoes per year. Greenhouse tomatoes are also reported to enjoy a shelf life of 21 days, which is seven days better than open farmed tomatoes, which have only 14 days shelf life.

Water utilisation is almost insignificant as it is released in drips under an environment of climate control where evaporation is minimised or fully eliminated. Evaporation accounts for up to 40% of water loss under open farming in rain-fed systems and 15% to 25% in sprinkler irrigation systems[230] – indeed greenhouse farming can be undertaken under a system of contracted water supply on commercial water rates. Susceptibility to diseases is reduced or controlled within greenhouses thus saving on the cost of pesticides, while labour needs are also tremendously curtailed by the intensity and controlled nature of the operations.

***

Under circumstances of heightening pressure on land use due to high and sustained population growth, a rise in food demand due to the said population explosion that is not abating, rapid urbanisation leading to less dependence on subsistence agriculture and more on commercial farming, as well as vastly reduced fresh water resources due to increased use and climate change, scientific agriculture is emerging as the most feasible option for producing larger crops with fewer natural resources (the most important being water).

Storage

> Initiatives by national and regional grain councils or industry associations are driving efforts to put in place warehouse aggregators for seeds, fertilisers and crop yields.

Whenever there is a bumper crop anywhere in Africa, predictably what happens next is that food goes uncollected in farms or poorly harvested and hastily stored in open structures exposed to the elements where it becomes unfit for human consumption in a much shorter time than it takes to grow it. Food prices then plummet and African farmers are poorly paid for their produce. The endemic problem is a lack of appropriate grain or cereal collection and storage facilities with ease of access by farmers. Where they are in place, they are government-run with chronic inefficiencies and stifling corruption.

Initiatives by national and regional grain councils or industry associations are driving efforts to put in place warehouse aggregators for seeds, fertilisers and crop yields.[231] A warehouse system where farmers deposit their produce and get a receipt with full descriptive details of their goods is what is urgently needed. The farmers can then wait for food prices to stabilise and enjoy the luxury of marketing their produce safely with the thought that it is hygienically secured in designated grain storage facilities.

Prices obtainable under these orderly circumstances are often more competitive as the system enables year-round market liquidity through the use of stored commodities as collateral for inventory finance and a wider geographical reach through *sight-unseen* transactions made possible by standardisation of products. The urgency of the need for massive storage for crop yields and the price advantage for farmers creates enormous scope for private sector investments in agricultural warehousing capacity across SSA.

Processing

Africa continues to hold the dubious distinction as home of primary commodities – be they hard or soft commodities. It seems to be perceived as a solicitous favour for well-disposed western and of late eastern merchants to relieve Africa of the *burdens* of its native

> **"An industry rule of thumb puts the value-addition at the first instance of processing at a staggering ten times, at the very least, of the value of primary commodities. "**

wealth. An industry rule of thumb puts the value-addition at the first instance of processing at a staggering ten times, at the very least, of the value of primary commodities. We can use simple logic to illustrate this situation. Two large potatoes are used to make a packet of potato chips in fast-food outlets dotted all over African cities and urban centres. The cost of two potatoes in a grocery market often a stone's throw away from an eatery could be some $0.03, while the price of the resulting potato chips is $0.63 – this is a price increase of 20 times.

Examples could also be given of the value that Starbucks wrings out of eastern African coffee, or that European packers squeeze out of its tea, or for that matter, that the European desserts and confectionary industry makes of western Africa's cocoa. At present, African fruits and horticulture are transported in planes whole, complete with skins and seeds. The day when they are transported packaged in bottles and sealed containers as the final product for consumption is when Africa's commercial agriculture will have come of age as a global end-to-end supply chain of food and nutrition solutions.

Before that day comes, the food industry can concentrate on processing African foodstuffs, beverage crops, fruits and vegetables for the swelling numbers of urbanites in African cities and towns.

Commodity exchanges

Alongside the warehouse receipting concept discussed above comes another opportunity for agricultural investors – that of commodities exchanges. Once warehouse receipting has caught on, farmers will hold more than a receipt in return for depositing their produce – that they will have created a financial instrument backed by the underlying physical assets of agricultural goods, such as maize, beans or wheat. It will be incumbent upon the warehousing companies to store and maintain the grains in the same condition without quality deterioration and to, as much as possible, ensure homogeneity between one bag of goods to another. They will also be expected to levy reasonable storage, handling and transactional fees per quantity of commodity deposited and time period of warehousing.

> **Alongside the warehouse receipting concept discussed above comes another opportunity for agricultural investors – that of commodities exchanges.**

Many African countries have tried to establish commodities exchanges since the 1990s and all of them, except the South Africa Futures Exchange (SAFEX), The Ethiopian Commodities Exchange (ECX) and the Zimbabwe Agricultural Commodity Exchange (ZIMACE), have had the same disappointing result – a lack of progress. This is mostly due to the absence of warehousing receipting and delivery systems.

A discussion paper for the Fourth African Agricultural Markets Programme (AAMP) policy symposium indicates that:

"Many of these [commodities exchanges] were initiated by private sector players, including the South Africa Futures Exchange (SAFEX), which is now owned by the JSE Securities, the now non-functional Zimbabwe Agricultural Commodity Exchange (ZIMACE), the Agricultural Commodity Exchange for Africa (ACE) in Malawi and the Kenya Agricultural Commodity Exchange (KACE). Others have been promoted with substantial government investment or direct support. Examples include

the Ethiopia Commodity Exchange (ECX) and Uganda Commodity Exchange (UCE). The Zambia Agricultural Commodity Exchange is one of the exchanges being promoted in the region with significant donor support – primarily from USAID. The UCE is also being supported by the EC. South Africa-based Bourse Africa is seeking to establish a pan-African commodity exchange. It has been licensed to operate from Botswana but is yet to make significant inroads in other African markets."[232]

The same paper suggests that the success of SAFEX has been underpinned by a credible delivery system, while ZIMACE had a receipt system in which the grain marketing board acted as the main warehouse operator with warehouse inspection conducted by ITS Socotec, a private inspection company.

Any warehouse receipt backed by the quality assurance and transactional integrity of warehousing and delivery systems will become a financial product, free to assume a life of its own. Then, and then only, will commodity exchange become a viable reality in Africa. The receipts will provide a basis for universal and transparent price discovery as the entire participating buy-side and sell-side will be able to at once weigh in their perceptions about the markets for grains and contribute to collective uniform pricing.

Commodity prices will reflect the dynamic changes or perceptions traders have of the underlying assets. These exchanges will once and for all end farm-to-market agriculture and smooth out demand and supply all year round through the mechanism of price guidance. They will provide and sustain year-round liquidity buoyed by the expectation of financial returns.

❝ The Ethiopian Commodities Exchange (ECX) established in 2008 is thriving. ❞

The introduction of commodities exchanges will beget an entire industry of traders, inspectors, warehouse operators, speculators, investors, market makers, regulators, advisors and other sorts of players, and of course the opportunities to make money.

The Ethiopian Commodities Exchange (ECX) established in 2008 is thriving – boasting a national infrastructure composed of 16 food warehouses, eight regional laboratories, 31 electronic price boards at markets across the country and 600 employees including product graders. After only three years of establishment it sold a staggering $1billion in coffee, sesame, wheat, maize, peas and haricot beans in 2010.[233]

OPPORTUNITIES IN REAL ESTATE

14

A fundamental part of identifying the opportunities in the real estate sector is being able to distinguish the drivers of growth and value for the next decade and into the foreseeable future. An analysis of the main factors follows. Either independently or interacting together, these factors will inspire and guide investment attraction and allocation for real estate in SSA.

Dominant themes in real estate

Population growth and demographics

As African populations continue to grow and families expand, demand for new homes is increasing. African populations are predominantly young and the baby-boomers of the 1980 and 1990s are now adults who are founding families of their own. The momentum of demand for new housing capacity, be it rental or owned, is only just beginning to gather speed, and the cumulative unmet demand should support a long-term underlying investment case for African real estate. The issues here are as follows:

• Increasing demand for materials

• Search for sustainable systems of materials realisation

Urbanisation

African populations are moving to urban centres and simultaneously urban centres are over-running African populations in their rural settings. Whichever happens to be true in any particular circumstance, the speed of urbanisation is the fastest ever recorded (the forces driving it were exhaustively tackled in Part I of this book). This dynamic alone is responsible for the rapid urban sprawl being witnessed in African urban centres.

New urban centres are popping up too. These new and expanding urban settlements are evidence of a critical demand for real estate. When new homes are built they are bought up quickly. This trend is only at its beginnings and the momentum can be expected to be maintained or increase in the future. The issues arising are:

• Growing demand for modern construction capability and technology

• The constraint of realising more properties with less land

GDP per capita

All independent estimates point to a continued expansion of wealth for the average African resident. It is estimated that GDP per capita should sustain a long-term growth rate of 4.5% per annum into the foreseeable future and that 128m African households will have discretionary income by 2020.[234]

❝ Next to automobiles, decent housing is normally very high up in the big ticket shopping lists of newly prosperous societies. ❞

Rising incomes, a growing middle class and an emerging culture of consumerism combine to make for quantum leaps in demand. Next to automobiles, decent housing is normally very high up in the big ticket shopping lists of newly prosperous societies. Accordingly, affordability for modern housing may have touched or be just about to touch critical mass in most African countries. The major issues arising here are:

- Upward spiralling demand for first homes

- Deepening of a secondary market in property as householders trade-up

Supply-side capacity constraints

The momentum of demand for new homes has not even gathered full steam yet, but the traditional real estate development and supply industry is already feeling the strain. In the Kenyan property market, for example, the effective demand, that which is backed by a demonstrated ability to pay, is a total of 150,000 new housing units per year. The construction industry has only been able to put out 35,000 new units per year to the market,[235] so far.

The story is not very much different in the rest of SSA. The mounting cumulative backlog was largely responsible for rendering African property markets recession-proof when the rest of the world property markets went into reverse, with some Western national markets glimpsing meltdown. It is also responsible for the relentless soaring of property values, first in big cities and now practically everywhere. Matters are compounded even further by the fact that annual demand has become a very fast moving consumer target.

The issues emerging here are as follows:

- Innovations on faster and higher capacity property delivery

- Long-term high returns act as a trap for new capital and capacity entry

Modernisation and urban renewal

Land is a fixed resource and fitting five to seven million people in a city that was designed for only 250,000 is a conundrum that calls for innovative systems of land use. This means that the old style of land use, when there was plenty of land to spare, cannot be maintained any longer. Whether commercial premises or residential estates, land has to be used intensively now. Another element to this is that the dilapidated state of some parts of old towns betray the fact they have seen better days.

Some effort is already going into urban renewal, redesign and modernisation of African cities, but what has been achieved so far hardly scratches the surface of what lies ahead. This phenomenon is expected to drive value in African real estate scene for the foreseeable future. The issues apparent here are as follows:

- Opportunities for shuffling underlying city real estate as it changes hands from city governments to private sector developers

- Employing modern architecture and design to increase cities' carrying capacities

Environmental concerns

It may take some time to get to the mainstream in terms of laws and regulations, but environmental and ecological issues and concerns will surely inform decisions, design and materials in the real estate sector in SSA going forward. When the Western world was developing, climate change was not a known concept, and development and industrialisation went ahead without thought to the cost to the environment. But it is the price for the industrialisation of the Western world that the whole world is paying now.

> **❝** It is not going to be possible for Africa to develop or industrialise at the same energy intensity as the developed world in the last century. **❞**

From the foregoing, it is not going to be possible for Africa, or indeed any other part of the world, to develop or industrialise at the same energy intensity as the developed world in the last century – these include the costs of material extraction and their attendant permanent effects on the environment; the energy cost of transporting materials; the energy costs of construction; and the energy costs of keeping buildings warm or cool and lighted. These ecological and environmental concerns will engender commercial opportunities in new, vast areas of real estate supply chains that investors will need to look out for. The issues arising here are:

- Finding sustainably-produced and environmentally friendly building materials

- Designing and delivering properties that are energy and carbon-neutral

Mortgage finance expansion

When the power of financial leverage has been brought to bear on the African real estate sector, it will be completely unrecognisable. Mortgage finance is becoming a standard product of commercial banks rather than a product available only in special purpose mortgage finance houses. Virtually every retail commercial bank now offers, or is soon to offer, a mortgage product. According to Shelter Afrique, a pan-African housing finance company:

> "The mortgage industry in Africa is in its infancy, except in South Africa. Mortgage loans in South Africa represent more than 30% of GDP while Kenya has the best ratio in Sub-Saharan Africa which is 2% of GDP. This means, beyond the gap, there are ample opportunities to grow this sector. The strategic thinking is encouraging in Africa. Many leaders in the banking sector in Africa are targeting the development of the mortgage industry whose annual growth is around 30% in countries like Kenya, Senegal and Rwanda."[236]

❝ When the power of financial leverage has been brought to bear on the African real estate sector, it will be completely unrecognisable. ❞

When mortgages have become just as ordinary as deposit products for people in Africa there will be an explosion in demand for real estate.

Another major current obstacle to property realisation is the challenge of raising the 20% to 30% down-payment, which still remains largely owner's equity. This stands in the way of the origination of millions of real estate property deals. When a solution to this issue is found demand for real estate will be boosted significantly. An emerging promising example is the concept of homes down-payment finance taking shape in some African countries.

The issues evident in this area are:

- Finding real estate development financing models that integrate with mortgage-powered property uptake

- Increasing construction and development capacity to match demand velocity resulting from the effects of mortgage finance leverage

Secondary property markets

As long as the only real estate demand in SSA was for permanent homes for first-time buyers who buy and hold, there was never going to be a property market to speak of. But, pleasantly, that is not the case anymore; a sizeable market in secondary properties is slowly developing, where people flip properties back to the market and go in search of upgrades either

> **"** The rising incomes of a bulging middle class, largely youthful and urban in character, are providing the fundamental underpinnings for a vibrant property market in the major SSA economies. **"**

of size, design or location. In so doing they create multiple transactions and inject liquidity into the property markets, promoting transparency and efficiency of price discovery.

The rising incomes of a bulging middle class, largely youthful and urban in character, are providing the fundamental underpinnings for a vibrant property market in the major SSA economies. Financial products are developing from these, as banks are also warming up to mortgage top-ups, home equity withdrawals and refinancing. This encourages real estate investments with a financial return motivation, adding dynamism to the property markets. The main issues arising here are:

- A market framework for secondary property trading

- Unitisation and securitisation of property income streams into financial products

Summary of the opportunities in real estate

Land banks

Just as with agriculture, the most strategic first move right now to position oneself to benefit favourably from the coming real estate bonanza in SSA is undoubtedly to acquire and hold on to choice locations. A lot of re-zoning and reclassification of land type and land use is already happening next to big cities and emerging towns – with agricultural land becoming commercial and residential. The value accretion here is astounding.

> **The most strategic first move right now to position oneself to benefit favourably from the coming real estate bonanza in SSA is undoubtedly to acquire and hold on to choice locations.**

Opportunities are emerging to plan state-of-the-art and ultra-stylish cities and residential complexes in unencumbered open spaces. In cities, the theme for remodelling and urban renewal is freeing up a great deal of real estate making it available to parties with the conceptual heft and financial depth to make the most of out it. With the model of Public-Private Partnerships (PPP) slowly taking root and catching on, opportunities for private investment or co-investment in public utilities are going to be in abundance in SSA cities.

Materials and aggregates

The next opportunity is to be found in the real estate construction supply-side. Cement consumption is expected to rise steeply. Investing in new cement manufacturing capacity or adding capacity for the existing companies becomes a great opportunity, as increased electricity generation and supply capacity becomes available and drives down energy costs in African economies,. In Kenya alone, there were only three cement companies in 2007. Two more were commissioned in 2009-10 and another three are set to come on stream by 2014. Just to illustrate the profound scale of the opportunity, one of the new cement companies vaulted to a 20% market share within two years of operation through innovative pricing in a market that is reportedly growing at 10% to 12% a year.[237]

Opportunities in coarse aggregates abound; for example in mobile concrete mixers, ballast supply and steel structures. There are also opportunities in supplying materials for civil works to connect to urban transport, sewerage and water supply systems. This role is increasingly being undertaken by private developers eager to enhance the value and facilitate the uptake of their developments in response to the failure of city governments to carry out their basic municipal duties. Cement companies are now diversifying into this area by manufacturing cement tiles, slabs and curbs, which are increasingly used for road and pavement construction.

The scale, capacity and diversification required to satisfy the rate of real estate development that will be necessary to fill the cumulative backlog and match future demand creates opportunities not only for existing players, but also for the major global players without a significant presence in Africa already.

Construction capacity

When the government of Kenya rolled out its infrastructural development programme in 2006-7, it quickly ran into construction capacity headwinds. Road projects were not started or stalled soon after inception even when they had been fully funded or provisioned, just because the existing construction capacity was lacking. There were just not enough construction companies with the right equipment and skills to undertake and deliver the assignments at the speed and to the standard of quality expected. This had to be addressed by opening up the field to international players.

The same scenario has long been playing out in private real estate development. The construction capacity, equipment and skills available are just not significant enough – this is a major reason for the persistent, chronic supply-side constraints. Academics G. Zawdie and D. A. Langford also came to this conclusion, arguing that "inadequate construction capacity (in Africa) gives rise to constraints on the supply side of the industry, which in turn affects the level of construction activity".[238]

The pressing need to substantially increase construction capacity is becoming increasingly evident. Many proposed development projects have to wait their turn for the attention and service of construction companies. Engineering and project management time is costly and expenses are soaring out of proportion to reasonable total construction cost models. As real estate development becomes more sophisticated, the need to renew the skills set and overhaul inventories of construction equipment becomes apparent. This too enhances investment opportunities and creates fresh entry points into SSA real estate development.

Soft timber

Vast sections of the USA and Canada are planted with soft timberland. Most, if not all, of these plantations are artificial, and were not there before the 1950s. They provide the physical backdrop to the biggest and most advanced real estate sectors in the world. The logic is simple – if they were to provide a home to every household in the USA built using stone, that would leave the landscape as an ugly series of mine shafts and quarries, laying waste to the countryside and more valuable real estate than that which has been built. Hence the industry-wide switch to soft timber.

> **Undoubtedly, the only feasible way to realise the vast amount of real estate Africa needs is to radically shift its view of housing and most importantly change the main building materials to soft timber.**

Soft timber recommends itself as the ultimate material for mass home building in a few ways. It is renewable – a replacement tree can be matured every seven to ten years; it leaves no permanent scars on the surface of the earth – tree stumps are easy to uproot and they can be put to a whole lot more diverse range of uses; it is easily accessible – timber plantations can be grown anywhere, even under irrigation as opposed to building stones which can only be found in specific places; it is cheap; houses are more liveable because they cost less in heating and air conditioning; and it is climate friendly – woodlands act as carbon sinks.

Undoubtedly, the only feasible way to realise the vast amount of real estate Africa needs is to radically shift its view of housing and most importantly change the main building materials to soft timber. In anticipation of this shift, some private timber plantations are already emerging. For example, the Global Environment Fund (GEF) in 2010 raised a $150m in the GEF Africa Sustainable Forestry Fund, which is "the first private equity fund to focus solely on sustainable forestry in Sub-Saharan Africa, in a pioneering investment to help develop and grow business in Africa's expanding forestry sector." CDC, the UK development finance institution, has committed $50m to the fund which is open to private sector investors.[239] However, for the moment these projects remain few and far between.

The opportunities in large-scale timber plantation business to supply the soon to become insatiable real estate construction demands are opening up, and the momentum to mainstream it should come along as international players begin taking interest in the market opportunities arising in this area. There are several countries within SSA which provide good opportunities for forest investments, including Mozambique, Tanzania, Swaziland, Uganda, Ghana, Malawi, Guinea and Zambia.

Consumer shopping experience

African shoppers are becoming worldlier; their tastes more eclectic and more varied. The cultural revolution I described in detail in megatrend two earlier in the book is now crystallising in a complete transformation of the African urbanite – nowhere is this more evident than in the shopping experience.

The emerging African shopping experience is shaped by the desire for variety, the psychological satisfaction of paying the lowest or most competitive price possible, and the new ability to buy all goods that are being shopped for under one roof. This third point is an especially important motivation because car parking is no longer free in city downtowns and, even worse, it is not available for most of the day.

> **“** The cultural revolution is now crystallising in a complete transformation of the African urbanite – nowhere is this more evident than in the shopping experience. **”**

Shopping malls meet these specifications perfectly well, both in design and presentation. For that reason, they are the latest trend in commercial real estate in Africa. Before the full shopping experience of each African with disposable income has been transformed, a considerable number of malls will have been built, so the opportunity here is opening up and will last for the long term.

Vertical real estate

There are two types of real estate that Africa so far has neglected to take advantage of. One is the real estate underground. It is vast, it is strategic and completely unexplored – but it is also extremely expensive to realise and for now remains outside the bounds of possibility either for African governments or private societies. The other is real estate above the ground, or more precisely above the ground floor. It is equally vast, abundantly accessible and supplies the classic example of real estate leverage, namely squeezing the maximum from one square foot of space by introducing an extra dimension – upwards.

The majority of residential estates in African cities are made up of old, low-lying single houses occupying vast real estate underneath. These are the epitome of under-utilisation. A convergence of forces is paving the way for the demolition of these structures and their replacement with high-rise apartment buildings. One of these forces is new urban regulations fostering urban renewal and modernisation, and the other one is the commercial logic of unlocking value from wasting assets.

Realtors and estate agencies

The field of real estate development and delivery is becoming more crowded with layers of professionals and technical experts. The marketplace is getting more sophisticated and navigation increasingly more difficult for private individuals and groups. At the same time there is the arrival on the scene of international players and their clients which calls for services in the real estate sector to be more formal and professional.

The increasing scale and liquidity, and the deepening investment options and motivations for participation, necessitate the roles of realtors and estate agents as facilitators, connectors, coordinators, managers and executors among other roles. The prospects are broadening and the market appeal has already lured some established international players.

REITs

Property values in most African markets have been on a long-term upward trend for more than a decade now. Capital gains are unparalleled by competing investment alternatives, underlying demand is durable, supply is being aided by financial leverage, and downside risk is minimised by rising asset values and the increasing liquidity in secondary markets. If the fundamentals are this

> **❝ REITs allow the greatest possible number of members of the public to lock in and benefit from the returns of rallying property markets without the headaches of physical participation. ❞**

attractive, it is pertinent to ask why people are not investing. The reason is that there are also constraints. The entry levels are just too high for many, with the cost of putting up real estate forbidding; there are not enough properties for each prospective individual investor; and the motions of real estate realisation are time consuming and too cumbersome for most.

The best route for aggregating partial savings and investments of individuals and groups with the appetite and risk tolerance for real estate exposure but without the depth to go it alone is real estate investment trusts (REITs). They allow the greatest possible number of members of the public to lock in and benefit from the returns of rallying property markets without the headaches of physical participation. The opportunities to establish REITs in some of the most advanced property markets of SSA are gaping. Positive financial contagion from these countries will create opportunities in other countries too where the stage of real estate development may still be low for now.

OPPORTUNITIES IN CONSUMER RETAIL

A perceptible change is happening in the theatre of the African consumer experience. A few major forces are responsible for this and these can be expected to continue to shape the context of the African consumer markets in the coming years. An analysis of the main factors and the opportunities they create follows.

Forces shaping consumer retail

Population growth and demographics

The fastest population growth rate in the world is adding numbers to the already bulging consumer base in SSA; it is now slightly under a billion (862m by 2010 estimates) strong and growing year on year. The demographics of a pyramidal shape – indicating an expanding number of children and young people – should continue to focus attention on where the main opportunities will be coming from across the consumer base.

Overall, a growing population means more demand for products and services. All in all an expanding population and a greater demand for goods and services of all types – including food, clothes, cosmetics, education, media and leisure – makes for a deep consumer proposition that is increasingly difficult to ignore.

Economy formalisation

Large sections of African economies still remain informal, operating outside of the money economy. Some estimates put the size of informal economy at between 42% and 45% across SSA (in nominal GNP terms), with most African countries tending towards having larger informal economies than formal ones.

The stalemate between formal and informal lasted for a considerable period of time, with both policymakers and businesspeople struggling to devise systems for taming and roping in the informal sector. That was until the late professor C.K. Prahalad released his seminal book *The Fortune at the Bottom of the Pyramid*, which exposed the viability of informal economies, and it found its way into boardrooms in African enterprises. The implementation of sustainable business models based on micro-economies articulated in this

" The demographics of a pyramidal shape should continue to focus attention on where the main opportunities will be coming from across the consumer base. "

book, has literally provided a basis for bridges across from the informal sectors of African economies to the formal sectors. The advance of the micro-economy in virtually every real sector of SSA economies is testament to this transformational trend that is opening up opportunities for new growth and market penetration.

GDP per capita/rising incomes

The past decade of business investments in new capacity and the deepening of the service and manufacturing bases in most African countries has had the desired positive effect of job creation, while the transformation from informal to formal status of many sectors and the enterprises therein is also resulting in more permanent, better paying jobs for African youths.

Government services are also being streamlined and the extension of these services to wider sections of society is no doubt generating more public sector jobs, which are now paying real living wages thanks to public sector reforms. Coupled with this, government infrastructural development has reached a new peak across SSA, creating many more construction jobs and a small number of high-paying specialised engineering roles.

In combination, these factors are putting an unprecedented amount of disposable income in the hands of an equally unprecedented number of African workers and contributing to the highest growth in GDP per capita ever recorded in SSA outside of plays on major resources.

Cultural revolution

By a strange twist of the cultural puzzle, Africa, the putative last bastion of cultural preservation, is also extremely receptive and adaptive to new cultural influences on styles, tastes, preferences and appetites, particularly those from the West. A large part of this is to do with the apparent success of Western consumer companies and cultural media in convincing the African youth that Western culture is hip, progressive and exotic, while everything else is drab and ordinary by comparison.

The other part of this *cultural revolution* that carries relevance to consumer markets is the steep rise in the propensity to consume of the average African consumer. A low savings culture among African youthful populations adds to the ever-swelling consumer proposition. The readiness of African youth consumers to try out new fashions, styles and trends means that there is a market here for consumer products companies from all over the world.

> **❝ The readiness of African youth consumers to try out new fashions, styles and trends means that there is a market here for consumer products companies from all over the world. ❞**

Infrastructure

A great challenge in the development and extension of retail networks across SSA has been the inability to establish and sustain tightly integrated supply and distribution chains. The absence or poor state of intercity road connections rendered many parts of countries inaccessible, making synchronous distribution impossible or very expensive. Countrywide supply of perishable commodities in most of Africa also remained implausible for the same reason. This has held back the growth of retail chains and grocery stores, which in turn has constrained the scale of suppliers, worsening the prospects for further investment in the sector.

This gridlock is being systematically broken down in many countries of Africa, through rehabilitation of collapsed road networks that connect the main cities, and by connecting new or expanding urban centres to national road networks. With every additional part of countries that is opened up and connected to the rest by modern road connections, the network effects of retail chains and other distributors are increased.

As an example, the complete overhaul and modernisation of Kenya's road transport network in the five years to 2011 has made it possible for

> **❝ As countries in SSA resolve their infrastructural deficits and interconnect among themselves with high speed, long-haul transport corridors, the resulting scale possibilities will increase opportunities for retail and distribution. ❞**

Nakumatt supermarkets, which hitherto only operated stores in three cities, to roll out a countrywide network with centralised distribution and an integrated system of suppliers across the country. This has seen it move from 17 stores in 2008 to 27 stores in 2010.[240] This pace of growth would never have been possible, finances permitting, without the enabling effects of good infrastructure.

As countries in SSA resolve their infrastructural deficits and interconnect among themselves with high speed, long-haul transport corridors, the resulting scale possibilities will increase opportunities for retail and distribution.

Urban systems

If you travel across cities in SSA you will almost certainly observe one common denominator; they are all being spruced up. City streets are being repaved, buildings have a fresh coat of paint, physical addresses labelling systems are being introduced, traffic lights are up again, sidewalks and parks are being fitted with benches and drinking fountains, and gardens are being replanted and well kept. Basically African cities are being made to function again.

Part of the process of installing and enforcing robust urban systems has contributed to a dramatic reshaping of the urban shopping experience. In redesigning downtown street systems a lot of parking space has disappeared and, further to that, commercial rates have been enforced for parking on the few that are left – street parking is no longer a realistic expectation for developers of commercial real estate. Yet, parking availability is perhaps the best trap for retail consumers – as they are encouraged to shop where they can park.

This has led to the emergence of mall systems on busy highways which either feed or evacuate the highest levels of vehicular volume in and out of cities – taking out the shopping experience to the suburbs or somewhere in between. It is for this reason that without exception, all new shopping malls are advertised in the press with *ample secure parking*. This trend is expected to continue, thus entrenching mall shopping across SSA and refreshing the whole urban shopping experience.

Credit expansion

All over SSA, banks have stopped regarding the African consumer as dangerous and not to be trusted. Consumer finance as a basic lending product has been around for more than a decade now. Credit cards, initially status symbols for the super-wealthy and employees of big corporations, have been transformed to extras given for the favour of "considering doing business with us".

Check-off systems with employers (arrangements where employers agree to deduct amounts owed by their employees from payrolls and pay directly to the parties owed) are being taken to another level – classes of qualifying employers are being expanded and the currently onerous eligibility profiles for borrowers are being relaxed. The credit referencing and credit scores systems expected to fully democratise credit in SSA are set to send credit availability and credit expansion to new heights. Take these evolutions in access to finance combined with the rising propensity of the African consumer to spend and the market proposition of SSA retail and consumer sectors is compelling.

Work ethic

As happens with all societies that become more prosperous, with growing middle classes and a larger formal economy, the cost of living normally rises in tandem with the expansion in money supply. This tends to affect the working population in low paying jobs who have to work longer to keep up with the pace of the rise in cost of living. Also, the democratisation of credit is expected to result in more indebted societies with its working populations having to work longer or take multiple jobs to keep up with their payment schedules and improve or maintain their credit scores. It is also worth considering the World Bank projection that SSA has the potential to become an increasingly important resource for global labour-intensive industries as real wages in China and its neighbouring countries continue to rise 7% a year, meaning they will double over the next decade.[241]

The Economist declared that "a number of economists believe that China has reached a turning-point in its development, having exhausted its supply of surplus labour," adding that "from 1995 to 2004, for example, labour unit costs in China's bigger firms tripled, and that is starting to show in the notorious 'China price'." The piece concluded that this "may leave room for

" It is worth considering the World Bank projection that SSA has the potential to become an increasingly important resource for global labour-intensive industries as real wages in China and its neighbouring countries continue to rise. **"** lower wage countries to enter industries China is graduating out of."[242] Dr Ngozi Okonjo-Iweala, former managing director at the World Bank posits that this mounting labour cost disadvantage for China is likely to default to SSA, bringing into the continent world class industries seeking wage arbitrage. The intensity of labour productivity that these industries demand is very high and should exact a huge toll on workers' time.

The point here is that workers will then spend more time in the offices and factories or in transit between home and work. This exacting work ethic should substantively impact their consumer character, and the consumer companies will then have to adapt to their conveniences. This upheaval should be expected to create new opportunities in retail and consumer markets.

Summary of the opportunities in consumer retail

Retail networks

The case for more investment in retail chains had never been stronger. The main features of expanding retail networks are as follows:

- Rehabilitated and expanding road networks are making efficient distribution possible

- Increasing employment opportunities mean more people have money to spend in retail stores

- The formalisation of the economy means millions of self-employed and informal sector workers have opened bank accounts and now have payment cards in their pockets

- Social modernisation and growing enlightenment is embedding sensibilities of hygiene, choice and convenience in shopping

- Rapid urbanisation is sending many more African youths into urban centres thereby swelling the consumer bases for organised retailing

- Improving personal prosperity is boosting the amount that people spend when they go shopping

- Urban authorities have pulled down illegal kiosks on roadsides and residential estates

As the economies and societies of SSA modernised, formalisation of shopping by shifting traffic to the supermarkets and grocery chains has lagged behind but most of the enablers are now in place and the momentum is just about to gather. That may explain Walmart's sudden interest in Africa – in 2011 it was successful in its bid to buy Massmart, a South African retail chain with presence in 13 African countries.

Retail supply chains

With the imminent explosive growth in retail chains, the ensuing effects of organising markets will trickle down to supply chains, fundamentally altering how they are structured and designed. What is most likely to happen is that a retail chain will retain one or a very small number of suppliers to supply a single item in long-term contracts and pricing. The suppliers may in turn subcontract other local suppliers or farmers at pre-agreed quality levels and prices under evolving advanced supply chain ecosystems. This will create huge opportunities to fully organise markets in terms of universalising quality and standardising product pricing across economies. The extended scale and reach of networks will surely enlarge suppliers' opportunities and boost investments in the retail supply chains.

Single brands retail

Along with the expected change in the retail experience and the formalisation of shopping through more supermarkets across SSA comes a welter of opportunities in *retail single brands*. The concept is simple – the crowds have already been pulled in as a result of the multiplicity of factors acting together as described above. While they are there, they may be tempted to buy other products.

There are two known versions of this kind of retailing. The first one is *in-store* stores, where small dealerships – such as for mobile phones, cosmetics or watches – are established in designated sections of supermarket floors. The other one is the mall concept, where adjacent to the supermarkets are shops selling designer products, butchers' shops, pharmacies, food courts, etc. They all target the crowds already attracted there by the supermarkets.

These opportunities can be expected to multiply as consumers shift towards formal shopping in supermarkets and shopping malls.

Branded clothing

Rising incomes coupled with increased fashion consciousness, especially among the youth and the bulging middle class, form the crucial basis for international names in the clothing business to establish in Africa. Local designs and clothes lines are also growing in popularity and regional distribution networks are taking shape. For example, the Nigerian Agbada robe, a clothing item that has long been ubiquitous in western Africa, is now easily available anywhere in SSA.

Child departments

Africa's population is now growing at a net sustainable rate of 3% per year, with around 50% of this in urban centres. A burgeoning, youthful middle class together with swelling ranks of employed young people with families and young children of their own are providing a fertile business area for producers of goods for children.

Successful public health awareness campaigns and commercially-laden advertisements on hygiene and sanitation are also sensitising African societies to the modern practices of child upbringing. The principal mechanism used by manufacturers is to say that children require new products often as they quickly grow, develop and change. The opportunities in merchandising children's sanitary products, nutrition, clothes, toys and toiletries are set to broaden.

Loyalty reward schemes

Retail chains all over the world encourage customer loyalty by use of reward schemes which award points redeemable for *free* products at their outlets. The essence of these programmes is to achieve customer ownership built on long-term business relationships and based on a reward incentive.

The ultimate is to make these points transferable, a sort of currency for buying a wide range of other products in retail or service outlets, or even to pay for holidays or the purchase of durable household goods. This level of flexibility can inspire impulse purchases and sustain consumption in the face of consumer price increases or economic downturns by altering or manipulating the reward system. Efforts to achieve points thresholds for qualifications to specified rewards, such as for aeroplane flights or colour TVs, could drive up sales against otherwise dull market conditions. Arrangements can be made with other companies which do not have their own programmes to buy points wholesale for their customers, creating new sales possibilities on the back of sales of other retailers.

Retail finance

Retail franchises process hundreds of millions of transactions every year and handle millions of customers, most of them repeat customers. Through their loyalty programmes they have been able to acquire and 'own' these customers as they can almost certainly count on them coming back again. The stores can therefore go to the bank and borrow against these customers' anticipated future purchases.

On the other hand, in collaboration with banks, retail stores process hundreds of millions of debit and credit card charges at their Point of Sale (POS) terminals for purchases made in their stores. Some have started joint ventures with commercial banks where they distribute pre-loaded charge cards ring-fenced only for shopping in their stores.

Very soon, as retailers in the developed world have long realised, SSA retailers will also realise that the entire purchase value chain can indeed be brought in-house, locking in the entire stream of cash flows and revenues generated. The leverage opportunity is in the data mining possibilities – they already own the purchasers' data, the loyalty reward schemes keep the shoppers on a short leash and the access to credit history through the charges on credit cards made at their POS terminals provides the requisite underlying rationale for a risk-mitigated retail finance business.

Big retail networks already enjoy long lines of credit from all their suppliers, anywhere between 45 and 60 days. In most cases they are able to turnover the products within 10-15 days. The remaining 30-50 days enable them to sit on cash belonging to their suppliers and herein lies the opportunity. Using the rich POS data retailers can lend funds that are part of the credit card portfolios of their customers. Not only does this generate new sales by supporting non-cash purchases, it also provides revenue diversification opportunities through the net-interest margins retained by retailers.

Fast food

The fact that future African workforces will be larger, busier and work longer has already been established. Their consciousness of hygiene and better public health is improving as a result of heightened awareness, while their palates and appetites are being sharpened by increased exposure to global culture. Another perspective to this is the growing number of children of the working middle class and youthful first time workers and their appetites for exotic tastes and predisposition to instant gratification.

From the foregoing, it is fair to conclude that the fast food craze will have to grip Africa, especially if or when it comes on the back of established global fast food brands such as McDonald's, Wendy's, Burger King, Le Pain Quotidien and Pret A Manger, among others. Suffice it to say, growth of the middle class anywhere is always closely associated with increased eating out for families and the salaried singles.

Global brands

❝ A sustained rise in GDP per capita across Africa, coupled with an almost fanatical relish for individual distinctiveness among the growing middle class, can underwrite adventures by global brands into Africa. ❞

By 2011 there are global brands without a presence in Africa as yet, however the McKinsey & Co projections that Africa's combined consumer spending will rise to $1.4 billion by 2020 – $740 billion in new spending power – should provide additional incentive for them to enter the continent. As if that is not enough, the same McKinsey report projects that up to 128m households in Africa will have discretionary income by 2020.[243] A sustained rise in GDP per capita across Africa, coupled with an almost fanatical relish for individual distinctiveness among the growing middle class, can underwrite adventures by global brands into Africa.

For example, General Motors of the US, which has had a presence in east Africa for a very long time, never assumed that there could be a market for the Hummer range of cars in SSA. That was until a handful of imports were brought into Kenya and shortly the flow of new imports turned into a mania to rival the tulip mania of Netherlands in the 1630s. This forced General Motors to go back to the drawing board and officially introduce the Hummer among its range of cars marketed and distributed locally. It is unfortunate that the global financial crisis gripped the world shortly thereafter, overturning the economics of the Hummer globally and spoiling the party for GM in Africa. But that brief and pleasant run was enough to prove that there are opportunities in Sub-Saharan markets and that global brands continue to ignore it at their cost.

Online shopping and home deliveries

The absence of technological hang-ups in Africa, as explained earlier, means that the marvels of broadband internet and democratisation of cyberspace in SSA are also set to revolutionise retail shopping among African households. Better quality streets, improving intercity road connections, maturing of regional common markets, and the incremental efficiencies of logistical companies have all paved the way for the arrival of online retailers in SSA. Once high-speed internet has penetrated Africa to a critical mass and reliable, acceptable online payment systems become widespread, retail should start moving online. In eastern Africa a local online payment system 3G Direct Pay launched in 2006 has clients in Zambia, Tanzania, Kenya and DR Congo.[244]

The limitations of physical stores – with finite space and constraints of physical separation – are well known in Western economies now and these realisations will come soon to SSA. The borderless virtual stores based on global sourcing

> **The absence of technological hang-ups in Africa, means that the marvels of broadband internet and democratisation of cyberspace in SSA are also set to revolutionise retail shopping among African households.**

will overhaul the economics of retail and move competitiveness to internet portals, with their intrinsic depth, dynamism and interactivity. E-commerce is the next *land grab* in the African consumer experience space.

OPPORTUNITIES IN FINANCIAL SERVICES

Banking and financial sector growth has been at the core of recent expansion in national economies in Africa. This expansion is a key driver of economic growth because it mobilises domestic savings, enhances credit expansion and availability, and broadens payment systems and service distribution. In almost every African nation the financial sector is outgrowing GDP – for example in Kenya between 2000 and 2008 GDP grew by an average of 4% annually, while its financial sector grew by 9%.[245]

Going forward, an acceleration of the prevailing growth momentum may be anticipated as banks, local and international, move to seize emerging opportunities in the SSA business landscape. The overlying themes that may be seen generating growth and influencing capital allocation in the banking and financial sectors of SSA in the coming decade and beyond are dealt with in this chapter.

Overlying themes in financial services

Scale

A major challenge that exercises bankers' minds all over the world is how and where to find the next source of growth. Just being successful is not good enough and the same is true of banks in SSA as elsewhere – the need for scale is imperative. Regional integration, larger and deeper common markets and increasing international trade are calling for banks of a size which, with the exception of a few, are currently not available in African markets. The costs of laying out country and region-wide operations, staving off competition from non-traditional sources and meeting the demands of customers are forcing banks to look for opportunities to scale up operations outside of the traditional route of organic growth.

Credit referencing

Credit referencing is a new concept of collateralising credit history through documented records of reputation in debt payback, honouring of hire purchase obligations, utility bill payment history and diligence in credit card debt settlements, among other criteria. This gives a customer a basis rating for unsecured borrowing in the future.

> **"** A credit democracy will be created, founded on accumulated credit quality, methodically breaking down the major barrier to credit access and leading to a quick expansion of consumer credit. **"**

Credit reference bureaus are being established with a primary mandate to raise and manage national databases of the credit history of every individual, company, institution or group association having accessed credit from any credit institution or reported records of all of their other financial obligations. Credit scores are awarded in a universal graduated system of credit quality much like the rating agencies' grades for firms and governments. It will be possible for a bank contemplating a loan application from anyone, even a non-customer, to call up the entire credit history of that individual at the touch of a button, for a fee. The momentum for getting this going should be vastly aided by the banks that are willing to share credit history and other relevant data in their possession.

This system will help substantially reduce the risk of lending, cut banks' credit risk premiums and quicken credit approval pipelines. It will create a kind of credit democracy, founded on accumulated credit quality, methodically breaking down the major barrier to credit access and leading to a quick expansion of consumer credit in the economies of SSA.

Search for long-term deposits

Banks the world over pay low rates of interest for retail deposits; deposit interest rates can range between 0% to 3% annually, which is not an enticing proposition for anybody with large cash assets. So banks are only able to attract very short-term deposits on a rolling basis – long-term funds generally tend to go elsewhere, where yields or returns are commensurate with the risk and size of investment. On the other hand, the very same deposits are used to generate long-term loans, generally three- to seven-year loans, chargeable to the loanee at exorbitant rates of interest under the argument that long-term deposits are difficult to come by. Up to this point, this describes global banking. The similarities between banks in Africa and those in the developed world end here.

African banks until now have insisted on originating loans to hold to maturity. This continues to limit the amount of loans they can generate according to the levels of long-term deposits they can lay their hands on at any given time, operating therefore within the limitations of their own balance sheets. In the rest of the world, the long-term deposits conundrum was cracked when banks started to generate loans and hold for trading purposes. The amounts of the loans they can generate are limited therefore to the depth and appetite of the markets, rather than their own finite internal sources of deposits – consequently they leverage and turn them over their balance sheets countless times. Basically the fundamental difference is that banks in the developed world discovered that long-term deposits had long moved elsewhere and, rather than just accept the situation, they devised ways of tackling it and bringing it back all over again.

> " It is therefore imperative that banks start to look for profitable ways of leveraging their balance sheets in a bid to lend more and work again with the long-term funds wherever they may be found in the economies. "

The cost of doing nothing and continuing to suffer serious limitations on funding is too much for African banks to bear long term. It is therefore imperative that they start to look for profitable ways of leveraging their balance sheets in a bid to lend more and work again with the long-term funds wherever they may be found in the economies. Their recent experiences of better yields realised in their treasury functions by trading bonds rather than holding them to maturity should soon start being brought to bear on their long-term lending functions. This new trend would unleash new opportunities.

Race to the bottom of the pyramid

> " One of the last remaining virtually unexplored territories is the unbanked section of society. "

The eternal search by African banks for the next marginal revenue, as long as the marginal cost incurred is lower, is taking African banks far and wide. One of the last remaining virtually unexplored territories is that dubbed the unbanked section of society. Less than a decade ago, this part of society was cynically sneered at as *unbankable* in mainstream banking circles. The unbanked are now the next big thing in African banking.

Banks have already begun to reach out to these unbanked sections of society by starting new branches in areas where there were none, or through agency banking. Electronic banking through mobile phone platforms is proving the fastest and most cost-efficient means of taking banking to unbanked masses across the continent.

Infrastructure plays

Infrastructural development programmes have just been restarted in many African countries in the 2000s. The themes may vary slightly, ranging from reconstruction after years of civil war; rehabilitation after decades of underdevelopment and neglect by oppressive minority regimes; or modernisation and capacity enhancements following years of sustained economic growth and fiscal expansion. Whatever the case, these programmes are long term in nature and the capital consumption involved is massive.

So far, in most cases, these programmes have been financed through bilateral (government to government) or multilateral (government to global lender) arrangements, or various permutations of these. The arrangements are all rooted in the ability of taxpayers to shoulder the ultimate burdens through government tax revenue streams. It follows that the capacity required to deliver these infrastructural solutions more quickly is circumscribed.

Infrastructure bonds, where national treasuries tap local and international capital markets for long-term infrastructure funding capital, have become a viable and robust option for delivering some of these projects. A few distributions have already been successfully closed in some SSA countries, including Kenya,[246] Ghana, Botswana and Nigeria.[247]

The Public Private Partnership (PPP) model of infrastructure delivery is also being tested in African countries and it is emerging as the clear favourite funding framework option, having been tried and proved elsewhere. PPPs are becoming more acceptable, easily deliverable and more practical as the best method for delivering multiple, big ticket infrastructural solutions in the shortest time possible.

A good number of the next phase of infrastructural development roll out is going to be organised as PPPs, such as the Lamu seaport in Kenya, Bugesera Airport project in Rwanda, Karuma Hydro-power project in Uganda, Mtwara seaport in Tanzania and the Grand Inga Hydropower project in DR

Congo.[248] These mega projects could have phenomenal transformational impact on banking and banks in the continent.

Home search

Demand for decent family housing in SSA is currently insatiable. A constant injection of new demand is coming from the forces driving an accelerating rate of urbanisation and is inspired by the ongoing modernisation and renewal of African urban centres. Rising wages and increases in the workforces are also boosting affordability among the swelling numbers of possible home seekers.

On the other hand, property values have maintained a long-term upward trend for a considerable time and this trend has not given any sign of abating, powered as it is by a backlog of cumulatively unmet demand and a sustained flow of new demand too. The two pressure points of rising demand and rising property values seem to reinforce each other, creating a sustainable basis for growth opportunities in mortgages.

Technology-inspired convergence

Banking in the 21st century is IT-platform centric. The vision is to be able to electronically deliver all services conceivable to an infinite size of customer-base at constantly lower costs. So, banks have heavily invested in core banking platforms. The first episode of this technological evolution has largely already happened – where banks have digitised their traditional services and now deliver them electronically through their own networks. The second episode is also largely figured out – where banks, after satisfactorily putting their core services on to their networks and delivering them electronically, are now looking to see what else they can deliver on their existing pipelines without much adjustment – they are looking for further technological leverage. This is what is inspiring the convergence between stock-brokerage and banks, or insurance and banks.

The third and final episode is where other technology-supported network operators look at traditional banking and innovate ways where they could, using their own pipelines, deliver banking services at lower costs than bank platforms would ever be able to achieve, to a wider consumer network that bank platforms would also never be able to address without massive investments in scale. The beginnings of this process can already be observed in the inchoate convergence between telecoms operators and banks, but it is only just the start. It is probably at this third stage that the real evolutionary metamorphosis will break through, and where the convulsions and opportunities will be identified.

All this is playing out in the African banking scene, chiefly because of the benefits of technological leapfrogging to which only Africa as a continent can lay claim.

Database mining

By the nature of the trust and fiduciary responsibilities that banks have to their clients and the wider public, they happen to have some of the richest databases of private individuals' information, including postal and email addresses, and telephone contacts. They also have data about peoples' financial histories through their banking activities, which can provide insight into people's characters, preferences, tastes, attitudes to money and life biases, including religious and political persuasions.

In the meantime, telephone call costs are falling through the floor as more and more calls are transferred to the internet, and call integrity improves as users demand greater dependability of the internet for e-commerce.

Putting the two points above together, the opportunities for profitable database mining and information weaving for banks becomes apparent. The opportunities are further developed in the next section.

Summary of the opportunities in financial services

Consolidation of banking services

There are far too many commercial banks in African countries for them to be sustained long term and profitably by the sizes of the national economies. The efficiency and scale needed for rapid economic development, by vastly lowering the costs of financial services to the economies, will only be achieved by having fewer, larger, banks. This has already been achieved in Nigeria, where by one stroke of regulatory fiat the number of banks was consolidated from 89 to 25, between 2004 and 2006. The resulting banks had the scale and capital base to both drive down their costs and penetrate large sections of the *unbanked* population. Total banking assets grew at an unprecedented rate for Nigeria, of around 60% annually between 2004 and 2008.[249] Other countries have not had the boldness to take these steps yet but market forces will achieve it either through natural evolution or external intervention.

Already in most countries, financial services sectors are highly concentrated, with about 70% to 90% of the sector profitability, total assets, deposits, loans and capital employed in the hands of 10% to 15% of the operating banks. Further concentration of market power among a very select group of local banks is to be expected, as the critical mass for consolidation builds up in the industry.

The other force behind faster consolidation is going to be giant international commercial banks. Some examples of firms that have already taken strategic positions in the few local banks with pan-African operations and a continental focus are as follows:

❝ Efficiency and scale needed for rapid economic development, by vastly lowering the costs of financial services to the economies, will only be achieved by having fewer, larger, banks. ❞

- ICBC, China's leading bank, bought 20% of Standard Bank of South Africa in 2007

- Bank of China, the country's most international outfit, entered into a pact with Ecobank which operates in 31 African countries, whereby Chinese staff will drum up business from local branches

- Brazil's Bradesco and Banco do Brazil created a new African holding company with Banco Espirito Santo (BES), a Portuguese bank active in Angola[250]

- HSBC of Shanghai and London in 2010 attempted to buy Nedbank of South Africa from Old Mutual, a pan-African insurance and investment group (this deal fell through in October 2010)

- Barclays of the UK bought 56% of ABSA, one of South Africa's biggest banks in 2005.

According to an article in the McKinsey Quarterly, from 2004 to 2009 some 430 M&A (merger and acquisition) deals involved financial institutions in Africa, and about 40% were cross-border with the acquirer originating elsewhere in Africa or from outside the continent.[251]

One of the main themes undergirding this push into the African banking scene by international players is their taking "a big bet on a booming economy – for instance Portugal's banks re-entered Angola after the civil war and are enjoying its oil bonanza. BES, Banco BPI and Banco Millennium BCP together have 170-odd branches, and made a staggering $440m of profit in 2009".[252] These international banks intend to use their African subsidiaries as vehicles for regional expansion to cover the whole of SSA. They are rugged consolidators and have the balance sheets to buy growth rather than wait for it. The parameters of competition will be taken notches higher and the majority of marginal players will be forced to sell and exit or fall by the wayside.

Consumer finance

Once credit referencing has fully caught on within well regulated regimes and with full co-operation and participation from all credit houses, utilities, retail and other entities with subscriber bases, sufficient data will have been accumulated over a wide enough base to enable short-term retail consumer finance to become as simple as making a phone call. Thus a rapid growth in credit card uptake and usage, and an upsurge in unsecured lending especially to the self-employed, can be expected.

Auto finance is another area with a huge upside, where banks will be more willing to lend. Generally banks will extend this concept and lend for any easily retractable and reclaimable goods as long as domestic and other kinds of insurance can cover them at the cost of the borrower, so for example computers, TVs, furniture, fridges, cookers and mobile phones. Basically consumer finance is set to become an area for long-term growth opportunities for the banks with the scale and skills to be involved. Substantively, it will provide a long-term answer to bank treasuries' recurring headache of finding profitable lending opportunities for the large stock of short-term deposits in their books against a backdrop of painfully low treasury bills and bond rates.

Securitisation

As described above in the themes section for drivers of value and opportunities in SSA banking, there is an ever-expanding business opportunity for banks to offer mortgage finance and other forms of long-term project finance lending to a growing, youthful middle class. The challenge, and where the real opportunity lies, is where to find enough long-term funds to go around.

In African markets the only accessible, organised, investible and large enough reservoir of long-term funds is the pension system and life businesses of insurance companies. Like banks, they too look at only traditional sources of investments – stocks, bonds and property. These investments are not always as high-yielding or liquid as they expect them to be; they can be either cyclical or unrealisable. Yet, pension funds and insurance companies receive new money every 30 days and they are under a lot of pressure to demonstrate how profitably they have deployed previous funds. According to their actuarial reports, they have fairly long periods of time to keep and invest the funds. However, they will have to return them one day with quite a few years of compounded returns. That word *compounded* can make fund managers' spines shiver.

> **The pension/insurance and banking sectors need each other, and urgently. One is holding a solution the other one is looking for, and the other is holding a problem the first one has a solution to – and vice versa.**

Banks, on the other hand, receive and evaluate numerous applications for mortgages, project finance, enterprise capital investments and other forms of long-term developments. They have invested in robust credit evaluation, assessment and risk identification systems and skills, and they have distinguished themselves as efficient allocators of capital. They have got in most cases long-approved and rolling pipelines they just cannot satisfy because they have insufficient funds.

It appears that the pension/insurance and banking sectors need each other, and urgently. One is holding a solution the other one is looking for, and the other is holding a problem the first one has a solution to – and vice versa. Securitisation – the process of packaging different financial assets to create a new instrument that is broken into tranches and sold to investors – does not have to be regarded as a dirty process as it has come to be seen in the West. It was originally a killer application created singularly to unlock financial gridlock such as banks and insurance firms in SSA are faced with. Well-regulated securitisation is inescapable if African banks are to get to the next level of lending. If employed, the opportunities it will open up are huge.

Full-scale securitisation will depend on the outcomes of the quest for a long-term funding solution for banks across SSA. Eventual successful securitisation of long-term debt will then pave the way and provide the template for securitisation of other categories of portfolios of consumer finance, such as credit card debt, auto loans, SME loans, etc.

Micro-banking

The viability of banking the *unbanked* having been proven beyond all reasonable doubt, all manner of mind-boggling figures are now being thrown about, some realistic, some stretching the imagination a little too far. But, they all underlie one particular truth about banking in SSA – that it has hardly begun.

> **"** Innovative methods of channel expansion, for example agency banking or indirect channel partnership, are the way forward for banks in trying to reach new markets. **"**

The realisation of the *fortune at the bottom of the pyramid* completely re-writes the thesis for banking in Africa. In 2010, only 12% of households in SSA were banked, or more specifically there were only 163 deposit accounts per 1,000 adults. Other developing countries have an average of 737 bank accounts per 1,000 adults, while high income countries have got 2,022 accounts per 1,000 adults (each adult having an average of two accounts).[253]

According to data from the Population Reference Bureau, the population of SSA is 57% adult, numbering 492m adults. If only 12% of these were banked (assuming proportionate age representation in households) then a huge number of adults – 433m – are without bank accounts. Just to put things a little into perspective, the 2010 listed Agricultural Bank of China, one of the many banks in China and not even the biggest, has over 24,000 branches serving 320m customers.[254] Sub-Saharan Africa's combined population is around two-thirds that of China's.

Obviously, to be able to penetrate and serve this section of society successfully and profitably, banks will have to completely overhaul their current retail franchises or erect parallel networks specially tailored for micro-banking. The cost of delivering banking services per customer has to be brought down substantially to a fraction of current costs for banking to be practicable in view of the lower revenues realistically expected per customer. IT platforms have to be stretched to the limit to realise more cost-effective methods of expedited penetration and sustainably profitable banking. Simply building new branches will not be sufficient on its own without tweaking the method of delivery.

Innovative methods of channel expansion, for example agency banking or indirect channel partnership, etc., are the way forward for banks in trying to reach these new markets. In Asia, Grameen Bank of Bangladesh and Bank of Madura (later bought by ICICI Bank of India) employ the model of indirect-channel partnership using Self Help Groups (SHGs) to reach millions of new individuals with fewer resources and staff employed.[255] People are organised into groups pulled together by an emotional common interest or bond, such as membership of a co-operative society, where they are taught the rudiments of banking, how to manage their own affairs of savings mobilisation, and how to underwrite each other for credit from banks, up to the point of aggressively collecting from defaulters from their membership contributions or co-operative shares.

The interface with the bank is only with one appointed official. This way banks are able to serve hundreds of thousands of customers, distribute their products to them collectively and leave the management of individual relationships and the attendant cost within the groups but, of course, with regular guidance and oversight from banks' own staff who are appointed as banking champions. This is the only imaginable way that ICICI Bank is able to reach more than 24m customers (2007), using 2,016 branches (2010) and a staff complement of 25,000 (2006).[256] As these figures are from different years, the 2007 figure of 24m customers is now even larger across the 2,016 branches recorded for 2010.

There is growing evidence of this phenomenon in SSA, with its own homegrown innovations. A report in *The Economist* said:

> *"In remote areas (of southern Africa) where delivering cash is hard, mini-machines have been installed in corner shops where customers print out a slip confirming they are in the black and present it to the shopkeeper, who provides the cash."*

> *"ABSA (a leading South African bank) meanwhile, is developing modern credit-scoring techniques for customers who have never been granted loans before. By keeping costs down and building up scale, it reckons micro lending is at least as profitable as other services."*

> *"In Ghana, Barclays works with susu collectors, who gather money from small scale market traders and keep it safe for them for a fee. The collector's clients are typically too small for high-street banks, but Barclays reckons that they collectively represent a market worth $154m. The bank offers savings accounts, loans and training to the susu collectors, and says they have helped it reach 200,000 market traders. In two years, there have been no defaults."*[257]

Despite the progress that has been made so far, the growth opportunities in this market space for African banks are so vast that they remain pretty much unscratched.

SME banking

Small businesses are the engine of private sector-led growth in any economy. They tend to be registered in large numbers and although early mortality rate is very high among them a few survive to become motors of economic activity and generators of the highest numbers of new jobs. In high-income economies they constitute on average 67% of formal employment in the manufacturing sector and 45% in low income economies.[258] The small businesses that do survive are usually successful implementations of new ideas about how to do things faster, easier, cheaper, or in a different way that makes better use of locally available resources. They may also be providing a badly needed service in accord with the changing dynamics of life. For investors, they normally provide the fastest and surest vehicles for wealth creation. By nature, they tend to be short of capital and long on bankable ideas.

However, their participation in African economies currently is very low at less than 4% of GDP, whereas for high-income economies it is 49% on average and 29% for other low-income economies.[259] As African economies continue to grow and their populations become more prosperous, demand for manufactured goods and a widening range of services will increase. As communities grow and develop, the need for systems to organise and make life orderly increases and as the culture of consumerism takes root in Africa, an explosion of diverse business opportunities will see small businesses rise on the tide. Opportunities to lend to these businesses and facilitate their banking transactions should equally lift banks' fortunes with the same tide.

Investment banking

Big ticket investment banking opportunities are already opening up with some of the ambitious infrastructure projects underway across the expanse of Africa. Most of these are in energy. To take a few illustrative examples:

- The world's largest hydropower project, the 39,000 MW Grand Inga III in DR Congo has a price tag of $80 billion, with the private sector financing component led by BNP Paribas and Fortis

- The 4,300 MW Inga III at a cost of $3.6 billion

- The ICBC, a leading Chinese bank, arrangement of financing for the $1.7 billion for the Gibe III 1,870 MW Hydropower Plant on River Omo, Ethiopia

- The $1.2 billion 700 MW Karuma hydropower project in Uganda tendered as a PPP with Standard Bank Group and Lonsdale leading the consortium

Power plants, toll roads, airports, sea ports, railway lines, fibre optic cables and oil pipelines are all candidates for private sector participation under the PPP framework of development and operation. Foreign banks are already spotting the opportunity in Africa and are beginning to show their interest. Others have chosen to focus on a wholesale or network banking approach to try to benefit from the wave of infrastructure and natural resources investments in Africa.

> *"Chinese firms that are building airports, roads and power plants are sought after clients. Standard Bank has a team of 40 bankers in an office opposite ICBC's headquarters in Beijing who are trying to woo the Chinese bank's clients. Citigroup seems set to reinforce its position in trade finance and investment banking."*[260]

It would be dreadful for African banks to sit out this infrastructural bonanza. Comfortingly, it promises to be a long-term process, which should enable African banks to develop the necessary scale, skills and experiences to be acquired and deployed.

Insurance

As banks in SSA find sustainable and market-deepening strategies for year-round medium and long-term lending, a business opportunity that will be open to them as a consequence of this is insurance. In a market environment without job security, low life-expectancy and scarce alternative savings the only way to convince secondary market off-takers of securitised bundles of loans receivables is if they are backed by a guarantee of full-term receivables, even in the event of an adverse outcome, such as death or full and permanent incapacitation of the borrower. Credit default swaps, or plainly borrowing-specific life insurance, can be used to provide this guarantee.

As mortgage finance, auto finance and any other form of securitisable debt obligations gather momentum in SSA economies, the volumes of insurance premiums generated as a by-product of lending will be huge and equally all-year-round. These revenue streams could grow large enough in size and dependability to suggest to any bank to keep them in-house. Captive insurance on all manner of securitisations should hasten the convergence between banking and insurance in SSA.

Database mining

Most banks already have in-house incoming call centres for customer care, and enquiry management and disposal. These are purely cost centres but they help banks service their clients better and therefore retain them. They will soon realise that these can actually become profit centres, by including outgoing calls sections to mine their client databases. This will come from the realisation that some of their existing customers may already, or are just about to become, customers elsewhere for products they can offer them with the ongoing diversification of product portfolios across the sector.

Bancassurance (product co-development arrangements and distribution contracts with insurance companies), for example, will enable banks to use their call centres to pitch life or other insurance products designed for mass distribution to their client bases. The same will be possible for mutual funds and unit trusts, with banks able to net handsome sales commissions.

Agency banking

The stark inadequacy of bricks and mortar banking is becoming clearer by the day. With advances towards 24-hour economies and demand for banking services becoming more widespread, channel expansion and diversification outside of physical branches has become the most viable route to extending banking services. So far this has been achieved through technological enhancements such as mobile and internet banking, but agency banking has also become feasible through accessing and utilising networks of savings and co-operative societies, retail and distribution chains, fuelling and gas stations, postal services, telecoms platforms and their supply-chains, and other feasible electronic-enabled networks. The banks which latch on to this opportunity will increase revenue opportunities and advance their market share. For retail and consumer-related banks, channel expansion will result in increases in fees and commission income.

Telecom-banking

The final consideration for the banking sector is the telecom-banking monolith. The telecoms business model as we know it is facing definite existential dangers and hurtling towards either a terminal situation or one where it will be reincarnated as something else altogether. Voice calls, the backbone of telecoms, are already largely free. The great majority of them are already routed free through the internet and for the remainder being carried on their networks, intense rivalry and competition is busily chipping away at call revenues to below full cost recovery.

Data, TV, SMS, and M-Commerce are good, but they can never replace the volumes and usage of voice calls, and even then competition is also quickly

❝ With advances towards 24-hour economies and demand for banking services becoming more widespread, channel expansion and diversification outside of physical branches has become the most viable route to extending banking services. ❞

rendering them uneconomic. In the meantime, telecoms firms are still erecting networks and will soon have extensive telecom networks with huge capacity that can deliver any digital content at fractional costs.

On the other hand, banks continue to face the challenges of scale imperative in a competitive environment where physical banking is the least available option, where daily transactions processed are multiplying astronomically, where turn-around-time is expected to be high speed, and where service delivery costs should exhibit profiles in cost innovation.

It seems that banks and telecoms companies both have problems that might throw them together and the resulting entity could be very impressive. To give a preview of the imminent possibilities we can take an example from India:

> "A Little World, an Indian firm, has combined several pieces of technology to create a 'branchless micro-banking system' to allow people in remote areas to withdraw cash. A fingerprint reader identifies them and the sum is deducted from their accounts via a special handset. A small printer produces a receipt. The system already has more than 3m users in India. In Andhra Pradesh it directly disburses welfare payments and pensions".[261]

Within Africa itself, Airtel Kenya, a telecom company, Standard Chartered Bank and MasterCard jointly unveiled an electronic credit card and online payment system in September 2011 that is " touted to be the world's first virtual card that operates off a wallet and residing on a mobile phone".[262]

OPPORTUNITIES IN TELECOMS

17

Telecommunication was without a doubt the fastest growing sector in Africa in the 2000s. When we talk about telecoms in Africa, it is principally mobile phones because fixed lines are insignificant in number. Telecommunication revenues have increased at a compound annual growth rate (CAGR) of 40% over ten years and the number of subscribers grew rapidly to stand at 453m at the end of 2008.[263] To meet the increased demand, investment in telecom infrastructure also grew massively to an average of around $15 billion per year between 2003 and 2008.

Overlying themes in telecommunications

In the coming decade and beyond, the overlying themes that may be expected to influence strategies and investment decisions in the SSA telecom sector are the following.

Rural penetration

Mobile coverage in Africa has grown at a very fast rate over the past decade – between 2000 and 2006 alone it increased more than ten times.[264] In terms of geographical signal availability, in 2006 there were 57% of Africans living under the footprint of the mobile networks, covered by at least one or all of their national operating mobile phone service providers.

“ Telecommunication was the fastest growing sector in Africa in the 2000s. Telecommunication revenues have increased at a compound annual growth rate (CAGR) of 40% over ten years and the number of subscribers grew rapidly to stand at 453m at the end of 2008. ”

However, most rural areas are not covered; with only 42% coverage as opposed to 91% for urban areas (figures again from 2006). Setting up calls from the remotest parts of Africa also still remains a dream – very few of those in rural areas have got handsets and to many of them wireless telephony remains a prospect for the future rather than a present reality. Roughly 58% of the adult population in SSA still remain outside of mobile phone networks and a majority of these are rural populations.

There appears to be a stalemate of sorts – telecom companies seem to think that the addressable market is largely exhausted, believing that the marginal subscribers who can use their services at rates and usage levels that make sense to them from a business point of view are now all catered for. As one report puts it:

> "All in all, the most essential problem of rural settings disfavouring the existing solutions for ICT rollout is the low income of the rural populations. Together with the relatively low population density and long distance between rural settlements, the ARPU (Average Revenue Per User) is normally too low for ICT operators to survive financially with respect to the commonly high CAPEX (Capital Expenditure) and considerably increased OPEX (Operational Expenditure)."[265]

The essence of the situation is that most rural inhabitants do not have the consumer power to sustain traditional breakeven ARPUs and so most telecom companies have declared them *unconnectable*.

However, the aggregate numbers are large and the collective impact of their participation is too big to ignore. Besides, the profound market potential when fortunes change or technological breakthroughs enable lower cost penetration is enormous. Further, internecine competition is leaving everybody badly wounded, with calling charges in free fall. This is what is going to make telecoms take another look at rural populations and search for cost-effective ways of reaching out to this new customer base and new source of revenue.

Revenue diversification

Voice calls typically make up anywhere in the range of 60% to 80% of the revenue mix of telecom companies, for some even higher. Pioneering providers had it easy when they were met by a flood of subscriber uptake owing to many years of underinvestment by the state-owned telecom incumbents. Along with the thrill and feel-good effect of making wireless telephone contact, a very alien proposition in Africa at the time, they could get away with charging anything; there were days when a one-minute call would cost $0.75 to $1.

Fortunes have since changed – the margins on voice calls are vastly shrinking in response to competitive pressures, regulatory fiat and economies of scale of delivery. In Kenya, for example, voice call charges came down by 50% to 75% in the market share contest between the two leading operators Safaricom and Zain Kenya.[266] Call costs now average between $0.025 and

$0.0375 per minute and there are indications that these rates could still come down further.

This realisation is well appreciated within telecoms circles and efforts to supplant plummeting voice call revenues have been put in place – but the fall is turning out to be far too abrupt and the replacement rate, dollar for dollar, too slow. The search to find revenue diversification initiatives that not only replace disappearing voice revenues but also grow the top lines of telecom companies in the future will continue.

Infrastructure ownership/sharing

Telecom companies own and operate extensive networks based on expensive physical infrastructure, including radio towers each fitted with a power supply or generator, various types of telecommunication installations mounted on these towers, micro-cells inside buildings to strengthen signal quality, fully fitted IT infrastructure, and so on. These are the technological backbone of telecom companies. They are extremely expensive to erect, extend and upgrade, and cost much more to maintain.

The physical hardware, especially radio towers, is the most expensive: it costs a lot to survey appropriate locations, install, and continually service and secure them. It can be duplicated effort when each provider has to erect and look after its own towers. It means service costs will never come down appreciably because if each provider has to recoup the capital expenditure of putting up, extending and modernising physical infrastructure from user revenues, the infrastructure premium will naturally remain very high.

Evolutions in the telecom infrastructure space are pointing to two major likely scenarios. The first one is where an operator incorporates a wholly or jointly owned infrastructure asset company, collapses all the infrastructure assets into it and then leases them back at ruling market capacity rates. It will also make excess capacity available to competitors or other services which require electronic carrier capacity. The second one is where designated independent telecom infrastructure companies take over all infrastructure assets in the sector and lease capacity on a need and ability to pay basis to any telecom operator without prejudice. It will be interesting to observe how these themes pan out in SSA and the resulting opportunities therein for telecom operators.

Capacity optimisation

A big challenge that constantly occupies the minds of many network operators in Africa is how to attain capacity utilisation full-time, or most of the time. They have invested in expensive networks, and incurred enormous daily costs to keep them operating around the clock. Yet, for most of the time, except during peak hours and the weekends, these networks lie idle with very light traffic passing through. Telecom companies in Africa have tried to address this by employing cost-lowering innovations such as variable call tariffs (*dynamic tariffing*) pioneered by MTN, which involved adjusting the cost of calls every hour, in each network cell, depending on the level of usage.[267] This used to help smooth out these variations in utilisation but only when the luxury of pricing power on voice calls was still intact. The short message service (SMS), which uses up minimal capacity by the nature and length of time of its delivery mode, continues to present enormous untapped capacity.

Technology neutrality in terms of transfers of voice, data and other forms of services from network to network would tremendously help boost usage. It will be interesting to follow how operators choose to align themselves to benefit from shifts in traffic flows.

Radio spectrum

Telecom companies use radio frequencies to transmit calls across the airwaves into handheld receivers or mobile phones. They also use lower-band frequencies to transmit wireless broadband internet using wireless data traffic technology (i.e. Wimax or LTE). The lower bands have stronger signal quality and do not suffer interference or cross-airs with other frequencies or types of microwave communication. Availability of the right bandwidth is crucial to the imminent growth of wireless internet across Africa.

The truth is that radio spectrum is a limited national resource – each country only has a finite range of frequencies which, when used up, create an obstacle to the growth of its telecommunication sector. In the majority of African countries radio frequencies are becoming an extremely scarce commodity, either because they were previously lavishly allocated to entities which do not require all of them, such as the military or individuals who hoard them to later rent them out for high rates. Telecom companies have ended up in a rat race hunting down any licence with a radio frequency attached to it that might be available. "Policy makers can help drive the data market in several ways, including making lower-spectrum bands available", suggested a McKinsey & Company report.[268]

Authorities have been sufficiently petitioned and the sooner lower spectrum bands are made available, so with them the practicality of wireless internet across Africa will improve considerably. The ongoing modernisation of TV delivery conventions in SSA countries from analogue to digital will release a large number of frequencies which telecom companies could then apply to deliver mobile internet which requires a very large range of frequencies.

Strategic partnerships

The costs of building telecoms networks is forbiddingly high. The average annual capital expenditure required just to sustain network quality and reliability can be punitive, let alone annual spends on network extension and upgrades which have to be conducted every so often because of technology obsolescence and demand for support of ever widening handset functionalities. Providers then have to recoup these costs as fast as possible, particularly because of lack of full visibility of the competitive environment beyond the medium term.

When on-net traffic is not at a high level, especially after efforts by operators to encourage it, then two parallel scenarios become clear. For networks running on leased capacity (MVNOs) from independent infrastructure owners or from infrastructure owning network operators, it is easy to fold up and move on, since all operating costs are variable costs to them. By contrast, infrastructure owning operators are forced to seek traffic off-net and this drives them into the arms of other players, such as banks and media companies, in strategic partnerships and operational alliances, such as have been discussed earlier in the book. The extent and scope of partnering is so fluid from both sides that a range of final outcomes seem possible.

Summary of the opportunities in telecoms

Bottom of the pyramid telephony

There is a proven very high acceptance rate for technology that is designed to make life easier among the poor in societies in Asia, as well as Africa. Taking India as an example, though mobile phone penetration in rural parts

❝ There is a proven very high acceptance rate for technology that is designed to make life easier among the poor in societies in Asia, as well as Africa. **❞**

of the country is still a long way from saturation levels, reaching only 32% of the rural populations, geographical coverage of rural India rivals that of developed countries at 91%. This is quite a coup for a country with 70% of its total population living in the rural areas.[269] This has been achieved against the backdrop of 76% of the population living below $2 a day (the internationally recognised measure of poverty) – a level that is higher than Africa's (74%).[270] It has been achieved through the erection of cheap but dependable networks in a process known as frugal innovation or the *Indian model*.

"Despite an ARPU of $6.5 and call charges of $0.02 per minute, Indian operators have operating margins of around 40%, comparable with leading Western operators," said a survey in *The Economist*.[271] The piece went on to point out the thrust of this innovation:

> "Outsourcing is at the heart of the Indian model, which was pioneered and now is embodied by Bharti Airtel, India's biggest mobile operator. All of Bharti's information technology (IT) operations are outsourced to IBM, the running of its mobile network is handled by Ericsson and Nokia Siemens Networks (NSN), and customer care is outsourced to IBM and a group of Indian firms. This passes much of the risk of coping with a rapidly growing subscriber base to other parties and leaves Bharti to concentrate on marketing and strategy."

Chinese network equipment makers such as Huawei and ZTE are also distinguishing themselves in the space of production and innovation. They have manufactured bespoke telecom network hardware and software with the same levels of reliability and scalability as the original equipment makers of Europe and North America, and which is capable of upgrades, but at discounts of as much as 50%. Now vendors are getting into outsourcing of construction under schemes known as *managed capacity* networks which "leave the vendor to handle the business of designing networks, putting up base stations and so on, giving it an incentive to build the network as frugally as possible".

With competition pushing down calling costs to untenable levels, coupled with the commercial realities of extending services to unserved sections of the economies, African telecoms will have to overhaul their networks and operate them from much cheaper platforms to remain relevant and profitable. To get this working, the other part of the equation involves putting handsets in the hands of the rural folk at fire sale prices to ensure uptake. And these handsets need to have alternative charging systems – for example solar phones – to ensure that battery power is available in rural Africa where there is not a reliable electricity supply. With developments like this it is estimated that ARPU will drop from $12 to $6 in SSA by 2013.[272] Sustenance strategies therefore have to be focused on expanding user numbers to make up for the shortfall in ARPUs as telecoms move to more and more marginal users.

Wireless broadband internet

Wireless internet is already emerging as the most feasible and effective way of extending internet to Africa because it is not realistic to lay cables leading to every house in the continent. Just like it is with traditional fixed-line platforms, it will be very expensive and uptake will be hampered by the high costs chargeable to recoup investments. Management and maintenance will also be a massive problem given the very high number of incidences of pilferage and vandalism being witnessed with the cable infrastructure. Redundancy (alternative routing for internet traffic) will be equally expensive (and duplicative) to provide. The cost of putting the necessary interface devices – computers and laptops – in the hands of users is prohibitive, while the constraint of a lack of electrification renders the devices unusable in vast swathes of Africa.

Wireless internet on the other hand has almost everything going for it: it will utilise existing wireless infrastructure in the form of telecom operators' sites and radio towers; it uses radio frequencies to broadcast to a wide area at once; the interface devices are in the main part the mobile phones already in the hands of users; and it is likely that advanced innovations in affordable laptop technology should result in a $100 laptop soon enough. On the development of these networks in Africa *The Economist* reported that "3G networks capable of broadband speed will soon be widespread and even faster 4G networks will be spreading rapidly in some places".[273]

Internet penetration in Africa now stands at 9% to 10%, most if not all of which is in urban centres.[274] The necessary backbone links – undersea and terrestrial fibre cables – are coming into place (for discussion of this see the chapter on technological networking). The main challenge for telecoms firms is to be able to acquire the right bands of radio spectrum with enough capacity to support the scale of roll out necessary to keep the projects viable. For full utilisation of the services, there will be a need for upgrade of mobile phones in the hands of users to 3G or 4G enabled sets, suitable for high-speed mobile internet.

Virtual networks

The cost of erecting network infrastructure from scratch is unthinkable now, especially since the per unit revenues of voice calls is trending down. Multiple players serving one market would ordinarily have to build their own separate infrastructure, an unnecessary duplication that costs economies dearly in capital outlay and renders telecoms companies high cost-base operators. Yet more of the African population is not served by telecoms than is already served, so more telecom infrastructure has to be put in place to reach these untapped markets. This residual unserved market segment is, however, marginal, with each new subscriber recruited potentially earning less the telecom companies and bringing down the average revenues per user. The penetration routes therefore have to be re-thought as the costs of roll out have to be rationalised to be recovered through the anticipated revenue streams.

There is an opportunity for network infrastructure companies to be established to take up the physical infrastructure of telecom operators, and lease back to them managed towers and sites as well as safeguard their electronics and other installations. This will address the issues of infrastructure duplication and will lessen the capital burdens on telecom companies by taking off their books physical infrastructure assets, freeing them to concentrate on service delivery.

World telecom equipment makers themselves are already diversifying their operations into this area, as with the example above of Ericsson and Nokia Siemens Networks building and operating a network for Bharti Airtel. This modus operandi converts telecom network costs from fixed costs – with debilitating depreciation, capex and amortisation charges – to variable costs, allowing expense only when necessary and to regulate it according to business performance. It will also make roll out faster and easier, as the infrastructure companies will manage and fund physical infrastructure roll out, including concerns such as new site viability and utilisation commitments, in co-ordination with the operators.

Separating infrastructure from service delivery should rationalise telecom companies' investment economics and put enough wind under their wings to hasten rural penetration and benefit from the expanded revenue opportunities therein. As if to prepare the ground

66 There is an opportunity for network infrastructure companies to be established to take up the physical infrastructure of telecom operators, and lease back to them managed towers and sites as well as safeguard their electronics and other installations. 99

for this inexorable evolution of networks architecture, "the Chinese vendors have shown that they can innovate by launching reconfigured base-stations, the functions of which are defined in software rather than hardware. That means the base station can be quickly *re-jigged* to support different mobile-network technologies or even several technologies at the same time".[275]

Mobile advertising and activation

The one thing that mobile networks have become as an unintended consequence of their vast, live and interactive networks is mass-broadcast media. The short message service (SMS) is hugely responsible for making this possible because of its many attributes and useful features. For example: SMS communication is instant – it delivers in seconds; it is traceable – delivery reports are available immediately; it is cheap – users do not think twice before using it; it is mobile – people wear their mobile phones like clothes; it is peremptory – it is impossible to ignore an incoming text; it is evident – there is an electronic trail; it is mass – a single text-shot to multiple recipients in one go is possible; it is ubiquitous – the mobile phone is the only device in the hands of multiple millions; and it is targeted – the sender knows in advance who a message is being sent to.

Companies already use SMS to send out communications to big groups of people, be they employees, suppliers or customers. Media companies use SMS to generate public opinions and responses to topical issues of the day. Charities and other non-profits use SMS to make appeals for funds. Some companies are now using SMS to run competitions or activations with financial or other attractive rewards wholly financed by the revenues generated from the messages – at premium charges above market rates – sent by the people who participate. Telecoms benefit from the upsurge in traffic instigated by the rewards incentive. Where the charge attracts a premium, a formula for premium sharing is pre-agreed with the responsible company. Telecoms have as yet only scratched the surface of the possibilities in this area and the potential for more corporate uses of SMS technology is tremendous.

All mobile lines are now being registered formally. With the digitisation of demographic data by governments, corporates and polling companies, it is becoming increasingly possible for telecom companies to take the challenge directly to mainstream media houses for a slice of the advertising windfalls they enjoy. Targeted and interactive marketing is the unique selling proposition enjoyed by telecoms which cannot be easily replicated by media houses even with digital set-top boxes. A BBC article on this subject suggested that "the marketing industry has decided the mobile is the platform of the future".[276] Arguing along the same lines, Kerstin Trikalis, CEO of Out There Media, said "we've seen triple digit growth in the last eighteen months (2010 and 2011) and this trend is continuing through 2011", in the same BBC report. Marcos Verinis, the President of Upstream, a mobile marketing consultancy, said that he believes the global mobile industry is set to hit $20 billion.[277]

Network leverage, such as by the marketing industry, allows telecoms to increase capacity optimisation, diversify revenue sources and boost their incomes without further capital expenditure.

M-Commerce

Thanks to Safaricom's M-Pesa technology, fund remittance by mobile phone is already accepted as an ordinary process. Subscriber uptake has been phenomenal – from zero to around 13.5m users on Safaricom's network alone by September 2010 – about 80% of its subscriber base in just three-and-half years.[278] A proliferation of mobile money applications is popping up everywhere in the world and the concept no longer sounds as exotic or unusual as when it first appeared. The challenge is to make these applications operable across networks within national boundaries first, and then internationally operable.

The next phase of this development is fully fledged mobile banking, in which all transactions receipts and payments, bills payments, standing instructions, online purchase payments, credit applications and all other communications and instructions to the bank are made electronically via a mobile phone. This is already available in Kenya in collaboration between Safaricom and Equity bank, M-Kesho.[279] The next phase will involve credit and charge cards going electronic with global usage and electronic authorisation and validation. The last will be loading other bank functionalities, such as foreign exchange transactions and trade finance facilities. Eventually, all personal and individual banking functions will have moved to the mobile phone and will be powered by telecom networks.

> **" Along with the growth in online shopping the mobile convergence will be complete and the number and speed of transactions will increase rapidly. "**

Along with the growth in online shopping which, as we have established above, will take place on wireless broadband internet on the mobile phone or electronic notebook devices, the mobile convergence will be complete and the number and speed of transactions will increase rapidly.

Progressive and favourable regulatory reform will be essential for this overlap between the telecoms and banking sectors, but market forces will continue to drive it within the spirit of *if it is not expressly forbidden, then allow it*. The number of daily transactions that will be generated once the last pieces of this evolutionary jigsaw have been put in place will make the figures we are witnessing currently look very small indeed.

Mobile services

It has been said that the greatest transformational effect of the railroads was not that they opened up long-distance travel to the public – which they did – but that they made possible vast and diverse mass markets in virtually any commodity. Likewise with the internet; its most notable effect on society has been the multiplicity of virtual and remote functionalities it has made possible. In the same breath, mobile telephony will not be complete till it has spawned capabilities that transform commercial, social and everyday life. A piece in *The Economist* argued that:

"Mobile phones are the world's most widely distributed computers. Even in poor countries about two-thirds of people have access to one. As a result, such devices and their networks, though mainly still much simpler than in the rich world, have become a platform on which many other services can be built."[280]

Mobile services in Africa are still embryonic but innovation and ever-increasing network strengths and advanced handset capabilities are allied to make every imaginable idea possible. So far in Africa the dominant categories of services are those that *connect the excluded*, i.e. provide information to those who would otherwise be out of the loop. For example, Farmer's Friend in Uganda sends out market prices and other agricultural information by text messages. Mobile trading platforms are also in this category, for example Esoko, a Ghanaian communication platform.

The opportunities to create compelling business models on any range of activities that can be commercialised around the increasing capabilities of mobile networks and the ever expanding functionalities of mobile devices make for exciting times ahead in telecoms.

OPPORTUNITIES IN TRANSPORT AND LOGISTICS

18

As was comprehensively described earlier in the book, the repair of African transport infrastructure is no longer wishful thinking. Several thousands of kilometres of roads have been relaid already and work to restore, expand, modernise or introduce new roads is continuing in virtually every country of SSA. Railways operations have mostly been concessioned to private sector operators and new standard gauge railroads are popular in transport and infrastructure ministries. The next phase of concessioning is international airports, which are not only increasing in numbers but also being modernised and receiving boosts to capacity.

From the foregoing, it can be seen that opportunities in transport and logistics business are opening up across Africa. These are driven by the following major themes.

Dominant themes in transport and logistics

Manufacturing for the world markets

Ambitious ongoing investments in power-generation capacity across Africa are set to stabilise power supply and bring down the cost of power to make it close to being internationally competitive. A steady rise in wages in China and eastern Asia as that region becomes more prosperous is unhelpfully (helpfully to Africa) increasing costs of manufactured goods from that region, forcing global supply chains to look for alternatives – Africa's average factory wages are still some of the lowest in the world, standing it in good stead to benefit from the shifts in wage arbitrage.

Some global contract manufacturing assignments have already arrived in Africa, for example under the African Growth and Opportunity Act (AGOA) apparel is manufactured for US brands in Africa. These include: Bodo Voahangy of Madagascar, which manufactures children's clothing under contract for Ralph Lauren; United Aryan of Kenya, which is a contract manufacturer for many US brands such as Levis, Jones of New York, Dickies and Haggar; and Wow Garments of Ethiopia, the only company in the eastern African region to export suits to the US.[281] A pesticide company in Nakuru, Kenya, is under

> **"** All the forces that are needed to be are in play for the eventual shift to Africa of global manufacturing for cheap, mass-produced manufactured goods. **"**

contract to manufacture mosquito coils, insect repellents, home and garden insect sprays, impregnated towelettes for international distributors, multinational chemicals and pesticides for companies in South Africa, Zimbabwe, Malawi, Tanzania, Sweden, Finland, Norway, Switzerland and Italy.[282]

Investments in more port capacity and improving efficiency, albeit gradual, in existing sea ports and the transport corridors that serve them is reducing turn-around time, freight costs per unit of exports and enhancing direct, and most importantly equidistant, maritime connections to all the parts of the world.

In short, all the forces that are needed to be are in play for the eventual shift to Africa of global manufacturing for cheap, mass-produced manufactured goods. How African economies position themselves and their private sectors to take full advantage of these tectonic shifts in world industrial architecture depends largely on what housekeeping plans they put in place from now on. These shifts will make possible great opportunities in transportation.

Growth in formal retail distribution

Better domestic and regional transport interconnectivity is perceptibly improving the prospects for deep, organised retail markets. Sustained underlying economic growth and expansion is putting more disposable income in the hands of more workers in African economies than ever before, while an equivalent pace of population growth as well as a fast rate of urbanisation ensures that consumption levels are high, if not increasing. At the same time sweeping lifestyle changes are resulting in heightened conspicuous consumption, more trips to the stores, and impulse buying. And, lastly, health-consciousness is leading to more formal (shopping in designated stores as opposed to backstreet kiosks) and hygienic (buying pre-packed goods as opposed to in-store re-packing) shopping practices in African societies. The retail revolution is indeed underway.

For the revolution to succeed, though, a lot of products, items and produce have to be moved around from point to point within the complex of networks of supply, distribution and delivery. This means there are great opportunities in transportation and logistics.

Rising intra-regional trade

Most regional governments have entered into expanded regional markets under elaborately detailed and delicately negotiated trading protocols. All pertinent trading conventions have been harmonised, bar a few substantive ones with profound financial and economic implications to government revenues and national budgets, such as VAT (value added tax). There are teething problems and full compliance is still a bit difficult to achieve, but clearly common markets are here to stay and reactionary forces are receding.

Saliently, labour markets have been liberalised and so have border crossings with single customs checks on behalf of the common market authorities. The natural outcome of this arrangement will be specialisation where each country's businesses will specialise in the goods, products and services where they have the natural or acquired competitive advantage, and will install capacity to serve the expanded hinterland of the common market from one or a few points in the market. Relative advances in transport and telecommunication infrastructure alluded to earlier will provide the basic underpinnings for these kinds of manufacturing and operating models.

Supply chains of suppliers, dealerships, distributors and agents will enlarge, and the networks to interconnect them will certainly be more complex than national networks. The resulting opportunities in transportation and logistics are bound to increase as regional trade grows and stabilises going forward.

Commuter connections

A useful bell-wether for a rise in economic fortunes of an economy and its people is changes in the rate at which

66 The 24-hour economy is inevitable in African cities. 99

people travel. Rising economies tend to have busier people, moving and travelling a lot. More and more workers everyday need to get to work and back home. Working shifts in industries, godowns, businesses, retail stores, eateries and other commercial enterprises tend to increase with the effect that crowds spill into the streets at regular intervals and need to be picked up from the streets by transport services. The 24-hour economy is inevitable in African cities as when the workers of the day depart the evening fun-seekers, date-makers and weekend shoppers appear, and they too will need transport connections to get them to and from their destinations. Someone has to ferry these people back and forth efficiently, securely and conveniently.

Urban renewal and modernisation, introduced in the real estate section, should result in more orderly re-zoning of city areas and re-classification of use, which will naturally lead to a need for new commuter connections. For example, schools may well be moved outside of residential areas where enough space is available for the necessary educational and extra-curricular activities, with the implication that children will have to be bussed to school and back every day.

Tourism

“ Successful documentation and broadcast far and wide of the magic of the African savannah by television channels with global reach continue to whet the appetites of global travellers for the inimitable African safari. ”

Annual tourist arrivals numbers in SSA grew 30% over the five years to 2010, from 23m to 30m, and 7% from 2010 to 2011. It was the only region to show positive growth in 2009.[283] New destinations in Africa are opening with the normalisation of order and security in almost all former war-torn countries. New concepts of tourism are also coming into being, such as gorilla tourism in the Rwanda Mountains; conference tourism in Arusha, Tanzania; golf and bird watching tourism in Nairobi; or the newest addition, *presidential tourism* in Kogelo, Kenya – the home of US President Barack Obama's father.

New source markets are compounding the numbers of arrivals as travellers from southeast Asia extend their travel itineraries and diversify their reason for travel beyond trade and scouting new business opportunities – consistent with the rise in their wealth, they have become holiday and fun seekers. At the same time, successful documentation and broadcasts of the magic of the African savannah by television channels with global reach – for instance *National Geographic* and *Animal Planet* – continue to whet the appetites of global travellers for the inimitable African safari. No doubt the recent growth of African markets and the perception of them as viable, expanding and investable is adding to the numbers of travellers induced by business and curiosity.

The problem facing any overseas traveller to Africa is the lack of direct flights to most destinations in Africa; and where the flights are there, the lack of enough seats. Foreign airlines are hearkening to the plaintive cries and filling the voids left by defunct African carriers. The demand will only grow further as the momentum of tourism increases.

Serving European markets with fresh produce

Africa's horticulture business model is to serve European consumers with a year-round supply of fresh, organic vegetables and fruits delivered within half a day of cutting. It is already happening in a small way but the growth trends are encouraging (export volumes having grown 107% between 1998 and 2009).[284] It takes a tightly-integrated supply chain to achieve and sustain such a business model, but the gridlock is not in the supply chain so much as it is in the marketplace. An explosion and proliferation of this model is set to unveil roaring horticultural farming in Africa, but one thing has still to happen – the successful repeal of the trade distorting practices of subsidising European farmers.

This is being agitated for collectively by the poor nations of the world within the framework of the Doha round of talks of the WTO. Europe is waking up to the truth, slowly but surely, of the ridiculous and indefensible aspects of its Common Agricultural Policy (CAP).[285] Year-round tropical weather, close proximity to Europe and some of the lowest wages in the world accord Africa unparalleled competitive advantage in horticultural and fruit production. The vast area of uncultivated arable land ensures that the turnaround time for a horticultural transformation will be as short as possible.

For this and other related reasons, demand for local air cargo capacity – for example for flowers – should be expected to trend higher than previously recorded.

The trap of competitive geo-location

Africa has an opportunity to offer the world the full benefits of its location at the centre of the world, logistically speaking. This is because from anywhere in the world it is possible to travel to Africa using only one direct flight. Currently aerial connections between North America and the Far East or southeast Asia have to fly through Europe. Those between western Europe and south East Asia or Australia and the oceanic islands have to fly through the Middle East or Persia. They take far longer to terminate, endure odd and inconvenient landing and take off slots in congested European airports and

> **❝ Africa has an opportunity to offer the world the full benefits of its central global location. ❞**

pay expensive fees to the airport authorities.

African airports can cut many hours of flight and airport time, grant convenient landing and take off slots, and charge low fees for them. The challenge, of course, is in finding the airports with the carrying capacity, ground handling efficiency and navigation capabilities to rival the competition. There is an opportunity right there for African airports and the ongoing airport developments across the continent are bringing this possibility nearer to fruition.

Looking at sea trade, maritime corridors between southeast and southern Asia and South America go through the Suez Canal across the Mediterranean, normally using trans-shipment ports in Spain or France and down the Atlantic to the ports of South America, and vice versa. The distance that would be saved by using the southern tip of Africa, rather than going through the Atlantic, would be around 18% (between around 8000 nautical miles for the trip via South Africa, and around 9500 nautical miles for the trip via the Suez canal and Mediterranean)[286] depending on the port of call on the eastern and northern seaboards of South America.

Again, the challenge here is to find sea ports that can fit Panamax-size ships for call and trans-shipment. An even greater challenge in fact is in finding enough cargo destined to African countries to share cargo space along with South American bound cargo in these ships. There is an opportunity for international trans-shipment business for African ports on the eastern seaboard and for African ocean liners.

The rise of online shopping

The case for online shopping was made in the retail experience section of this book. This will only be possible with an efficiently operating logistical system to co-ordinate and make deliveries of items bought and paid for online. Indeed, the very nature and structure of online shopping alone promotes logistical systems and companies through the shipping fees that are paid by online shoppers with every purchase made. Aggregated together these fees should sustain the growth of logistical businesses or divisions of integrated logistical businesses specialised in catering to online shoppers across Africa.

Summary of the opportunities in transport and logistics

Logistics outsourcing

African logistics companies are most likely to be very busy in the days ahead. They will have to cater for:

- moving finished manufactured goods from the emerging regional industrial heartlands to the ports for onward trans-shipment to world markets

- rising intra-regional trade as trading blocs and common markets come of age

- distribution needs of the retailers and grocery chains

- the call of online shoppers and the overnight delivery needs of enterprises

Industrial and commercial companies are already averse to ownership of fleets of distribution vans and trucks on their books, and are resorting to outsourcing these services from logistics companies. The organising effects of new business design and operating models has independent logistical arrangements right at the core of the strategy, and any growth in industrial and commercial activities has a direct correlation with the growth in demand for logistical services. Scale, efficiency, dependability and cost of operation are necessary to be able to thrive in this industry.

Warehousing

The concept of outsourcing logistics and handling of goods and products goes hand in hand with the business of warehousing. As retailers, manufacturers, traders, exporters and importers across Africa grow bigger and their networks become more expansive and sophisticated, logistical outsourcing will initially combine both transportation and warehousing services. However, with the anticipated growth in volumes and scale of operations, warehousing business will find prospects grow either as direct linkages to logistical services or as standalone outfits, especially at seaports and international airports where major trans-shipments take place. The opportunities have a natural correlation to the growth in retail, international trade and logistics outsourcing.

At another level, there will also be warehousing opportunities created by the introduction of the concept of the warehouse receipting system for agricultural produce which I described under the commodities exchanges opportunities in agriculture.

Commuter transport

African cities are already abuzz with activity; they are dynamic and pulsating with traffic congestion, teeming pedestrians, noise, pollution and street humour. Yet, room has to be made for economic growth. The traffic situation in the bigger cities is of such alarming proportions that something has to be done in a hurry to fix it. To make African cities absorb and cater to greater millions of populations in constant motion than they already do, efficient public transport systems will have to be provided for these people.

Space is a challenge already at street level and the capital requirements for underground commuter systems mean they are impractical – at this stage – leaving bus companies as the most plausible answer, followed by over-ground commuter rail in phased roll out. Street surfaces need to be smoother to reduce wear and tear, and priority entry into the city centres needs to be granted for effective termination and collection.

Opportunities for bus companies to carry schoolchildren are also emerging, initially in the bigger cities, as traffic conditions increasingly undermine the ability of parents to drop their children to school and still make it to work in time, while fluctuating demands at the workplace also affect their availability to do this.

Airline business

Air travel in Africa has been expanding rapidly in the past decade for a number of different reasons. Increased contact for trade, business conferences, sporting and cultural activities is bringing African people together in more ways than had ever been experienced previously. Recent availability of direct aerial connections between major African cities has catalysed growth of intra-African contact and travel. The momentum generated so far has uncovered the need for more intra-African aerial connections and airline capacity deployment.

Sustainable growth in tourist flows to Africa could also be enhanced by, among other factors, the establishment of more direct flights from the points of origination for new source markets, supported by seamless transfers to any destination within Africa from the main international hubs. A lot is still to be done in the area of more intercontinental direct flights originating or terminating in Africa. Boeing and Airbus are not necessarily helping African carriers by their incessant delays in new aircraft manufacture and delivery, especially with the Boeing 787 dreamliner[287] and the Airbus A3450,[288] which are definitely the most suitable equipment for intercontinental deployment.

Horticulture is an agro-business activity for which Africa enjoys tremendous competitive advantage, not least in terms of location. This is already being experienced on a small scale in Kenya, Ethiopia, Uganda, Zambia and Tanzania, and

> **❝ To make African cities absorb and cater for greater millions of population in constant motion than they currently do, efficient public transport systems will have to be provided. ❞**

the pace of growth is gathering momentum on the wheels of factors already touched on above. Cargo business for airlines is already getting tighter in terms of available cargo space in aircraft, such that business cases for dedicated cargo freight planes are no longer unthinkable. The impetus for this rides on Europe's anticipated thawing to competitive agriculture and exploding African contact with Asia. Also, with the expected shift in world industrial capacity to Africa, global logistical prospects should brighten for carriers operating to or from Africa.

International air traffic

African airports are receiving a facelift. Without tying specifics to any particular airport, this is what is going on generally in airport improvements across the continent:

- New runways are being added where they are needed and the length of existing ones being increased to land bigger planes, e.g. the Boeing 747- 400 and Airbus A380

- Terminal capacity is also being increased to facilitate speed of passenger handling as well as boost the numbers of passengers processed per hour

- More aircraft parking slots are being provided

- Navigation and guidance systems are being improved to international levels

- Security is being improved

- Operations are being concessioned to established private PPP operators

Basically, African airports, at least the established hubs in Nairobi, Addis Ababa and Lagos, should be getting prepared to handle any major positive shifts in global flight-paths. The opportunities range from landing fees, transfer traffic and code-sharing for local carriers, to ground handling, re-fuelling and in-flight amenities.

Trans-shipment ports

The Suez Canal is increasingly perilous as a sea trade route because of the presence of the Somali pirates and the apparent inability of world navies to curb hijacking of ships off the coast of Somalia. Yet transit of freight originating from Asia or the gulf states, through the southern tip of Africa, substantially shortens the travel distance to the eastern seaboard of South America. In addition, the expected rise in the profile of Africa as an emerging manufacturing base for world markets should increase the volumes of cargo terminating and originating from African ports. The case for more international trans-shipment ports in Africa is becoming ever stronger.

OPPORTUNITIES IN MANUFACTURING AND PROCESSING

19

To satiate the demand for deeper and more regionally interconnected consumer markets – which are being shaped by a growing and progressively more sophisticated clientele, forces to better organise and structure the markets, and the commercial effects of globalisation and global sourcing – vast new manufacturing and processing capacity is going to be required. The following are some of the factors that will fundamentally shape the landscape of manufacturing in SSA in the coming years.

Themes shaping manufacturing opportunities

Demographics

Africa continues to have the highest birth rate in the world and is expected to defend this position for the long term, underpinned by the driving forces that were discussed in the demographics section in Part One of this book. Approximately 39 new children per 1,000 of population are now being born in SSA annually according to the Population Reference Bureau – that is approximately 34m births per year.

Compounding this is the highest rate of urbanisation in the world, ensuring that the majority of the children being born are to families living in urban centres. As African economies become more prosperous, (urban) families are acquiring the habit of pampering and spoiling their children with new, even designer, things. Growing and sustainable demand for new children's products should shape investments in manufacturing capacity for these products in SSA economies in the days ahead.

Entertainment

Youth and entertainment are both sides of the same coin. They define each other, shape each other and reinforce each other. Youth is what African population is all about and this will become even truer in the future. The rate of consumption of entertainment in African countries has been rising steadily in tandem with the coming of age of batches of the population spikes of the 1980s and 1990s. This is escalated by the embrace and adoption of popular Western culture.

❝ The rate of consumption of entertainment in African countries has been rising steadily in tandem with the coming of age of batches of the population spikes of the 1980s and 1990s. ❞

So far the African entertainment industry has depended largely on imported hardware to kit out entertainment joints that have been proliferating in cities and urban centres, put entertainment systems in homes and automobiles, and place mobile entertainment gadgets in the hands of African youth. However, some basic industrial capacity has been springing up in a few countries – namely Ghana, Nigeria, Kenya, Namibia, Uganda and Zambia[289] – to manufacture or assemble simple entertainment gadgets like speakers, leaving advanced engineering gadgets to manufacturers in America, Europe and Asia.

Work ethic – opportunities in food processing

The argument for a busier and more indebted workforce, leading to longer working hours or multiple jobs, has already been set out in the retail experience section; it was summarised how this will shape consumer experiences of the workers and thereby the design of consumer solutions to cater to them. By the same token, these expected changes in workers' circumstances, in particular their time and time-consciousness, should be expected to create and shape opportunities in food processing.

Health and hygiene

There is no doubt African societies are becoming more educated and more enlightened. Above all, public awareness of health and hygiene matters has been sharpened. Consequently, therefore, concerns about handling of foods and other consumables are becoming mainstream, providing underpinnings for the evolution and sustenance of a wide range of businesses in formal or industrial handling and packaging in environments that are regulated, supervised and certified and which also provide a definite trail for recourse in circumstances of public backlash to the products distributed or consumed. The transition from informal to formal economies should provide a long-term basis for the establishment of more manufacturing, processing and packaging industries that provide products for the entire human life spectrum.

Preservation

The problem of a lack of appropriate storage as one of the major hindrances to the growth and commercialisation of agriculture in Africa, confirming it as perhaps the most urgent opportunity in that sector, has already been

> ❝ The transition from informal to formal economies should provide a long-term basis for the establishment of more manufacturing, processing and packaging industries. ❞

highlighted. An additional challenge is what to do with gluts of agricultural produce which cannot be stored properly for future consumption in lean times.

With climate change causing unpredictable and unseasonable weather patterns in Africa, creating more frequent pendulum swings between swamping floods and flattening droughts, feast and famine can no longer remain random variables to food security; they are now preponderant factors. Consequently, therefore, the need for preservation of essential food commodities whose fortunes rise and fall with the pendulum swings should spawn whole new industries in the emerging African manufacturing landscape.

Capacity optimisation

Installation of industrial or manufacturing capacity is never an exact science. With just sufficient capacity you run into big problems when demand increases even slightly; with too much capacity you have excess idle capacity for which you incur financing costs and depreciation without utilisation. That said, it is preferable to have some idle capacity in growth markets where annual increases in demand and consumption are almost assured. Besides, the logistical costs, hazards and hassle of importing and installing plant in Africa aren't something industrialists want to repeat in a hurry. There are also scale benefits to buying larger capacity equipment.

Unsurprisingly, therefore, operating industries which have been adding new capacity in Africa tend to have large unutilised capacity, which when aggregated together presents a convincing case for optimisation innovations in industries such as dairy processing in Ethiopia[290] and Kenya.[291] Capacity can be harnessed for capacity optimisation and leased under contract

❝ As more entrepreneurs come forward searching for unutilised capacity to manufacture or process their products, the more compelling is the business case for pure-play contract manufacturing capacity. **❞** manufacturing or processing to firms which have no industrial capacity of their own but market their own brands. In turn this provides a basis for the establishment of own-brands or product marketing outfits without the costs and hassle of manufacturing infrastructure. This trend is already being observed in African economies and is gathering pace as it opens up numerous manufacturing opportunities that were hitherto unimaginable.

Indeed, these two factors can be self-reinforcing. As more entrepreneurs come forward searching for unutilised capacity to manufacture or process their products, the more compelling is the business case for pure-play contract manufacturing capacity. Industrialists will emerge whose only business is to sell industrial capacity to operators without the scale and wherewithal to produce their own brands or consumer products.

Global dynamics

Global sourcing and outsourcing have been around for some time now as the most dynamic concepts for pulling together segments of global competitiveness. The challenge is to assemble them in some form of distributed business model to realise the best global products at the lowest world costs. This process is the soul of global supply chains and it has so far eluded Africa – if you strip out mining. Obviously there are a few exceptions like pharmaceuticals, apparel, currency notes and industrial crops. But this is about to change.

❝ Global sourcing and outsourcing have been around for some time now as the most dynamic concepts for pulling together segments of global competitiveness. **❞** The World Bank has already expressed fears the future sustainability of the Chinese industrial model as the cheapest producer of simple, mass manufactured products for the world markets. Wages continue to increase there as the economy crosses into developed status, lifting the cost of living with it, so workers are demanding better real wages. Labour is also becoming short in supply, as workers get more skilled and one-time poorly developed regions that provided migrant workers are being transformed into bustling investment destinations.

There are also genuine expectations that the Chinese authorities may not continue to artificially keep the Chinese currency undervalued, in response to persistent calls for its appreciation from its main trading partners the US and Europe. The *Financial Times* has stated that "the Chinese central bank said that it would increase the flexibility of the exchange rate, an indication that it will resume a policy of gradual appreciation of the Yuan Reminbi".[292] It has also been reported that "Wage inflation coincides with Beijing's drive to push infant industries out of the nest. China is shedding manufacturing jobs in its most labour-intensive sectors to low cost alternatives elsewhere". It then posed the question 'Can Africa join the party?'[293]

It looks as if the baton of cost competitiveness is slipping slowly from China's grasp, or it could be the case that China is a runner which has finished its race.

Summary of the opportunities in manufacturing and processing

Children's products

The retail opportunities in products for children have already been adequately introduced in this book. The real question now is whether to import these products or to establish local industrial capacity to manufacture them. The factors traditionally militating against a globally viable industrial base in Africa continue to be addressed, eliminated or mitigated as described in Part Two, while the relative slide of cost competitiveness of China and its neighbourhood on account of rising wages and strengthening local currencies is also helping to make the proposition of manufacturing goods within Africa more attractive.

An important determinant is that Africa will remain the last continent with a population willing and able to continue producing children at the highest rate in the world into the foreseeable future. It just seems a needless logistical challenge to continue catering to such a market from external sources. Every conceivable aspect of a child's life cycle is beckoning for products, for capacity, for service. The market is there, so where are the manufacturers?

Consumer electronics

Nearly every leading consumer electronics manufacturer in the world now has strong marketing and service presence in Africa. That is a good start. However, anybody who still thinks that the African market should continue to receive cursory attention as a segment of miscellaneous international operation does not get the point. Just as there is a large children's market, there is a large youth market too. Many of these youthful consumers have more prosperous parents than generations before them, plus they may also have casual or permanent jobs of their own.

Their propensity to consume entertainment and leisure activities is unparalleled. They have, without any external help, established entertainment as one of the fastest growing industries in Africa. For example, the concept of the sports bar was virtually unknown in Africa before the early 2000s, but now even village trading centres with neither electricity nor stone buildings have them. The unrelenting pace of urbanisation is set to augment this trend even more in the future.

This situation more than merits the establishment of advanced manufacturing capacity to serve the vibrant African entertainment industry. As an early example, one of the special economic zones being established in Zambia is planned to host manufacturers of electrical goods and mobile phones.[294]

Processed foods

Longer working hours, shorter nights and often non-existent weekends: these are the patterns of industrious societies, particularly those breaking out into periods of long, unpunctuated economic expansion. The pressures of entrepreneurs and business enterprises for constant improvements in labour productivity as they stretch to satisfy ever-expanding demand in the face of fixed short-term capacity place greater burdens on workforces to produce more by working harder and longer. They will also be forced to work back to back to meet credit card payments, forgoing all manner of pleasures, including that of preparing a decent home made meal.

These scenarios create fertile ground for the growth of processed food industries.

Packaging

A direct beneficiary of the formalisation of shopping is the packaging industry. Virtually everything that is retailed is packaged; even furniture and white goods are delivered in cartons and Styrofoam. Private label

> 66 Whichever way you look at it, the packaging business is highly connected to retail and packaging industries have got a very selfish interest in the formalisation of shopping. 99

brands, ready to eat foods and all manner of other products must all come in packages. Health consciousness is making people cautious about the handling of their groceries and other food items, leading to an incipient but growing trend where vegetables and meat products come pre-packed in punnets.

At the same time, consumer and health activism are succeeding in changing consumers' expectations about what they consume; therefore, increasingly, they want and demand to see the contents, ingredients and breakdown of food components prominently labelled on the products – hence another need for packaging of almost every consumer product.

So whichever way you look at it, the packaging business is highly connected to retail and packaging industries have got a very selfish interest in the formalisation of shopping.

Food preservation

Two glaring opportunities need to be singled out in the food preservation space. During rainy seasons, which admittedly are becoming a rare occurrence in large parts of Africa, flash floods cover large expanses of land, bursting river banks and laying siege to civilisation and all its manifestations. But another kind of flood takes place contemporaneously in farms triggered by the external flood; that of a milk glut. Milk prices come crashing down and retailers are forced to give incentives for shoppers to pick more milk off their shelves in case it goes bad and gets discarded and written off. A lot of milk goes to waste either uncollected in farms rendered inaccessible by the floods or in cooling plants gridlocked by saturated markets. No sooner does the rain dry up than the milk spigots reduce to a trickle before running dry thereafter.

In dry seasons, which are never more than three months away from the last drop of rain, milk becomes rare and prices soar back to high levels, each time exceeding the last recorded high. To be sure, shifts to formal retailing and increasing populations and urbanisation are also contributing to the impending milk crisis in African markets. There are opportunities to collect this surplus milk when it is available, convert it into powder, store it for as long as is reasonable and put it back to the market when it can fetch a good price across SSA. There are not many powdering plants in Africa so a lot of milk still goes to waste.

A similar cycle runs in beef and ranching, where spot market demand is not always able to consume a constant supply in normal weather conditions, but craves and pays top dollar for even a pound of flesh during famines where drought decimates entire herds. Opportunities in beef canning are there to be taken.

Contract manufacturing

A lot of new manufacturing capacity is being installed in many African countries, be it in food processing, printing, extractive industries, pharmaceuticals, etc., and idle capacity is being created as a result. As the pace of economic growth and expansion gathers momentum, these circumstances should be replicated across other industries. It is therefore no longer an excuse not to get into manufacturing just because one does not own a factory or have the capital to invest in one. The trends for contract processing/manufacturing in dairy, bread, garments, pharmaceuticals, cosmetics and so on are very encouraging of an emerging permanent overhaul of the whole industrial model of manufacturing and processing.

> **It seems that, knowingly or unknowingly, Africa is putting its house in order for some kind of global role.**

Roche, a Swiss pharmaceutical firm, has outsourced production of HIV drugs in Africa to CAPS Holdings of Zimbabwe, Shelys Pharmaceuticals of Tanzania and Regal Pharmaceuticals of Kenya.[295] Protex Kenya, a garment company operating in the Export Processing Zone (EPZ), taking advantage of the US government Growth and Opportunity Act (AGOA), imports textiles from Asia to transform them into clothes that are sold predominantly to Walmart.[296]

The opportunities even extend to *pure-play* contract manufacturing – businesses established purely to manufacture or process under contract on behalf of others – where economies of scale and non-competition agreements allow the plant owners to reduce the unit costs of manufacturing substantially enough to shift the dynamics of competitiveness and establish contracted production as the model of the future.

Global outsourcing

African governments, aided primarily by the Chinese, are pulling out all the stops to improve transport infrastructure, extend and unclog transport corridors, deepen and modernise seaports, and streamline customs procedures. Vast new power capacity is scheduled to come on stream in phased commissioning of long pipelines of power plant developments, and telecoms (wireless) and ICT (terrestrial) networking is nearing final stages with continent-wide connection to the world through multiple undersea fibre-optic cables with unimaginable redundancy (spare capacity).

At the same time academic and training (technical and professional) institutions are churning out ever more hundreds of thousands of relatively better educated and appropriately trained youths eager for engagement and ready for the travails of the job hunt. It seems that, knowingly or unknowingly, Africa is putting its house in order for some kind of global role.

In all likelihood, China seems eager to pass on the badge of being *factory to the world* and Africa is positioning itself to receive it. Whether it gets it in one piece or a part of it, Africa is unarguably poised to service the world from a manufacturing perspective. It will not unfortunately go to every African country indiscriminately, but rather will cluster in zones with the vision and drive for industrial excellence and world-class infrastructure to ply the logistical aspects of it. Special Economic Zones (SEZs) are already springing up in select African countries.

> *"Africa has seven [SEZs] that are nearing readiness: two in Nigeria, one each in Algeria, Egypt, Zambia, Ethiopia and Mauritius. In Kenya's EPZ at Athi-River, 23 companies are busy making everything from clothes and tarpaulins to pharmaceuticals, dartboards, batteries and various agro-processing products. And a new business incubator is being built, with the current one fully occupied by Nestlé."*[297]

The manufacturing capacity and opportunities these shifts in global outsourcing entail are huge.

CONCLUSION

This book has attempted to analyse the business and investment opportunities currently obtaining and those expected to emerge in Sub-Saharan African countries between 2010 and 2030. To achieve this, it has depended on carefully identified and rigorously developed major trends and their underlying driving forces. The book has presented the emerging opportunities on the back of relevant and independently computed prognoses and predictions into the future.

I acknowledge that there are many opportunities not discussed in this book but at the same time the facts and trends developed and presented in the first and second parts should provide a complete reference basis for many more conclusions for other businesses and commercial enterprises across SSA economies to be independently made by readers.

It is a fact that technological evolution is difficult if not impossible to predict. In view of this, there may be technological changes either not being considered at present or which are existing but in experimental scale and in fields out of the business sphere that might be commercialised in the future and impact business in ways that cannot be conceptualised at present. There exists therefore a possibility that some of the sectors or opportunities addressed in this book could be either accelerated, or completely overhauled and revolutionised by new technological capabilities.

African societies continue to evolve both socially and politically. However, like all progressive societies, the potential for policy reversals and public sector bureaucracy is inherent, particularly in policy implementation. African governments are working hard to provide an environment conducive to business, but their civil services are not necessarily the best implementers of policy, and variances between the spirit and letter of the law do occur. Because of this, there could be variations between the ideal and the reality which can cause delays and increase costs of doing business.

Finally, the investment case for Africa and its economies which are opening up becomes more compelling every day. Investment momentum is building – the early adopters have a unique and singular opportunity to secure assets at zero or minimal premium. Visibility on the investment radar screen continues getting clearer as new and higher thresholds of business viability and competitiveness are attained through improving business environments and the network effects being generated by the interactions of previous investments.

The horizon is getting pushed further by better relative stability and predictability of the environment and by the constant emergence of new opportunities.

I wish every investor a long and prosperous investment run in Sub-Saharan Africa.

APPENDICES

Transportation corridors in Africa

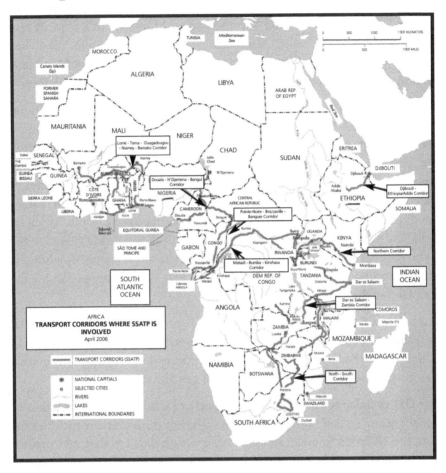

The **Walvis Bay Corridor Group** caters for the countries of south western Africa, including Namibia, Botswana, Zimbabwe and western Zambia, as well as markets in the hinterland of DR Congo and South Africa's Gauteng region. It incorporates three major trans-continental highway systems: the Trans-Cunene-Highway which is comprised of the northern part of the Namibian national highway from Otavi to Oshikango and joins the Trans-Caprivi Highway at Otavi to Walvis Bay; the Trans-Caprivi which connects Grootfontein in Namibia to Katima Mulilo on the River Zambezi in Zambia, via north west Angola; and the Trans-Kalahari Highway which connects Johannesburg and Pretoria to Walvis Bay through Botswana. These are all served by the Walvis Bay port of Namibia.

The **Northern Corridor** comprises the transport facilities and infrastructure linking the landlocked countries of east and central Africa – Uganda, DR Congo, Burundi and Rwanda – to the port of Mombasa in Kenya. It also serves northern Tanzania, southern Sudan and Ethiopia. The key infrastructure is the Mombasa-Kampala-Kigali Highway, the Mombasa-Kisumu-Kasese railway line and the Mombasa-Nairobi-Eldoret pipeline.

The **North-South Corridor**, also known as the **Great North Road**, is by far the longest trans-African highway system of roads. Stretching 10,228km, it connects Cairo in Egypt to Johannesburg in South Africa, sewing together the countries of Egypt, Sudan, Ethiopia, Kenya, Tanzania, Malawi, Zambia, Botswana, Zimbabwe, Lesotho and South Africa. The southern parts connect the countries of Malawi, Zambia, Botswana, Zimbabwe, Lesotho and eastern South Africa to the port of Durban on the eastern coast of South Africa by road. The northern parts connect Sudan, Ethiopia, Eritrea and Djibouti to the Cairo metropolis and onwards onto the Mediterranean sea ports, while the middle section forms the vital north-south axis of interconnection for the countries of the COMESA region.

The **Maputo Corridor** connects the city of Maputo to Gauteng, the industrial heartland of South Africa. It comprises a concessioned road (or toll road), where service has been privatised and the concessionaire company levies a charge on road users, a railway line and a gas pipeline.

The **Dar es Salaam Corridor** links the port of Dar es Salaam in Tanzania to Lusaka, Zambia, and Lilongwe, Malawi. The key infrastructure includes the port, the TAZARA Railway and the Tanzam Highway. The **Central Corridor** connects the port of Dar es salaam to the central African nations of Burundi, Rwanda and DR Congo. It is comprised of the port at Dar es salaam, the Kigoma-Dar es Salaam Railway; the Lake Tanganyika waterway; and a highway linking Dar es salaam to Burundi and Rwanda through Dodoma, Nzenga and Lusahunga.

The **Lagos-Abidjan-Dakar Corridor**, also known as the **Trans-Coastal West Africa Corridor**, traverses all the 11 coastal countries between Senegal and Nigeria. It links Lagos in Nigeria to Dakar in Senegal through Abidjan in Côte d'Ivoire, connecting the countries of Nigeria, Benin, Togo, Ghana, Côte d'Ivoire, Liberia, Sierra Leone, Guinea, Guinea Bissau, Gambia and Senegal. The main infrastructure is a highway.

In Dakar it connects to the **Trans-Sahelian Corridor** and the **Cairo-Dakar Corridor**; in Lagos it links to the **Trans-Saharan Corridor** that connects Lagos to Algiers, Algeria, as well as the **Lagos-Mombasa Corridor** that connects east Africa to west Africa by road. It provides the most direct, and sometimes only, road connection between the capitals of the countries along its alignment. It also provides the starting points for the roads leading from the ports to the landlocked countries in the hinterland. It stretches for 4,010km, of which 3,260km is paved in various conditions, while a total of 750km, or 18% of the network, is gravel and earth roads.

The **Dakar-N'Djamena Corridor**, also known as the western **Trans-Sahelian Corridor**, covers 4,500km in seven countries – Senegal, Mali, Burkina Faso, Niger, Nigeria, Cameroon and Chad. Its alignment is largely determined by the five capitals that it passes through – Dakar, Bamako, Ouagadougou, Niamey and N'Djamena. It intersects with four other trans-African highway systems: in Dakar – the **Lagos-Dakar Corridor**, and the **Cairo-Dakar Corridor**; at Kano in northern Nigeria it meets the Trans-Saharan Highway linking Lagos with Algiers; and at Ndjamena it abuts the Tripoli-Windhoek Highway, and at the same time connects to the N'Djamena-Djibouti Highway (the eastern leg of the **Trans-Sahelian Corridor** running from N'Djamena to Djibouti).

It also provides the main connection to the highway which leads to the coast and the ports in west Africa for the landlocked countries of central and western Africa. Parallel to it, at the Dakar-Bamako stretch, is the Senegal-Mali railway, a 1,200km single track, narrow gauge, non-electrified line, which provides year-round access to the port at Dakar for Mali. This becomes important during the rainy season when highway missing links between the two countries become impassable. Of the 4,500km highway, 20% is unpaved, though for about one-third of this there are alternative alignments made up of fairly high-class paved roads.

The **Trans-Cameroon Corridor** connects the two landlocked central African countries of Chad and Central African Republic (CAR) to the Atlantic Ocean sea port of Douala in Cameroon. The main transport infrastructure is a road which forks into two legs, one connecting to Bangui in CAR and the other to N'Djamena in Chad. The transport is either fully road or a combination of road and rail between Douala and Belabo (CAR) or between Douala and N'Goundere (Chad). In addition, a pipeline from Chad to Kribi (Cameroon) has also been completed. The Douala-Bangui leg is a 1,500km road link, with two shorter alternatives – the Douala-N'Goundere-Bangui which is 867km with a parallel rail link of 922km, and the Douala-Belabo-Bangui, a 670km road. The Douala-N'Djamena leg is a 2,100km highway, with a 750km alternative link going through N'Goundere, running parallel to a 922km rail road.

Other smaller, point to point, direct link corridors include the **Trans-Equatorial Corridor (Point Noire-Brazzaville-Bangui Corridor)** which provides an alternative sea link by road for the Central African Republic and the republic of Congo through the port of Point-Noire in Congo or Matadi in DR Congo. It is a 640km road, with a parallel railway line covering 512km to Point-Noire. The alternative is 1,200km river navigation on river Oubangi which drains into river Congo and onwards into the Atlantic Ocean at Matadi, DR Congo.

The **Djibouti-Ethiopian/Addis Corridor** connects Addis Ababa in Ethiopia to the Red Sea port of Djibouti in Djibouti. The main infrastructure is a road in good condition, supplemented by an old railway line in a state of disrepair.

References

Part I: The Megatrends

[1] ssl.csg.org/Trends/Megatrends%20Definitions%20and%20Categories.pdf

[2] www.infinitefutures.com/resources/glossary.shtml

Chapter 1. Population Growth and Demographic Shifts

[3] www.futurepundit.com/archives/004914.html

[4] en.wikipedia.org/wiki/Demographics_of_Africa

[5] PRB 2010 World Population data Sheet.

[6] History of Small Pox and its Spread Around the World, "Mortality rates of 80% were reported among the Griqua people in 1831, and as late as 1899 smallpox almost exterminated some tribes in northern Kenya. A similar pattern was observed as central Africa was opened up to European trading from the west, and some parts of the eastern Zaire river basin were completely depopulated."

[7] Exploring Africa (exploringafrica.matrix.msu.edu/teachers/curriculum/m18/activity1.php): "Central Africa, was impacted by great epidemics, in addition to the more chronic endemic diseases like malaria, yellow fever and sleeping sickness. The high mortality rate caused by these diseases reduced considerably the size of the population and the growth rate. But after the 1930s, very vigorous medical measures were taken by the colonial administration, including improvement in hygiene. Eventually, these measures stopped the decline in the size of the population and brought the growth rate to a normal level."

[8] Jacob Adetunji and Eduard R. Bos, 'Levels and Trends in Mortality in Sub-Saharan Africa: An Overview', in Dean Jamison, *Disease and Mortality in Sub-Saharan Africa*.

[9] Population Prospects: The 2008 Revision Population Database, United Nations (www.un.org).

[10] Keneth Hill and Agbessi Amouzou, 'Trends in Child Mortality, 1960-2000', in Jamison, *Disease and Mortality*.

[11] 'Levels & Trends in Child Mortality Report 2010', by UN Inter-agency Group for Child Mortality Estimation IGME).

[12] CIA World Factbook (2009 estimates).

[13] www.en.wikipedia.org/wiki/Nairobi#Population

[14] www.populstat.info/Africa/congokip.htm

[15] 'Regional Fact Sheet from the World Development Indicators 2009', Sub-Saharan Africa.

[16] 'Uganda: Teenage Pregnancies Dilemma to System', *Daily Monitor* (Uganada), 27 September 2010.

[17] 'Rising teenage pregnancy top of the agenda as contraception day marked', *Daily Nation* (Kenya), 3 November 2010.

[18] Data sourced from iLook China (**www.ilookchina.net/tag/teen-pregnancy**), 30 April 2011.

[19] 'Genesis of Eden' (**www.dhushara.com/book/diversit/extra/popb/popb.htm**): "In many African countries average families still have six or more children, while in Kenya in recent years there have been four times as many births as deaths. The country has had the world's fastest population growth rate, exceeding 4% per year during the 1980s. At the United Nations population conference in Cairo in 1994, 28 countries reported that their fertility rates had risen since the previous population conference in 1984, twenty of those countries were in Africa."

[20] R. A. Wortham, 'Population Growth and the Demographic transition in Kenya', *International Sociology* 8:2 (1993).

[21] John Blacker, 'Kenya's Fertility Transition: How Long Will it Go?', (**www.un.org/esa/population/publications/completingfertility/RevisedBlackerpaper.PDF**).

[22] Worldometers, real-time world statistics (**www.worldometers.info**).

Chapter 2. Cultural Revolution

[23] 'Goal 2: Achieve universal primary education', (**www.afdb.org/en/topics-sectors/topics/millennium-development-goals-mdgs/goal-2-achieve-universal-primary-education**).

[24] 'Engendering Education Sector Budget: Reforming Future Education Sector Budgets', Institute of Economic Affairs (IEA), (**www.ieakenya.or.ke/documents/EDUCATION%20PP%20IEA%20_2_.pdf**).

[25] Sunny Bindra, 'Lessons in Competition from the demise of GTV', (**www.sunwords.com/2009/02/23/lessons-in-competition-from-the-demise-of-gtv**).

[26] 'Lights, camera, Africa – Movies are uniting a disparate continent, and dividing it too', *The Economist*, 18-31 December 2010.

[27] *The Economist*, 18-31 December 2010.

[28] 'Communication Statistics Report 2008', (**www.cck.go.ke/resc/statistics/Communications_Statistics_Report_2008.pdf**).

[29] 'UN-HABITAT report projects steep growth of African urban population', (**www.unhabitat.org/content.asp?cid=6041&catid=357&typeid=6&subMenuId=0**): "It is projected that by 2050 there will be more than 1.2 billion African city dwellers. That means that by 2050 there will be more people living in African cities than the combined urban and rural populations of the Western hemisphere."

[30] Kenya Population and Housing Census Report 2009.

[31] www.en.wikipedia.org/wiki/Democratic_Republic_of_the_Congo

[32] www.lagosstate.gov.ng/index.php?page=subpage&spid=12&mnu=null

Chapter 3. Regionalisation: evolution of intra-African markets

[33] The Lomé Conventions (**www.acpsec.org**).

[34] Denise Prevost, 'Sanitary, Phytosanitary and Technical Barriers to Trade in the Economic Partnership Agreements between the European Union and the ACP Countries', Maastricht University.

[35] Salma Maoulidi, 'Contemporary Africa and Pan-Africanism: Articulation, unity and inclusion', *Pambazuka News* 427, (**www.pambazuka.org/en/category/comment/55476**).

[36] *Exporting Africa: Technology, Trade, Industrialization in Sub-Saharan Africa*, UN University Press (**www.unu.edu**).

[37] Munyae Mulinge and Margaret Mulinge, 'The Persistent Growth in Size and Importance of the Informal Economy in African Countries: Implications for theorizing the Economy and labour Markets', *African Sociological Review* 2:2 (1998).

[38] **www.bidco-oil.com/regional/index.php?conid=1**

[39] 'Bidco oil – For Africa, by Africa', (**www.developtechnology.co.za/index.php?option=com_content&task=view&id=20298 &Itemid=57&PHPSESSID=9ad5b0e718eb2e614c65a60f17490808**).

[40] Pauline Dibben, 'Transport, Trade and Economic Development in Mozambique: An Agenda for Change'.

[41] **www.en.wikipedia.org/wiki/Uganda_Railway**: "Although almost all of the rail line was actually in the colony that would come to be known as Kenya, the original purpose of the project was to provide a modern transportation link to carry raw materials out of the Uganda colony and to carry manufactured British goods back in."

[42] **www.en.wikipedia.org/wiki/TAZARA_Railway**

[43] **www.en.wikipedia.org/wiki/Chad#Economy_and_infrastructure**

[44] *Information And Communication Technologies For Development In Africa: Volume 1*, 'The context of ICTs in Africa: The cases of Kenya, Senegal, South Africa, and Uganda', (**www.www.idrc.ca**).

[45] 'Telephone Lines in Malawi', (**www.tradingeconomics.com/malawi/telephone-lines-wb-data.html**).

[46] Tokunbo Ojo, 'Wiring Africa for Development', *International Journal of Education and Development using Information and Communication Technology* 1:3 (2005).

[47] James Macharia, 'Telkom Kenya to cut 10,000 jobs', *Business Day*, (**www.hartford-hwp.com/archives/36/156.html**).

[48] World Bank infrastructure indicator data, Mobile and fixed line telephone subscribers per employee, (**www.data.worldbank.org**).

[49] 'Telkom clashes with staff on new round of layoffs', *Business Daily*, (**www.businessdailyafrica.com/Company%20Industry/Telkom%20clashes%20with%20 staff%20on%20new%20round%20of%20layoffs/-/539550/908466/-/view/printVersion/- /ij29cp/-/index.html**).

[50] 'Communication Commission of Kenya, Quarterly Sector Statistics Report', (3rd quarter June 2010), (**www.cck.go.ke/resc/downloads/Sector_Statistics_Report_Q4_09010.pdf**).

[51] **www.nationmaster.com**

[52] PRLog, 'African Mobile Voice Market and Major Network Operators', (**www.prlog.org/10867609-african-mobile-voice-market-and-major-network-operators.html**).

[53] C. Chipeta, and M.L.C. Mkandawire, 'Monetary Harmonization in Southern Africa', African Economic Research Consortium (AERC), (**www.aercafrica.org/documents/RP30.pdf**).

Chapter 4. Rapid Urbanisation

[54] 'Facilitating Urbanization', in Vivien Foster and Cecilia Briceño-Garmendia (eds.) *Africa Infrastructure: A time for transformation* (a co-publication of L'Agence Française de Développement and the World Bank).

[55] 'Africapolis: Urbanization trends in West Africa 1950-2020', L'Agence Française de Développement.

[56] GTZ Eastern Africa Energy Resource Base, Hydro (Kenya).

[57] 'Mozambique – The country with unrealized potential', *25 Degrees in Africa* 1:1 (2006), (**www.25degrees.net/index.php?option=com_zine&view=article&id=337:mozambique&Itemid=81**).

[58] 'Nigeria-Electric Power', (**www.mongabay.com/history/nigeria/nigeria-electric_power.html**).

[59] Global Network on Energy for Sustainable Development (GNESD), (**www.gnesd.org**).

[60] 'Rate of electrification in Africa', (**www.ezega.com/News/NewsDetails.aspx?Page=news&NewsID=1484**).

[61] **www.unesco.org/new/en/natural-sciences/environment/water/wwap/facts-and-figures**

[62] **en.wikipedia.org/wiki/Land_reform_in_Zimbabwe**

[63] 'Kenya: landlessness is a ticking time-bomb', *Daily Nation*, 10 July 2007.

[64] "Nairobi quickly became a tent city and a supply depot, and soon enough developed into the administrative nerve-centre of the Uganda Railway. The place became a convenient and relatively cool place for the Indian railway labourers and their British overlords to pause midway before tackling the arduous climb into the highlands." (**www.africa.com/nairobi/city**).

[65] Julius Olujimi, 'Evolving a Planning Strategy for Managing Urban Sprawl in Nigeria', Department of Urban and Regional Planning, School of Environmental Technology, Federal University of Technology, Akure, Ondo State, Nigeria.

[66] Jacob Songsore, 'The Urban Transition in Ghana: Urbanization, National Development and Poverty Reduction', Department of Geography and Resource Development, University of Ghana. "This period also saw the mass influx of immigrants from other African countries into especially mining towns and the areas of cocoa production in Southern Ghana."

[67] 'Urbanization in China and the Market Potential', Li & Fung Research Centre, October 2002 (**www.lifunggroup.com**).

Chapter 5. Commercialisation of Essential Services

[68] 'Africa's Excellent Growth Prospects for the 21st Century: What Just Happened?', speech by South African Deputy President Kgalema Motlanthe to the Emerging Markets Summit 2010: The New Reality. "Africa has experienced growth spurts before. Some of us are old enough to remember that in the 1960s and 1970s, a growth acceleration, mainly driven by a sustained commodity price boom, helped make some newly independent African countries complacent."

[69] 'The Exposure of African Governments to the Volatility of International Oil Prices, and What to Do About it', AU Extraordinary Conference of Ministers of Trade on African Commodities, Arusha, Tanzania, 21-24 November 2005.

[70] Roger Kubarynch, 'How Oil Shocks Affect Markets: consider the five most recent scenarios', in *The International Economy*, "Over the next year and a half, the price of Saudi light crude oil soared from $2 per barrel to over $13 per barrel. The price subsequently leveled off to trade in a narrow range just under $15 per barrel until the next geopolitical shock in 1979, the Iranian revolution."

[71] Kubarynch, 'Oil Shocks', "By the time the market peaked in 1980-81, the price of Saudi light crude oil had climbed to just below $40 per barrel, a rise of about $25 per barrel and almost a tripling of the 1978 average price."

[72] Martin Khor, *The Commodities Crisis and the Global Trade in Agriculture: Problems and Proposals* (TWN, May 2005).

[73] F. E. Ogbimi, 'Structural Adjustment is the Wrong Policy', African Technology Forum (**www.africantechnologyforum.com**).

[74] Paul De Grauwe and Filip Camerman, 'How Big Are The Big Multinational Companies', January 2002. Table 2: Countries and Corporations Classified According to Value Added/GDP in 2000.

[75] Friedrich Schneider, 'Size and Measurements of the Informal Economy in 110 Countries Around the World', July 2002.

[76] A statistical picture of the workforce, Women in Informal Employment (**wiego.org/informal-economy/statistical-picture**).

[77] 'Improving Tax Administration in Sub-Saharan Africa: The potential of Revenue Agencies and Electronic Service Delivery', Ad Hoc Expert Group Meeting on Strategies for Improving Resource Mobilization in Developing Countries and Countries with Economies in Transition Montreal, 2-6 October 2000.

[78] Mathew K. Jallow, 'Foreign aid and Underdevelopment in Africa', (**www.probeinternational.org**).

[79] Tonny Killick, 'The Developmental Effectiveness of Aid to Africa', International Economics Department, World Bank (1991).

[80] Sulemana Braimah, 'Why foreign Aid has Failed to Develop Africa', March 2009 (**sulemana-braimah.suite101.com**).

[81] Refer to Martin Meredith, *The State of Africa*, (Free Press, 2005). Chapter 13: The Coming of Tyrants, and Chapter 22: The Lost Decade.

[82] **www.standardandpoors.com/ratings/articles/en/us/?assetID=1245226449301**

[83] Hadewych Hazelzet, 'Suspension of Development Cooperation: An Instrument to Promote Human Rights & Democracy?', European Centre for Development Policy Management, Discussion Paper No.64B, (August 2005).

[84] Mutizwa Mukute, 'Experiences and Lessons From a Regional African NGO Network: Tracing PELUM's Developmental Journey', (2004).

[85] Samuel Uwhejevwe-Togbolo, 'The Role of Non-Governmental Organizations (NGOs) in Development', (**www.nigeriavillagesquare.com/articles/samuel-uwhejevwe-togbolo/the-role-of-non-governmental-organizations-ngos-in-development.html**).

[86] Patrick Bond and Horacio Zandamela, Governance and Service Delivery in Eastern and Southern Africa: Issues for Debate, Directions for Research', IDRC conference on Governance Ottawa, Canada, September 2000.

[87] Robert J. Barro and John Wha Lee, International Measures of Schooling Years and Schooling Quality, World Bank, 2001.

[88] Earnest Harsch, 'Schools struggling with crises: Financial constraints hamper expansion of primary education in Africa', July 2000
(**www.un.org/ecosocdev/geninfo/afrec/subjindx/childpdf/childed4.pdf**).

[89] Igor Kitaev, 'Private education in sub-Saharan Africa: A re-examination of theories and concepts related to its development and finance', International Institute for Educational Planning, UNESCO (1999).

[90] Yannis Kamokolias and Jacob Van Lutsenburg Maas, 'The Business of Education: A Look at Kenya's Private Education Sector', IFC Discussion Paper Number 32(1997).

[91] **www.nationmaster.com**

[92] See Transparency International website (**www.transparency.org**).

[93] Police and Private Security in Africa and Dangerous Partnerships – an article by Mary Kimani who writes for the UN Africa Revival magazine.

Chapter 6. Deregulation and Liberalisation of Manufacturing and Services

[94] **www.un.org/ecosocdev/geninfo/afrec/vol18no3/183industries.htm** Africa Renewal: Africa strives to rebuild its domestic industries – Gumisai Mutume (October 2004).

[95] John Nellis, 'The Evolution of Enterprise Reform in Africa: From State-owned Enterprises to Private Participation in Infrastructure – and Back?', Center for Global Development, Washington, USA, September 2005. "Other measures from a number of African studies and surveys in the 1970s and1980s show the economic importance of state-owned enterprises (henceforth SOEs): SOEs accounted for about one-quarter of total formal sector employment in all reporting African countries, and more than 18% of all non-agricultural employment; SOEs accounted for more than 20% of gross domestic investment; more than 14% of total external debt, and more than one-third of domestic

credit; In 15 of 22 francophone African countries surveyed, SOEs ranked first in sales. Clearly, Sub-Saharan African states relied heavily on SOEs to achieve their economic objectives."

[96] Gumisai Mutume, 'Africa strives to rebuild its domestic industries', *Africa Renewal* 18:3 (October 2004), (**www.un.org/ecosocdev/geninfo/afrec/vol18no3/183industries.htm**).

[97] Capitalism – Africa – Independence, State-led Development, and Import-Substitution Industrialisation (**www.science.jrank.org/pages/8525/Capitalism-Africa-Independence-State-Led-Development-Import-Substitution-Industrialisation.html**).

[98] Roelof Jacob Van Der Veen, 'The disintegration of states in Africa : the interaction of politics, economics, culture and social relations, 1957-2003', (2004).

[99] 'Reviving Investment in Africa: Constraints And Policies', UN Economic and Social Council, Addis Ababa, Ethiopia, March 2005. "Although there are several explanations for the continent's poor economic performance since 1980, the low levels of domestic investment are a major causal factor. Gross fixed capital formation has declined in Africa, from a total of $76.3 billion in 1980 to $58.9 billion in 1989."

[100] 'Public Enterprises: Unresolved Challenges and New Opportunities', United Nations, Department of Economic and Social Affairs, Division of Public Administration and Development Management (2008). "The investment decisions of government agencies were constrained by special laws and by central government planning criteria and procedures; they rarely considered the needs of communities or the preferences of consumers."

[101] 'Public Enterprises', United Nations. "Their inefficiencies were seen clearly in their limited abilities to satisfy the rapidly growing needs for commercial and social services that were becoming crucial for economic growth and for widespread participation in a globalising economy."

[102] Deborah Potts, 'The State and Informal Sector in Sub-Saharan African Urban Economies: Redefining Debates on Dualism', King's College London, October 2007.

[103] Osman Suliman and Ghirmay Ghebreysus, 'Determinants of Privatization in Selected Sub-Saharan African Countries: Is Privatization Politically Induced?', *Journal Of Economic Development* 26:2 (December 2001).

[104] Nellis, 'Enterprise Reform in Africa', Centre for Global Development. "The recognition of the magnitude and depth of African SOE problems coincided with the launching, in 1979, of the World Bank's 'structural adjustment' lending operations. These operations differed from the Bank's traditional bricks and mortar projects that built dams, roads, schools or airports. Adjustment loans provided large resource injections in return for which the borrower committed to taking measures designed to correct unstable 'imbalances' in the economy. Invariably, the recommended measures involved 'reductions in expenditures to bring about an orderly adjustment of domestic demand to the reduced level of external resources available to the country.' Since financial losses in African SOEs, especially infrastructure SOEs, tended to be substantial, they became a natural focus of the adjustment process."

[105] Suliman and Ghebreysus, Determinants of Privatization. "The motives behind privatisation are complex and controversial. Importantly, the bulk of researchers are more inclined to believe that most African privatisations take place as part of a broader structural adjustment program under the auspices of international development agencies

or the so-called 'donors', including the World Bank and the International Monetary Fund (IMF). Both the World Bank and the IMF are concerned with the necessary macroeconomic stability as they see it, which usually entails fiscal discipline and privatisation."

[106] Suliman and Ghebreysus, Determinants of Privatization. "…as independence came to Africa in the late 1950s, political rather than economic logic prevailed. … a new political class began to emerge that used the state as its instrument of action and source of power, status, rents, and other forms of wealth. The state was used to begin building an economic base for itself. Thus, in contrast to the onerous private capitalist activity, all groups concentrated on the weak and vulnerable, newly autonomous state to reach power and wealth. The result was a formation of networks to build support through rent distribution, creation of a large parastatal sector, and purchase of urban support via state welfare services and subsidies."

[107] Nellis, 'Enterprise Reform in Africa', Centre for Global Development.

[108] T. Ademola Oyejide, 'Taking Stock of Sustainable Development Finance in Sub-Saharan Africa', University of Ibadan, Nigeria. "During the 1970s and 1980s, ODA flows were as high as 10% of the GNP of African countries. By providing half or more of the total investment in many African countries, ODA flows financed significant proportions of the budgets of many African governments."

Chapter 7. The Growth of Credit

[109] Financial Sector Reforms in Africa: Realities and Problems (www.uneca.org/eca_resources/Major_ECA_Websites/6finmin/cmffin1.htm).

[110] Danny Zandamela, 'Banking in Africa: The big picture', First National Bank of Botswana Limited, February 2009.

[111] Central Bank of Kenya, Monthly Economic Review, August 2010.

[112] National Bank of Rwanda, Annual Report 2009.

[113] 'COCOBOD raises one billion dollars to purchase cocoa', (www.ghanaweb.com/GhanaHomePage/economy/artikel.php?ID=149474).

[114] According to statistics from the Uganda Securities Exchange website (www.use.or.ug).

[115] Tom Minney, 'New bond listing on Rwanda's Capital Market', January 2010, (www.africancapitalmarketsnews.com/244/new-bond-listing-on-rwanda%E2%80%99s-capital-market).

[116] 'Fixed Income – Nigeria – Bond Rush', Vetiva Capital Management Limited, January 2010.

[117] Martin Mbewa, Rose Ngugi, Angela Kithinji 'Development of Bonds Markets: Kenya's Experience', Kenya Institute for Public Policy and Analysis (KIPPRA), Working Paper 15 (December 2007).

[118] 'Banking Sector Stability, Efficiency, and Outreach in Kenya' World Bank Development Research Group, October 2010.

[119] According to IFC (International Finance Corporation), the World Bank's private sector financing and advisory arm.

[120] Anupam Basu, Rodolphe Blavy and Murat Yulek, 'Microfinance in Africa: Experience and Lessons from Selected Countries', IMF Working Paper, September 2004.

[121] Alexia Latortue & Audrey Linthorst, 'Sub-Saharan Africa Microfinance Analysis and Benchmarking Report 2010', a report from Microfinance Information Exchange (MIX) and Consultative Group to Assist the Poor (CGAP), April 2010.

[122] Anne-Lucie Lafourcade, Jeniffer Isern, Patricia Mwangi and Mathew Brown, 'Overview of the Outreach and Financial Performance of Microfinance Institutions in Africa', April 2005.

[123] *The Banking Survey 2010*, a Think Business publication.

[124] According to statistics from *The Banking Survey 2010*.

[125] 'Banks Reluctant to Lend to Small Companies', *African Business*, May 2008.

[126] 'Salaried Employees Regain Sparkle in Kenya's Lending Market', *Africa Investor*, (**www.africa-investor.com/article.asp?id=7809**).

[127] Razia Khan, Head of Macroeconomics and Regional Head of Research for Africa at Standard Chartered Bank, 'Africa Finance Forum: Credit Growth in Africa'. "Prior to the recent global crisis, Africa's economic upswing – which went beyond the usual commodities boom – was noted for a number of factors:.. Unsurprisingly, rising levels of household consumption and, in many countries, an increase in private-sector credit extension also featured heavily."

Chapter 8. Development of Capital Markets

[128] List of African Stock Exchanges (**www.en.wikipedia.org/wiki/List_of_African_stock_exchanges**).

[129] Cyril Nkontchou, 'Recent Evolution of The African Financial Markets', *Proparco*, March 2010 (**www.proparco.fr**).

[130] 'Broadening Local Participation in Privatization of Public Assets in Africa', United Nations Economic Commission for Africa Working Paper.

[131] IFC backs training program to strengthen East African Securities Markets (**www.ifc.org/ifcext/media.nsf/content/SelectedPressRelease?OpenDocument&UNID= C36169BC9A9D6EAA852577ED00587A00**).

[132] IFC Helping Rwanda Create New Sources of Capital (**www.ifc.org/ifcext/africa.nsf/Content/Rwanda_securities_markets**).

[133] Uganda Securities Exchange website (**www.use.or.ug**).

[134] Malawi Stock Exchange (**www.mse.co.mw**) and Privatization Commission (**www.privatizationmalawi.org**).

[135] Lusaka Stock Exchange (**www.luse.co.zm**) and Zambia Privatization Agency (**www.zpa.org.zm**).

[136] Nkontchou, 'African Financial Markets', *Proparco*, (**www.proparco.fr**).

[137] Ecobank Transnational Incorporated Rights Issue and Offer for Subscription Prospectus, August 2008; 'Ecobank Transnational Incorporated Announces Share Offer Results', article on Modern Ghana, an online news portal (**www.modernghana.com/news/203527/1/ecobank-transnational-incorporated-announces-share.html**).

[138] Global Credit Rating Company (**www.globalratings.net/page.php?p_id=39**).

[139] See Uganda Securities Exchange (**www.use.or.ug**).

[140] See Botswana Stock Exchange (**www.bse.co.bw/listed_companies/foreign_companies.php**).

[141] F.M. Mwega, S.M. Ngola, N. Mwangi, 'Real Interest Rates and the Mobilization of Private Savings in Africa: A Case Study of Kenya', AERC Research Paper 2, November 1990.

[142] Ruling Deposit Interest Rates: Kenya – 3.58% (December 2010) (**www.centralbank.go.ke**), Nigeria – 4.32% (October 2010) (**www.cenbank.org**), Ethiopia – 4.5% (March 2010) (**www.nbe.gov.et**).

[143] Mahmudul Alam, Gazi Salah Uddin, Relationship Between Interest Rates and Stock Prices: Empirical Evidence from Developed and Developing Countries, March 2009. "In such cases, if the rate of interest paid by banks to depositors increases, people switch their capital from share market to bank. This will lead to decrease the demand of shares and to decrease the price of shares, and vice versa."

[144] National Social Security Fund website (**www.nssf.or.ke**).

[145] National Social Security Fund (Uganda) (**www.en.wikipedia.org/wiki/National_Social_Security_Fund_(Uganda)**).

[146] See: 'Reviving Investment in Africa: Constraints and Policies', United Nations Economic and Social Council, Economic Commission for Africa, March 1995.

[147] 'Collective Investment Schemes', Making Finance Work for Africa, (**www.mfw4a.org/institutional-investors/collective-investment-schemes.html**).

[148] *Kenya Gazette*, 30 April 2010.

[149] CMA Quarterly Statistical Bulletins, September 2009 and September 2010.

[150] **www.en.wikipedia.org/wiki/Frontier_markets**

Chapter 9. Infrastructure Imperative

[151] Uganda Railway (East African Railway) **www.en.wikipedia.org/wiki/Uganda_Railway** "The original purpose of the project was to provide a modern transportation link to carry raw materials out of the Uganda colony and to carry manufactured British goods back in."

[152] Frost & Sullivan, 'Strategic Analysis of the DRC Electricity Industry', (2006).

[153] 'Water and Sanitation in Sub-Saharan Africa', a progress report by ONE (**www.one.org/c/us/progressreport/779**), (2009). ONE is a grassroots advocacy and campaigning organisation that fights extreme poverty and preventable disease, particularly in Africa, by raising public awareness and pressuring political leaders to support smart and effective policies and programmes that are saving lives, helping to put

kids in school and improving futures. Co-founded by Bono and other campaigners, ONE is non-partisan and works closely with African activists and policy makers.

[154] Bloomberg Business Week, October 2010.

[155] 'Economic growth hinges on infrastructure', **www.constructionkenya.com/901/infrastructure-development-to-boost-construction-growth**

[156] See Kenya Budget Speeches from 2006-10.

[157] ICA Financial Commitments 2008, ICA Annual Report 2009.

[158] 'Africa's Path to Growth: Sector by Sector', *McKinsey Quarterly* (2010).

[159] 'Lamu port set to be a growth catalyst', an article in the 15 June 2009 issue of *The East African*, a weekly publication of the Nation Media Group.

[160] Regional Programme of Action: Economic Development and Regional Integration, Lobito Corridor Project (Feasibility Study), March 2006.

[161] Mtwara Development Corridor: Regional Development Initiatives, National Development Corporation of Tanzania, and Mtwara Development Corridor SDI.

[162] 'Logistics In Africa: Network Effects', *The Economist* (18 October 2008).

[163] 'Concessionaire of port container terminals', (**www.bollore-africa-logistics.com/pages-savoir-faire/metiers.aspx?id_metier=1**).

[164] *Africa Infrastructure: A Time for Transformation*, co-publication of L'Agence Française de Développement (AFD) and the World Bank (2010).

[165] 'Significance of deep sea port to Nigeria's economy', *Africa Investor*, Wednesday 24 February 2010 (**www.africa-investor.com/article.asp?id=6430**).

[166] See **www.infracoafrica.com/projects-kenya-nairobirail.asp**

[167] 'Priority Infrastructure Projects of Kigali City', (**www.kigalicity.gov.rw/IMG/pdf/Program_of_road_construction_for_the_next_5_years _in_the_City_of_Kigali.pdf**), March 2007.

[168] 'Decongestion Abuja: A memo to the new FCT Minister', *BusinessDay*, 30 April 2010.

[169] Abstract on the Projects and Operations page of the World Bank website (**web.worldbank.org**).

[170] See the company websites for
Kenya Airways (**www.kenya-airways.com/home/default.aspx**),
South African Airways (**www.flysaa.com/Journeys/home.action**) and
Ethiopian Airlines (**www.ethiopianairlines.com**).

[171] **www.airport-technology.com**, the website for the airport industry.

[172] Anna Tomová, 'PPP Projects and Airports: Experience and State in World Regions', Department of Air Transport, University of Žilina, The Slovak Republic.

Chapter 10. Technological Networking

[173] Afeikhena Jerome, 'Infrastructure in Africa: The Record', University of Ibadan, Nigeria.

[174] 'Mobile communication the most powerful technology to end poverty', **www.africagoodnews.com/infrastructure/ict/2153-mobile-communication-the-most-powerful-technology-to-end-poverty.html**, (September 2010). "Currently, there are 5 billion mobile subscriptions worldwide. Out of those, 450m are in Africa, which represents 43% of the African population. In Sub-Saharan Africa, the penetration is 42 percent, representing 297m. By 2013, analysts estimate that Sub-Saharan Africa will increase its mobile penetration to 65 percent."

[175] 'Africa's Path to Growth: Sector by Sector', 'Telecoms: From Voice to Data', *McKinsey & Company Quarterly* (June 2010).

[176] Jenny C. Aker and Isaac M. Mbiti, 'Mobile Phones and Economic Development', (June 2010).

[177] **www.intomobile.com/2010/12/20/china-climbs-to-833-1-million-mobile-subscribers**

[178] **www.en.wikipedia.org/wiki/SAT-3/WASC_(cable_system)**

[179] **www.mainonecable.com/index.php**

[180] Itai Medaimombe, 'New cable to connect eastern africa: NEPAD pushes for cheaper, faster telecommunications', *Africa Renewal*, October 2007, **(www.un.org/ecosocdev/geninfo/afrec/vol21no3/213-cable-connecting-africa.html)**.

[181] **www.en.wikipedia.org/wiki/TEAMS_(cable_system)**

[182] **www.eassy.org**

[183] **www.kdn.co.ke/index.php/content/products/fiber.xhtm**

[184] Jevans Nyabiage, 'Three more years of expensive internet costs in Kenya despite fibre optics cables?' 29 September 2009, **(www.africanewsonline.blogspot.com/2009/09/will-kenyans-be-subjected-to-three-more.html)**; and The African Regional Communication Infrastructure Program, World Bank Group.

[185] *The Little Data Book on Information and Communication Technology*, World Bank (2010).

Chapter 11. Human Resources Development

[186] **www.wikigender.org/index.php/Primary_Education_in_Sub-Saharan_Africa**

[187] Kitaev, 'Private education', UNESCO (1999).

[188] Kitaev, 'Private education', UNESCO (1999). "Profit-making institutions have arisen as a result of a diversified and/or unmet demand and are particularly developed in central urban areas (to serve middle and high income families)..they may provide more expensive and better quality education than public or other types of private schools."

[189] UNESCO Institute for Statistics **(www.uis.unesco.org/ev.php?ID=2867_201&ID2=DO_TOPIC)**.

[190] Economic Survey, 1996.

[191] 'Public universities to enroll 24,000 students this year', *Daily Nation*, 19 August 2010.

[192] Pamela Marcucci, D. Bruce Jonhstone and Mary Ngolovoi, 'Higher Education Cost Sharing, Dual Track Tuition Fees and Higher Education Access: The East African Experience', *Peabody Journal of Education* 83:1 (2008).

[193] See Tiyambe Zeleza and Adebayo Olukoshi, *African Universities in the Twenty-first Century. Volume One: Liberalization and Internationalization (CODESRIA, 2004).*

[194] UNESCO, 2004.

[195] Damtew Teferra and Philip G. Altbach, *African Higher Education: International Reference Handbook* (Indiana University Press, 2003).

[196] 'Nokia reaches out to learning institutions to enhance mobile development', *Ratio Magazine* (8 November 2010). *Ratio Magazine* is an online magazine reporting on financial and economic trends in eastern Africa (**www.ratio-magazine.com**).

[197] 'China's Huawei Opens Training Centre in Angola', IT News Africa (29 October 2008), (**www.itnewsafrica.com/?p=1581**).

[198] 'Mitigating the risk of inadequate managerial capacity', Frontier Market Intelligence (12 May 2009), (**www.tradeinvestafrica.com/feature_articles/150100.htm**).

[199] **www.globalcareercompany.com**

Chapter 12. Reform of the Business Environment

[200] *Doing Business 2010*, World Bank report.

[201] *Doing Business 2011.*

[202] *Doing Business 2010.*

[203] *Doing Business 2010.*

[204] *Doing Business 2011.*

Part III: Opportunities

[205] Ngozi Okonjo-Iweala, 'Fulfilling the promise of sub-Saharan Africa', *McKinsey Quarterly* (June 2010).

[206] 'Demographia World Urban Areas Population Projections' (July 2010).

[207] Munir Nanji, 'The Corporate Scramble for Africa', *Journal of Corporate Treasury Management (JCTM)* 2:4 (2009).

[208] Acha Leke, Susan Lund, Charles Roxburgh and Arend van Wamelen, 'What's Driving Africa's Growth', *McKinsey Quarterly* (June 2010).

[209] Maurice Mubila, Mohamed-Safouane and Ben Aissa, with Charles Leyeka Lufumpa, 'The Middle of the Pyramid: Dynamics of the Middle Class in Africa' (April 2011).

[210] Charles Roxburgh, Norbert Dörr, Acha Leke, Amine Tazi-Riffi, Arend van Wamelen, Susan Lund, Mutsa Chironga, Tarik Alatovik, Charles Atkins, Nadia Terfous and Till Zeino-Mahmalat, 'Lions On The Move', McKinsey & Company (June 2010).

[211] Stephanie McCrummen, 'In Africa, a New Middle-Income Consumerism', *Washington Post* (2008).

[212] 'Africa 2' was coined by Vijay Mahajan, business professor at the University of Texas and author of *Africa Rising: How 900m Consumers Offer More than You Think*.

[213] Adapted from the McKinsey & Company article, 'Lions on the Move'.

Chapter 13. Opportunities in Agriculture

[214] 'The Parable of the Sower: The debate over whether Monsanto is a corporate sinner or saint', *The Economist* (21 November 2009).

[215] 'The Miracle of the cerrado: Brazil has revolutionized its own farms. Can it do the same for others?', *The Economist* (28 August 2010).

[216] 'Africa Blossoms: A continent on the Verge of an Agricultural Revolution', *Time* (31 October 2011).

[217] 'Buying Farmland Abroad: Outsourcing Third Wave', *The Economist* (21 May 2009).

[218] **www.g77.org/doc**

[219] 'African Agricultural Finance Under the Spotlight', Reuters Africa News Blog (**www.blogs.reuters.com/africanews/2010/08/24/african-agricultural-finance-under-the-spotlight**).

[220] 'African Agricultural Finance', Reuters.

[221] 'African Agricultural Finance', Reuters.

[222] Giulio Boccaletti, Merle Grobbel, and Martin R. Stuchtey, 'The Business Opportunity in Water', *McKinsey Quarterly* (2009).

[223] Hugh Grant quoted in 'The Parable of the Sower: The debate over whether Monsanto is a corporate sinner or saint', *The Economist* (21 November 2009).

[224] 'Dams in Africa: Tap That Water', *The Economist* (8 May 2010).

[225] G. Denning, P. Kabambe, Z. Sanchez, A. Malik, R. Flor, et al, 'Input Subsidies to Improve Smallholder Maize Productivity in Malawi: Toward an African Green Revolution', *PLos Biol* 7:1 (2009). "Farmers welcomed the availability of seed, fertiliser, and extension services. Aided by a better than average rainy season, the intervention package resulted in unprecedented productivity improvements. In Mwandama Village, 1,000 farmers obtained an average yield of 6.50 t/ha—more than four times the officially estimated national average for 2005-2006."

[226] 'Factors Affecting Supply of Fertiliser in Sub-Saharan Africa – agriculture and Rural Development', World Bank discussion paper (2006). "…production in SSA was only 177,000 tons of nutrients. This represented 3% of Africa's total and just 0.1% of global production. Fertiliser production in SSA peaked at 572,967 nutrient tons in 1992/93, comprising 407,111 tons of nitrogen and 165,856 tons of phosphate. The steady decline in production since then has been due to the closure of the National Fertiliser Company of Nigeria, Ltd. (NAFCON) ammonia/urea plant in Nigeria in 1997 for political reasons and the declining production in Tanzania, Zambia, and Zimbabwe".

[227] 'Climate Change and Variability in the Southern Africa: Impacts and Adaptation Strategies in the Agricultural Sector', World Agroforestry Centre (ICRAF) and United Nations Environment Programme (UNEP).

[228] www.mumias-sugar.com/index.php?page=Future-Products

[229] 'Kenya Starts Greenhouse Tomato Farming', (www.freshplaza.com/news_detail.asp?id=8859).

[230] Pasquale Steduto, Jacob W. Kijne, Munir A. Hanjra, Prem S. Bindraban, 'Water Use and Productivity in A River Basin: Pathways for Increasing Water Productivity', February 2007.

[231] See Gideon E. Onumah, 'Implementing Warehouse Receipts Systems in Africa: Potential and Challenges', discussion paper for the Fourth African Agricultural Markets Programme (AAMP), Lilongwe, Malawi, September 2010, organised by the Alliance for Commodity Trade in Eastern and Southern Africa (ACTESA) of the Common Market for Eastern and Southern Africa (COMESA).

[232] Onumah 'Warehouse Receipt Systems'.

[233] 'Africa Blossoms: A Continent On the Verge of An Agricultural Revolution', *Time* (31 October 2011).

Chapter 14. Opportunities in Real Estate

[234] McKinsey & Co.

[235] 'Housing Prices Steal Limelight at HF bond Trading Ceremony', *Standard* (Kenya) (10 March 2010).

[236] 'Housing in Africa: The new revolution to come in Africa', Shelter Afrique (January 2011).

[237] Jevans Nyabiage, 'New Kenya Cement Makers Shake Up Building Industry' (24 November 2010), (www.cementchina.net/news/shownews.asp?id=8099).

[238] G. Zawdie and D.A. Langford, 'The State of Construction and Infrastructure in Sub-Saharan Africa and Strategies for a Sustainable Way Forward', Department of Civil Engineering, University of Strathclyde.

[239] 'GEF Africa sustainable forestry fund' (14 August 2010), African Capital Markets News (www.africancapitalmarketsnews.com/551/gef-africa-sustainable-forestry-fund).

Chapter 15. Opportunities in Consumer Retail

[240] 'Top Grocery Chains Around the World', Food & Drink Digital (22 December 2010) www.foodanddrinkdigital.com/industry-focus/retailing/top-grocery-chains-around-world

[241] Ngozi Okonjo-Iweala, 'Promise of Sub-Saharan Africa'.

[242] 'The Next China', *The Economist* (31 July 2010).

[243] 'Lions On The Move', McKinsey.

[244] www.3gdirectpay.com/index.html

Chapter 16. Opportunities in Financial Services

[245] Hilary De Grandis and Gary Pinshaw, 'Banking: Building on Success', in 'Africa's Path to Growth', *McKinsey Quarterly* (2010).

[246] See **www.centralbank.go.ke/nps/Reforms/ModernizationFramework.aspx**

[247] 'State Gears Up For Infrastructure Bonds', The Kenya Engineer Online, (**www.kenyaengineer.or.ke/index.php/kenyaengineer/article/viewFile/229/249**).

[248] Africa Public Private Partnership Database (**www.geoinfo.uneca.org**).

[249] De Grandis and Pinshaw, 'Banking', in 'Africa's Path to Growth', *McKinsey Quarterly*.

[250] 'Africa's Banking Boom: Scrambled in Africa', *The Economist* (18 September 2010).

[251] De Grandis and Pinshaw, 'Banking', in 'Africa's Path to Growth', *McKinsey Quarterly*.

[252] 'Africa's banking boom', *Economist*.

[253] 'Financial Access 2010', a survey on financial inclusion in the world by CGAP and the World Bank Group.

[254] 'Agricultural Bank of China: Listing or Capsizing?', *The Economist* (10 June 2010).

[255] C.K. Prahalad, *The Fortune At The Bottom of The Pyramid: Eradicating Poverty Through Profits* (Prentice Hall, 2005).

[256] ICICI Bank Wikipedia page **www.en.wikipedia.org/wiki/ICICI_Bank**

[257] 'On the frontier of finance: Taking advantage of more stable economies, banks are venturing deep into Sub-Saharan Africa', *The Economist* (17 November 2007).

[258] 'Financial Access 2010'.

[259] 'Financial Access 2010'.

[260] 'Africa's banking boom: Scrambled in Africa', *The Economist* (18 September 2010).

[261] 'Mobile Services in poor countries: Not just talk', *The Economist* (29 January 2011).

[262] 'Airtel Kenya unveils new online payment system', *Business Daily* (14 September 2011).

Chapter 17. Opportunities in Telecoms

[263] 'Telecoms: From Voice to Data' in 'Africa's Path to Growth', *McKinsey Quarterly* (2010).

[264] 'Information and Communication Technology in Sub-Saharan Africa: A Sector Review', World Bank report (June 2008).

[265] Yrjö Neuvo & Sami Ylönen, 'Bit Bang II: Energizing Innovation, Innovating Energy', (2010).

[266] 'Kenya Mobile Price War Cuts Calling Costs', *Guardian* (7 September 2010). "In recent weeks a brutal price war has broken out between the mobile operators, slashing the cost of calls between networks by at least 50%, and in some cases 75%. The cuts have come so fast and are so deep that they caused Kenya's August inflation rate to drop, along with the jaws of some mobile executives complaining that they are now losing money."

[267] 'Mobile Marvels: A special report on telecoms in emerging markets', *The Economist* (26 September 2009).

[268] 'Telecommunications' in 'Africa's Path to Growth', *McKinsey Quarterly*.

[269] 'Telecom Penetration in Rural India' an article on India Telecom Online (25 December 2010), (**www.indiatelecomonline.com/telecom-penetration-in-rural-india**).

[270] Population Reference Bureau.

[271] 'Mobile Marvels: A special report on telecoms in emerging markets', *The Economist* (26 September 2009).

[272] 'Mastering the $4 ARPU Challenge: A tale of India and Sub-Saharan Africa', Oliver Wyman paper (communication, media and technology consultancy).

[273] 'Special report on telecoms in emerging markets', *The Economist* (26 September 2009).

[274] According to statistics from *Online Africa*, a website that tracks internet progress in Africa one day at a time, for 2010.

[275] 'Special report on telecoms in emerging markets', *The Economist* (26 September 2009).

[276] 'Mobile Mad Men: Advertisers want to dominate your phone', BBC (20 February 2011).

[277] 'Mobile Mad Men', BBC.

[278] Safaricom Limited – Investor Roadshow Presentation (November 2010).

[279] **www.equitybank.co.ke/products.php?subcat=128**

[280] 'Mobile service in poor countries', *The Economist* (29 January 2011).

Chapter 18. Opportunities in Transport and Logistics

[281] 'Discover the Magic of Africa with East African Companies at Sourcing at MAGIC, the Largest Apparel Trade Show in the US' (5 February 2007), (**www.eastafrica.usaid.gov/%20(S(b4pwlof5vvgllertsj5haquo))/en/Article.1046.aspx**).

[282] Kapi Kenya, Contract Manufacturing Opportunities (**www.kapikenya.com/contract.htm**).

[283] United Nations World Tourism Organization (UNWTO), *World Tourism Barometer*.

[284] A. Barno, B. Ondanje and J. Ngwiri, 'Dynamics Of Horticultural Export To European Union Market: Challenges And Opportunities In Sub-Saharan Africa', *Acta Hort. (ISHS)* 911:61-72 (**www.actahort.org/books/911/911_7.htm**).

[285] WTO Doha Round: Agricultural Negotiations – updated September 2006.

[286] Google Maps Distance Calculator (**www.daftlogic.com/projects-google-maps-distance-calculator.htm**).

[287] 'Boeing 787 Dreamliner Deliveries Delayed Again', Airport International News (19 January 2011), (**www.airport-int.com/news/boeing-787-dreamliner-deliveries-delayed-again.html**).

[288] 'Airbus A350 Deliveries May Slip a Few Months, EADS say', *Bloomberg* (12 November 2010), (**www.bloomberg.com/news/2010-11-12/airbus-a350-deliveries-may-slip-a-few-months-eads-says.html**).

19. Opportunities in Manufacturing and Processing

[289] www.consumerelectronics1.com/consumer-electronic-suppliers/africa.html

[290] 'Dairy Investment Opportunities in Ethiopia', Tam Consult, Addis Ababa (July 2008). "Most dairy plants in the country are operating under capacity, i.e., less than 40%. Excess processing capacity, where accompanied by abundant low priced milk, is one of the 'low hanging fruits' for increased domestic business and cross border trade into COMESA."

[291] Andrew M. Karanja, 'The Dairy Industry in Kenya: The Post-Liberalization Agenda' (2003). "Only 22% of the installed milk processing capacity is currently being utilized."

[292] 'China vows increased currency flexibility', *Financial Times* (19 June 2010).

[293] 'Manufacturing Made in Africa', in *The Africa Report* issue of December 2010/January 2011 titled 'Africa in 2011: A brighter spot in a changing world'.

[294] 'Manufacturing Made in Africa', in *The Africa Report*.

[295] 'Into Africa: Roche Expands Tech Transfer' (January 2008), (**www.outsourcing-pharma.com/Contract-Manufacturing/Into-Africa-Roche-expands-HIV-tech-transfer**).

[296] 'Manufacturing Made in Africa', in *The Africa Report*.

[297] 'Manufacturing Made in Africa', in *The Africa Report*.

Index

J

Japan
  population, 20, 32
  teenage pregnancy rates, 15
Johannesburg
  aviation networks, 149
  consumer market, 200
  multinational corporations (MNCs) in, 41
  urbanisation, 32
Johnson Sirleaf, Madame Ellen, 182
Juba, 141
judicial reform, 192

K

Kaduna, 148
Kafue River, 138
Kampala, 200
Kano, 200
Kapichira, 131
Kasese, 58, 131
Katanga, 142
Kenya
  agriculture, 206
  automated teller machine (ATMs) in, 102
  aviation industry, 149
  banking and finance sector reforms, 95
  bond market, 98
  bootleg operations in, 25
  business reforms, 182, 183, 185
  cement companies, 230
  city development plans, 146
  collective investment schemes, 121
  commercial bank branches, 101
  construction reforms, 186
  corporate governance, 189
  credit reforms, 187, 188
  customs administration, 190, 191
  dairy processing, 299
  domestic savings, 96
  education, 77, 166, 168, 169, 170, 173, 174
  electricity generation, 53, 56
  fertility rates, 17
  financial inclusion, 99
  graduate employment, 176
  greenhouse farming, 217
  horticulture, 293
  industry, 38
  infrastructure development, 133, 231, 256

land dispossession, 55
land subdivision, 60, 206
Maasai people, 11
manufacturing, 39, 40, 285, 298
ministry of education, 23
mobile banking, 281
mobile phone use, 30
mortgage industry, 228
outsourced production in, 304
pension funds, 117
police officer ratios, 78
population figures, 9, 15, 19, 32
power generation, 138
private sector, 83
property market, 226
railways, 51, 131
recapitalisation strategy, 113
smallpox epidemic, 11
Special Economic Zone (SEZ), 305
stock exchange listings, 112–113
sugar cane production, 216–217
technical training institutions, 173
teenage pregnancy rates, 15
telecommunications, 43, 44, 158, 159
tourism, 288
transport infrastructure, 141, 241–242
urbanisation, 51
Kenya Agricultural Commodity Exchange (KACE), 220
Kenya Horticulture Development Programme (KHDP), 217
Khambata, Farida, 121
Khartoum, 200
Kigali, 147, 151
Kigoma-Dar es Salaam Railway, 314
Kimberley, 58
Kinshasa
  consumer market, 200
  population figures, 14, 32
  telecommunications, 44
  urbanisation, 32
Kisii highlands, 60, 206
kitchen supplies, 38
Kogelo, 288
Konza City, 147
Kruger, 151
Kuwait Fund for Arab Economic Development, 135
KwaZulu-Natal, 151

U

United Nations
  G77, 212
  Millennium Development Goals (MDG), 12, 163, 165
universities, 168–177
  coverage and capacity, 168
  enrolment, 174, 175
  faith-based, 170
  graduate employment, 176
  parallel degree programmes, 169
  privatisation, 170–171, 173
  skills-specific, 172–173
urban centres *see also* rural-urban migration
  banking services, 96
  modernisation and renewal, 227, 242
  public services, 51
  real estate demand, 225
  slums, 56
  town planning, 57–58
  utility development, 54
urban renewal, 227, 230, 234, 288
urbanisation, 14, 18, 32–33, 202
  background and perspective, 51–52
  business and economic implications, 61–62
  commerce and entrepreneurialism, 32, 54–55
  conurbations and metropolitan sprawl, 57–58
  demands on infrastructure, 146–148
  driver of African economy, 4
  impact on agriculture, 206–207
  impact on household consumption, 62
  influence on economic growth, 198
  land tenure and ownership systems, 59–60
  landlessness and settlements, 55–56
  mining sector and, 58–59
  and population density, 60–61
  real estate demand, 225
  rural Africa, 51–52, 56–57, 61, 207
  utilities in urban centres, 53–54
  youth migration, 52–53
USA
  farming policies, 211
  negative population growth rates, 20
  popular culture, 25
  teenage pregnancy rates, 15
USAID, 72
utilities, 53–54

V

value added tax (VAT), 190, 287
Varghese, N.V., 170
Verifies, Marcus, 280
vertical real estate, 234
very small aperture terminal (VSAP), 99
Victoria Falls, 151
Vietnam, 65
vigilante groups, 78
village banking, 100
village systems, 60
virtual networks, 278–279
Voice over Internet Protocol (VoIP), 45

W

wages, 102, 243–244, 285, 301
Walvis Bay Corridor Group, 136, 313
warehouse receipt system, 218–219, 220, 221, 292
warehousing, 291–292
water, 53, 54, 57, 132, 213–215 *see also* hydropower
  government failure to provide, 76
  greenhouse farming, 217–218
  purification, 76
Water Efficient Maize for Africa (WEMA), 208
welfare systems, 74–75
West African Power Pool, 139
Westernisation, 15, 23, 24–27, 240
What is Driving Africa's Growth?, 197
white goods, 31
wholesale sector, 54–55, 198
wind power, 138, 139, 140
Windhoek, 200
wireless technology, 277–278
work ethic, 243–244, 298
World Bank, 12, 72, 109, 134, 182
World Health Organisation (WHO), 12
World Trade Organisation (WTO), 211–212

Y

Y2K scare, 200
Yaoundé, 25
Yom Kippur war 1973, 65
young people *see also* children
  consumerism, 241, 302
  education, 23–24, 33
  the generation gap, 29–30
  global brand ownership, 31